History of Metals in Eastern India and Bangladesh

History of Metals in Eastern India and Bangladesh

Pranab K. Chattopadhyay
Gautam Sengupta

Series Editor
O.C. Handa

PENTAGON PRESS
in association with
INFINITY FOUNDATION

ISBN 978-81-8274-512-4

Published: 2011 by

PENTAGON PRESS

206, Peacock Lane, Shahpur Jat,
New Delhi-110049
Phones: 011-64706243, 26491568
Telefax: 011-26490600
email: rajan@pentagonpress.in
www.pentagonpress.in

Typeset by
The Laser Printers
New Delhi-110027

Printed in India by
Swan Press, New Delhi

Dedicated to
Prof. R. Balasubramaniam
(15th April 1961 – 9th Dec. 2009)

The distinguished Archaeometallurgist, who
contributed significantly
to
research in
Corrosion Metallurgy

CONTENTS

FOREWORD TO THE SERIES

INDIA HAS HAD A LONG HISTORY OF CIVILISATION GOING BACK SEVERAL thousand years. In the global mind this civilisation is largely associated with spiritualism, philosophy and religiosity. There is also appreciation of great traditions that have continued: of performing arts in dance and music; of magnificent works in architecture, sculpture, painting; and of artisanal output of quality relating to the crafts. Over the last couple of centuries the image has been significantly one of poverty: surprising when John Milton in *Paradise Lost* had referred to 'the wealth of Ormuz and of Ind'. For many, it is a land of magicians and snake-charmers; of wild animals, like tigers and elephants; of mendicants, and mystics. This image is changing today with India moving powerfully into the knowledge economy and becoming a power to reckon with. What is not known and appreciated is the extent to which a whole knowledge system, and particularly scientific thought, has been inextricably linked to the development of this ancient and continuing civilisation.

There are many reasons for this. An important one is that there has been no major work on the history of science and technology in India. This is not to say that no work has been done in this field; there is a great deal available relating to specific areas, and involving specialised discussion, more so concerning technology. But there is nothing covering science and technology as a whole, dealing with the many diverse areas that it covered, and particularly its very different conceptual foundations, as also the extent to which it has underpinned the development of Indian society and civilisation. Because of this, in authoritative encyclopaedias, (such as Encyclopaedia Britannica), Indian science and technology is dealt with in a few hundred words. This must be contrasted with the situation in respect of China, following the great work of Dr. Joseph Needham, who produced thirty odd volumes on the history of science and technology of that country.

This made a monumental impact in the academic repositioning of China as a scientific, rational and progressive civilisation. There is need for a similar effort with regard to Indian science and technology.

A further reason for the rather poor appreciation of the history of Indian science is that, in the public eye, the development of science and technology is manifested through its innumerable technological artefacts that affect daily lives in society, and great scientific discoveries, both of which rapidly followed the developments that took place around a few hundred years ago in Europe with the birth of the modern, ongoing Scientific and Industrial Revolutions. As a result, the image of western science is so overwhelming that it swamps all earlier history.

In the West, there is major reference to the Greek origins of western philosophy and scientific thought. There was a strong coupling of Arab and Greek science, particularly as manifested in the historical Library of Alexandria. It must be remembered that India was an open country, and had significant interactions with the Arab world. Also, western scholars of the pre-Christian era had information on India through reports of Greek origin. It is, thus, that the 'Zero' and the 'Decimal place value system' became international and got referred to as the Arabic numerals; but these had their origins in India. Indeed 'Zero' had a deep philosophical meaning, that was characteristically Indian, denoting 'nothing or emptiness'.

There are many who, without a deep appreciation of the character of indigenously developed knowledge structures in India, often propagate the idea that science (which was so intimately interwoven with these knowledge structures) came to India from the outside through Islamic and Western conquests. The fact is that India absorbed all that came in from the outside (whether by invasion or otherwise) and gave freely of itself to the East and to the West; it was an open society.

The following reasoning may provide an indication why it has been difficult to compile a meaningful and reasonably comprehensive history of science and technology in India.

A great deal of knowledge transmittal in India has been through the oral tradition, having been conveyed through chants, hymns, poems and the like; this has been true even in mathematics. These do not remain in the written record, and much of it has probably been lost with the cataclysmic changes in Indian society.

What has been written has invariably been on palm leaf and such other materials, followed by paper recordings; this is particularly the case for the earlier period in history prior to the advent of printing. A great deal of the source material on which writing has taken place, would have been subject to ravages of weather and insects, since India is located in the tropics characterised by high temperatures and humidity. After printed books came into existence, which ensured the availability of many copies of a text, India has not had a great history in science and technology, except in the last century.

Even when written, this was in the language then prevailing, namely, Sanskrit, particularly of the archaic variety and other related languages; there was also the problem of scripts. In recent years, one finds that those who know these scripts and languages, particularly their older forms, have little knowledge or interest in matters that are scientific. Their interests largely lie in areas of literature, philosophy, religion and the like. In contrast, those who know science, and could contribute to a meaningful analysis of recorded history, have scant knowledge of the language and the scripts of the past and often little interest.

Finally, what was transmitted, even on matters that were scientific, was mixed up with a great deal of philosophy, religion and mysticism; often practitioners of science of those days were philosophers or those high up in the socio-religious hierarchy. Knowledge in ancient India was much less compartmentalised; it was characterised by a holistic approach. To extract that which would be regarded as science, from this totality, is not an easy task.

For all these reasons, the overall effort relating to writing of the history of science and technology in India has been a limited and scattered effort.

From what we know already, it is clear that there was a significant development of science and technology, covering a wide range of areas, with high creativity and originality, and over a long time-span. It is important to record and understand this. The purpose would not be to go back to the past from the viewpoint of claiming how great India was. Whilst there were many great discoveries made in India, which predate the same ones later made in the West, and now named after western scientists, the purpose would also not be to claim priorities or demand changes in attributions. What is important is to carry out proper historical work to understand the developments that had taken place and to record them appropriately.

There are two important reasons why this should be done. The first is from the viewpoint of understanding the nature of society in which science can flourish. Ultimately it is a thinking questioning society that can give rise to science. It is from this angle that Jawaharlal Nehru constantly spoke about the need for society to be imbued with scientific temper, namely, society functioning on a rational objective basis, which can give rise to the development of science – with innovation, originality, and creativity. These qualities cannot arise in a society which is hierarchical and authoritarian. On this aspect Gautama, the Buddha had remarked:

> 'Believe nothing
> merely because you have been told it
> or because it is traditional
> or because you yourself have imagined it
> Do not believe what your teacher tells you,
> Merely out of respect for the teacher
> But whatever after due examination and analysis
> You find to be conducive to the good, the benefit,
> The welfare of all beings,
> That doctrine believe and cling to,
> And take it as your guide.'

It is important to understand why, with so much creativity and originality that had characterised Indian science and technology of the past, those developments did not last or takeoff on a self-sustaining basis.

The second reason why one needs to look at the history of science and technology in India is that, to a great extent, the conceptual approach in it has been different from which has characterised western development. It has tried to examine problems on a holistic basis. It has dealt with complexity. Thus the fundamental basis of the Indian system of medicine, referred to as Ayurveda, is very different from that which characterises the allopathic system. Ayurveda is a holistic system, which attempts to ensure harmony among the different components of the human body, and aspects of its functioning, including relationships with the outside world and inputs received. The approach is to ensure that the mind-body system remains in health, rather than in the treatment of disease. This involves a complex many body synergy (including the treatment with medication, body discipline of *yoga, meditation* and the like) rather than the deductive, reductionist 'active principles' approach of allopathy; the latter has certainly yielded a plethora of miraculous results.

One is also amazed at the dimensions with which the ancients grappled with, and their many speculations on issues such as origins of the universe and cosmology that are still with us. There is a great deal that one can learn from these excursions into ancient thoughts.

It is, therefore, important that any such history deals not only with narrow technological issues that related to societal needs but to science as a whole.

There have been a number of efforts to cover the history of science and technology in India. The Indian National Science Academy publishes a journal entitled *Indian Journal of History and Science* under the guidance of the Indian National Commission for History of Science of the Academy. One of the other very ambitious ongoing projects in this area is that on the 'History of Science, Philosophy and Culture in Indian Civilisation' of which the General Editor is Prof. D.P. Chattopadhyaya. The series is projected to cover approximately seventy-five volumes, of which twelve have already been published. There are also many individual efforts such as the Sandeepani Science Gallery in Porbunder and innumerable publications that cover specific topics in science and technology such as 'copper and its alloys in ancient India'; works on 'Indian medicine and medicinal plants'; works on logic, where India was particularly strong, and so on.

I am glad that the Infinity Foundation has considered it appropriate to produce a series on the History of Indian Science and Technology (HIST). It is important that this effort covers not only areas of technology but also of science. It will have to bring together for this, scientists and historians of science, along with those concerned with philosophy, anthropology, religion, ancient Indian languages and many such other disciplines, who will have to interact strongly among themselves on the basis of available textual and other material. It has to be a holistic, interdisciplinary approach. This is a major task but well worth doing.

Prof. M.G.K. Menon, FRS
Advisor, ISRO (Department of Space), New Delhi

NOTE ON INFINITY FOUNDATION

Facilitating Research, Publishing and Education in:
History of Indian Contributions to Science and Technology (HIST)

'In 1750 China accounted for almost one-third, India for almost one-quarter and the West for less than a fifth of the world's manufacturing output . . . In the following decades . . . the industrialisation of the West led to the de-industrialisation of the rest of the world'.

Samuel Huntington, *Clash of Civilisations*, 1997: 86-87.

It is now largely forgotten that India held its prominent economic position referenced above because of its accomplishments in science and technology. The commonly taught history of India emphasises mostly kings, invasions and conflicts. The history of Indian ideas, if taught at all, is limited to religion, philosophy and popular culture. What is being often ignored is the well-documented evidence of India's significant contributions in metallurgy, civil engineering and architecture, water harvesting, shipping and ship building, textiles, medicinal plants, medicine, agriculture, forest management, management, astronomy and linguistics, among other disciplines. By way of comparison, Joseph Needham's 30 odd volumes on Chinese history of science and technology have made a monumental impact in the academic repositioning of China as having a rational and progressive civilisation. This work is a premier reference in China Studies world-wide. But no such equivalent exists for India, as explained below:

'Fear of elitism did not, happily, deter Joseph Needham from writing his authoritative account of the history of science and technology in China, and to dismiss that work as elitist history would be a serious neglect of China's past . . .'

'A similar history of India's science and technology has not yet been attempted, though many of

the elements have been well discussed in particular studies. The absence of a general study like Needham's is influenced by an attitudinal dichotomy. On the one hand, those who take a rather spiritual — even perhaps a religious — view of India's history do not have a great interest in the analytical and scientific parts of India's past, except to use it as a piece of propaganda about India's greatness (as in the bloated account of what is imaginatively called 'Vedic mathematics', missing the really creative period in Indian mathematics by many centuries). On the other hand, many who oppose religious and communal politics are particularly suspicious of what may even look like a 'glorification' of India's past. The need for a work like Needham's has remained unmet.'

— Amartya Sen, 'On Interpreting India's Past' in *Nationalism, Democracy and Development* (Ed.) S. Bose and A. Jalal, 1997: 32

HIST is an important part of India's story because it has been the substratum of its civilisation's rationality and secular progress, the basis for pre-colonial Indian Ocean global trade, the foundation for building India's future knowledge society, and a key element in projecting Brand India.

Infinity Foundation, a private non-profit foundation based in Princeton, USA, launched the HIST project with the following objectives:

- Document and discuss the history of scientific and technological achievements in the Indian subcontinent until the end of the 19th century, because the period after that has already been well documented.
- Inspire creativity and self-confidence among our youth, refuting the popular notion that Indians were irrational and mystical. Replace colonial notions of intellectual dependency and revive India as a premier knowledge exporter.
- Bridge the socio-economic divide: it is often the rural and the underprivileged in India who have preserved key aspects of traditional knowledge, such as in medicinal plants, or traditional civil engineering and home building. By restoring legitimacy to traditional knowledge, which is decentralised and less capital-intensive, we empower local/rural cultures, lifestyles and economies. If India hopes to create genuine alternatives to rural migration and the burden of high-density metro lifestyles, we need to re-engage with, and build upon, the strengths of traditional knowledge systems.
- Build India's brand, cultural capital and soft power: Ancient India's higher education and technological genius attracted the cream of Asian students to Nalanda, Taxila and other Indian centres of learning. The alumni and visiting scholars spread India's cultural capital across Asia. Today, USA has a strategy to educate the future leaders

of the world to gain influence globally. China has also embarked upon a strategy to export its higher education for geopolitical influence. If India hopes to preserve and expand its role in the information economy or in engineering design, she needs a civilisational or 'cultural brand' in the same sense as the following culture specific brands:

Japanese-ness	Quality
French-ness	Beauty/aesthetics: cosmetics, fashion, wine, Cannes, tourism
Italian-ness	Design, art, cuisine
British-ness	Justice, law, rationality
German-ness	Precision, manufacturing
Chinese-ness	Efficiency

In each of these cases, the soft power wielded by the country's brand has fuelled economic expansion using its civilisational advantages. It is important to restore a realistic counter-balance to India's negative branding brought about by some of the thrusts of the social sciences until now. The following table is not intended as a generalisation but merely as indicative of some differences between two ways of seeking Indian culture — the one by social scientists and the other, by technocrats such as those pursuing HIST research.

Social Sciences on Indian-ness	HIST on Indian-ness
Mystical and otherworldly	Rational, innovative and creative
Frozen in time and backward	Pragmatic and progressive
'Caste, dowry, sati, conflict'	Multicultural and interdependent
Knowledge came from invaders	Indian knowledge systems
British made us a nation	Many prior nations existed
Lacking self-esteem and afraid of future	Confident and competitive
Defensive and closed	Open and globalised

Once again, Indians are increasingly being acknowledged worldwide for their brainpower, but the civilisational brand is dominated by 'caste, cows, curry' images from anthropology. Furthermore, many Indians have distanced themselves from what they see as 'baggage', bringing about disconnects with their own past. HIST is a secular and all-encompassing shared past for nation-building.

It is important to bring scientists and technologists into this historical research so as to stay focused on the evidence and not the politics. The goal is not to glorify but analyse objectively, in order to use the knowledge for present and future growth and to learn from past mistakes.

INFINITY FOUNDATION'S HIST PROJECT

Although Infinity's vision is to implement this unprecedented, composite and inclusive series, we would like to acknowledge and applaud many pioneering research and contributions made in this field, such as the following, and work with them to expand the discipline:

- Five volume series on traditional agricultural practices by Indian Council for Agricultural Research;
- Multi-volume series on History of Science by Dr D.P. Chattopadhyay;
- History of Indian medicine by Valiathan;
- Works of Indian National Science Academy; and
- Many others.

The HIST project was started in 2002, after being conceived at the Foundation's Colloquium in Woodstock, that was jointly convened by Infinity Foundation and Columbia University. So far, only the series on Materials and Technologies has been started. Two other series, one on Life Sciences and another on Theoretical Sciences, are envisioned for the future.

Annual project meetings have been held all over India to review progress, share research and foster collaboration. These meetings — in places as varied as Indian Institute of Technology, Kanpur, India International Center (Delhi), Kumaon University (Nainital) and Banaras Hindu University (Varanasi) — have also served as outreach to local colleges and to the general public by giving them a chance to interact with our academic scholars. It takes approximately three years to develop each volume (the final manuscript) and involves a team of scholars, in addition to the author(s).

TOPIC SELECTION CRITERIA

The following criteria were applied in selected topics for the series:

- Time period of focus should be sciences and technologies developed until the end of the 19th century.
- Topics must have empirically verifiable and significant Indian contributions.
- Subject matter experts should be available, especially within India. This helps the growth of research communities invested in such investigations and secures the roots of this work in India over time.

- Religion and 'stories' should be avoided as evidence, that is, no 'Pushpak Viman' to be included. The goal is an honest exploration, not glorification.
- The sources and scholar must be internationally credible.

It takes approximately three years to develop each volume (the final manuscript) and involves a team of scholars in addition to the author(s). The steps include rigorous peer review and editorial review at each step, and project administration by Infinity Foundation. Infinity Foundation owns the copyright.

ABOUT INFINITY FOUNDATION (IF)

Infinity Foundation is a 501 (c) (3) non-profit tax-exempt private foundation that was started in 1995 as a vehicle for its founder to give back to the Indian and American societies. For further information, please contact:

Project: http://www.indianscience.org/
Foundation: www.infinityfoundation.com
Address: 53 White Oak Drive, Princeton NJ 08540, USA
Email: infinityfoundation@gmail.com

Rajiv Malhotra
President, Infinity Foundation

EDITOR'S NOTE

The 'traditional knowledge system' is an accepted phrase coined by the anthropologists to explain various scientific systems of the indigenous communities the world over. Centuries before the science of scripting the oral tradition developed in India, the common folks of this country had been transmitting the inherited knowledge to the next generation by words of mouth through the oral traditions, or *orature* as apposed to the literature, or what in the ancient India was known as the *shruti* and *smriti* tradition, supplementing that with their own empirical experiences. Therefore, the extant popular belief systems, traditions, arts, folk sciences and folklore of the ethnic communities and the rural folks are the most authentic and valuable source material to discover that knowledge system. Is it not an irony that the well-tried and ancient *Ayurvedic* and other indigenous medical systems that have sustained generations of people through centuries are dubbed as the 'alternative' medical system against the modern westernised allopathic system? This is but one instance of how the traditional knowledge systems have been lost to the oblivion under the western pressures, and under that euphoria, our attitude towards all that traditional Indian knowledge system has become very callous, casual, and derogatory. Why such disinterest in the traditional Indian knowledge system, is a provocative question, which must be addressed objectively and urgently. There is an urgent need to remove the queer dichotomy between the traditional and modern knowledge systems to generate a rational knowledge system.

The traditional Indian knowledge system provides a wealth of wisdom, for it is the repository of philosophical, social, religious, cultural, technological, and behavioural human response to the complexities of life and nature. The Indian traditional folk and elite sciences are interlaced with their quintessential ancient cultures and universal vision. Therefore, the holistic traditional Indian knowledge system holds key for most of the maladies of the so-called modern technologies.

The Infinity Foundation (IF) has been striving to rediscover those traditional technologies and the ancient scientific systems through the 'History of Indian Science and Technology' (HIST) series with the objective not only to establish their relevance in the modern scenario, but also to make the works on the Indian 'traditional knowledge system' (TKS) available to the general readers throughout the world. Thus, these hardbound and immaculately published volumes have been heavily subsidised.

Under the HIST series, five volumes have already been published. Three books — Harappan Architecture and Civil Engineering authored by Jagat Pati Joshi, Marvels of Indian Iron Through the Ages written by R. Balasubramaniam and History of Iron Technology in India authored by Vibha Tripathi appeared in 2008. In 2009, two books: Harappan Technology and Its Legacy by D.P. Agrawal and Himalayan Traditional Architecture authored by O.C. Handa were released. Indian Zinc Technology in a Global Perspective of J.S. Kharakwal is soon to be released. This book – *History of Metals in Eastern India and Bangladesh* — jointly authored by Pranab K. Chattopadhyay and Gautam Sengupta is latest in the HIST series. In this volume, Dr Chattopadhyay and Dr. Sengupta have studied in depth the metallurgy in the eastern part of Indian subcontinent in the historical context, right from the earliest period to our times. They have also studied in detail the various traditional techniques of extraction of metals from the ores. Besides, different traditional methods of preparing metallic objects, including cannons, images, utensils etc., have also been discussed in great detail.

Thus, the Infinity Foundation has brought out seven comprehensive authoritative volumes on the Indian traditional knowledge system under the HIST publication programme. Many more such volumes on various aspects of the Indian 'traditional knowledge system' are in different stages of preparation by various accomplished authors, and many more topics of may follow. Of course, this achievement is a matter of great satisfaction to us.

However, there also have been the moments of grief to the IF fraternity. We lost our two great friends and accomplished authors. On 27th June 2008, Shri Jagat Pati Joshi (born: 14th July 1932) left for the heavenly abode. Shri Joshi had a very long inning in the Archaeological Survey of India at various positions. He retired as its Director General. He was the senior most author of the HIST series. Then, on the 9th Dec. 2009, one the most erudite authority on the Indian iron technology at IIT Kanpur and a very good friend, Prof. R. Balasubramaniam (born: 15th April 1961) suddenly left us. In their death, the Infinity Foundation in particular and the scholastic world in general have lost two distinguished authorities of their respective specialities.

I hope that the scholars and general readers shall find the HIST volumes very interesting and informative. Our objective is to rediscover the Indian traditional knowledge system and to establish its relevance in the modern technological and scientific scenario. How for we succeed in that endeavour, only future can tell, but we shall continue to strive to achieve our goal.

O.C. Handa,
Series Editor

PREFACE

The Indian subcontinent has a long, rich tradition of metallurgy. In the recent past, significant researches on the origin and development of metallurgy in this region have taken place. However, no exclusive work on the wonderful metallurgical traditions of the Eastern India and Bangladesh has so far been done. This book focuses on the important metal objects unearthed in excavations and explorations. From a tiny coin to the massive iron and brass cannons, and the use of metals by the people in this part of the subcontinent has been very interesting. In this book, the valuables metallic object — the images and other finds preserved in temples and monasteries — have been discussed in detail. There is information with regard to the massive iron beams used for building monuments, along with the filigree crafts of Orissa. The traditional ornaments, the utensils of everyday use and the manufacturing techniques of those have also been discussed.

The main objective of this book is to encourage young readers to know about metallurgy and requisite skills that the common artisans of this part of the subcontinent posses. At the same time, an effort has also been made to convey to the enthusiastic non-Indian readers the information about the wonders of metallurgical skills in the eastern part of this country.

This book furnishes original researches of the first author on the archaeometallurgy in Eastern India and Bangladesh, and of the second author on the Eastern Indian images and sculptures. It is hoped that this volume will serve as a comprehensive introduction to the metal technology in this part of the subcontinent.

Pranab K. Chattopadhyay
Gautam Sengupta

ACKNOWLEDGEMENTS

Numerous people helped us in this project from the outset. We are immensely grateful to Prof. D. P. Agrawal, Dr Basudev Narayan, Dr Asok K. Bhattacharya, Dr K. K. Basa, Dr Shamsul Hussain, Prof. Mozammel Haque, Prof. Prasanta Dutta and Buddhadev Bhattacharjee for their help at every step during the course of this book project.

Dr Vincent Lefevre, National Museum for Asian Arts Guimet, has supplied the photographs of bronze images of Mainamati and Varendra Research Museum, Rajshahi. Thanks are also due to Pratip Kumar Mitra, Dr Sutapa Sinha, Dr Sharmi Chakraborty, Dr Suchira Roychowdhury, Jibanananda Basu, Raju Mitra and Surajit Lahiri of the Centre for Archaeological Studies & Training, Eastern India, who were, throughout, associated with this work. The maps in the book have been drawn painstakingly by Sharmistha Chatterjee. We are grateful to her for professional services.

We are thankful to Mr Rajiv Malhotra and other members of the Infinity Foundation for funding the crucial field research for writing this book. We have got laboratory support from the Department of Metallurgy, Jadavpur University; Indian Institute of Technology, Kharagpur and Bhabha Atomic Research Centre.

We also acknowledge the support of authorities of the State Archaeological Museums of Assam, Orissa and West Bengal; along with the support of Tai Museum, Sibsagar; District Museum, Jorhat; Archaeological Survey of India, Guwahati Circle; Director, Indian Museum; Directorate of Research, Government of Arunachal Pradesh, Itanagar; Director General, National Museum of Bangladesh; Director, Varendra Research Museum, Rajshahi and Director General, Department of Archaeology,

Bangladesh. The Birmingham Museum & Art Gallery has permitted us to use the photograph of the Sultanganj Buddha. Special appreciation goes to Prof. R. Balasubramaniam for his unfailing support, and a range of helpful comments and also for many suggestions for improvement.

The manuscript of this book has been entirely checked by Dr. O. C. Handa. We are grateful to him for his guidance and painstaking editorial advice.

Pranab K. Chattopadhyay
Gautam Sengupta

LIST OF TABLES

LIST OF FIGURES

(The figures, without source indicated against these, are from the author's collection.)

LIST OF ABBREVIATIONS USED IN THE TEXT

ASI	Archaeological Survey of India
BRW	Black-and-Red Ware
CASTEI	Centre for Archaeological Studies and Training, Eastern India
EPMA	Electron probe micro analyses
GSI	Geological Survey of India
MAH	Mahasthan
NBPW	Northern Black Polished Ware
PIXE	Proton Induced X-ray Emission
SAIL	Steel Authority of India Limited
SEM	Scanning Electron Microscope
TEM	Transmission Electron Microscope
TISCO	Tata Iron & Steel Company
XRF	X-ray Fluorescence

1

INTRODUCTION

THE HISTORY OF METALLURGY IS CLOSELY LINKED TO THE HISTORY of the development of human civilisation. It is perhaps one of the earliest branches of technology that was developed by mankind, which singularly led to the introduction of enormous changes in the socio-economic life patterns of human beings. It is unconceivable to think of the growth of man to his present level, without the knowledge of science and technology of metals and alloys. Having mastered the extraction of metal from its ore, the process of refining and processing it had to be understood. In addition, the physical properties of metals had to be mastered. The main objective was to produce the desired objects using metal. Traditionally, it had been thought that metallurgy and metal crafts originated in the Middle-East. That was a strongly held belief until recently, but the archaeological discoveries since 1960 have upset such traditional theories concerning the origin of copper and bronze technologies. However, Michael Cheilik, in his article 'Bronze Age' in the Microsoft Encarta 2007, has mentioned that the discoveries near Ban Chiang in Thailand, indicate that bronze technology was known there as early as 4500 BCE. That preceded the bronze working in the Middle-East by several hundred years. In this light, it becomes important that a fresh look be taken at the development of metallurgy in the South-East and Near East. The present work is an attempt to look into these areas, especially, Northeast India.

Unless specifically mentioned, the term 'eastern Indian subcontinent' mentioned throughout this volume refers to the states of Bihar, Chhattisgarh, Jharkhand, Orissa, Sikkim and West Bengal, along with a vast stretch of land in the northeast, encompassing the states of Assam, Arunachal Pradesh, Manipur, Meghalaya, Mizoram, Nagaland, Sikkim and Tripura in eastern India. Bangladesh is also included because of its topographical location and common history.

ORIGIN OF METTALURGY

There is no coherent record of the pattern of development of metallurgy in the eastern part of the subcontinent. The exact location where metallurgy originated in this area cannot be identified with certainty. However, with the help of recent archaeological findings and scientific analysis of data, a better understanding of the metallurgical heritage of eastern India can be obtained. Eastern India populations witnessed a gradual transformation from the Neolithic to Chalcolithic cultural and civilisational stages of human development.

The first excavated Neolithic phase (Period IA) was established at Chirand, and it has been dated to 2500-2300 BCE (Verma 2007:17). The Neolithic phase was that cultural stage of human development, during which the people learnt to improve upon their stone tools (which they had been using since thousands of years), and began turning them out with excellent finish. An overall development in the human index can be noticed with the discovery of farming and firing of pottery. Fire was used in Neolithic Period to burn earthenware into pottery. Firing of pottery was the beginning of pyrotechnology – the science and technology of intentional use and control of fire by humans. The main industry of the Neolithic or Pre-Chalcolithic period was the production of food through (the discovery of) agriculture, manufacturing of polished stone tools and bone artefacts. Mankind learnt manufacturing of objects, like scrappers, chisels, needles, points, awls, and so on, that were made of stone. A well-developed microlithic industry was also initiated during the Neolithic Period. Bone was also used as the raw material for ornaments that were popularised as objects of everyday use. In the Neolithic Period, mankind had become aware of minerals and and while working with minerals, stumbled upon and discovered native metals.

The next development in the application of pyrotechnology was the beginning of metallurgy. Mankind discovered native metal and subsequently learnt how to convert some specific ores into copper. Pyrotechnology helped the conversion of minerals into metals. The beginning of metal craft is known from the transition phase of the later Neolithic to the Chalcolithic phase. This transformation basically was underlined by the introduction of copper in a limited quantity (Singh 1999: 509-529). Mankind used newly discovered copper, and at the same time continued with the stone and bone artefacts. That period is known as the Chalcolithic.

Copper

The Chalcolithic culture implies both copper – 'chalco', and stone – 'lithic', being used simultaneously. The use of copper was established through the discovery of copper artefacts in the excavation at Senuwar, in a layer dated to 1950 BCE. Along with other artefacts, a crucible with copper slag clearly identified that copper smelting was carried out at the site itself (Singh 1999: 509-529). That is still the earliest evidence of copper and lead in eastern India. This has been reported from Senuwar IB (supported with a ^{14}C date, BS-755). The date 1950 BCE can be accepted as the beginning of metallurgy, as well as for the Chalcolithic culture in eastern India. The Period IIA of Chirand, where a single piece of a copper object was reported (Verma 2007:12), has been dated to 1600-1000 BCE.

Copper tools slowly replaced bone tools and microliths, even though a simultaneous occurrence of both continued to be noted in this part of the country. The appearance of copper rewrote the curse of human civilisation, to a great extent. The people not only learnt extraction of metal (mostly copper), but also the casting and forging of copper objects. They prepared small artefacts like, fishhook, bangles, needles and other simple metallic objects.

In this part of the subcontinent, in the present geographical context, a number of sites have been located where copper artefacts were uncovered. The examples of Chirand, Pandu Rajar Dhibi and a few other sites may be cited.

In the beginning of the Neolithic-Chalcolithic (transition from Neolithic to Chalcolithic) Period, copper was used in its pure native form. However, after a short period, evidence of alloying was noted. From Senuwar, one copper object (Sp. no. 323; analysed by R. N. Singh (Singh 2007: 67) indicated alloying with arsenic up to 1.422 percent. From Senuwar, Period II (Chalcolithic), 5.208 percent tin was reported in a bangle (Sp. no. 1656) (analysed by R. N. Singh, in Singh 1999: 593). The layer was dated 1210 ± 110 BCE (BS-915). From the same site Senuwar, a needle (Sp. no. 1112) indicated 15.162% tin. The specimen was collected from the NBPW Period, dated between seventh to sixth century BCE. The metal smiths had learnt that addition of tin and arsenic improved the strength of copper.

In this manner, the knowledge of alloying was gradually improved by constant effort at innovation, and also through trial and error in producing utility items. It is also likely that the knowledge of alloy was a chance discovery – the alloy was found to be the outcome of extraction using mixed ores. For example, the mixing of a small amount of tin ore – cassiterite – along with copper ore in the extraction process resulted in bronze alloy. That continuance of alloying proves that the artisans had acquired the knowledge and skill of alloying. This is an important development in technology.

From 300 BCE onwards, the use of additional amount of tin in copper alloys was noticed. This bronze with high amount of tin is called 'high tin-bronze', where tin increases from 15 to 30 in weight percentage. Alloying with tin meant that by increasing the tin contents, the artisans initially found useful changes in the properties of artefacts. However, this posed a problem in manufacturing. Later, they applied the technologies known as the 'thermo-mechanical treatment' (both forging and heat treatment together). This shall be discussed in a later chapter on copper.

In a vast area of north and peninsular India, hoards of copper implements have been found. All these implements are chance finds. These cannot be securely dated. In eastern India, a number of implements of different shapes, weighing even up to a few kilogrammes were identified. The size and weight of those artefacts often brings into question their suitability for everyday use. Some of the important sites are located in the Ranchi District, Jharkhand; Mayurbhanj District, Orissa and the West Medinipur District, West Bengal. The available hoards are interesting and pose many questions. These shall be dealt with in the relevant chapter.

Chalcolithic culture has some regional identities, which are primarily based on the typical kinds of ceramics used, like the Black-and-Red Ware (BRW). Archaeologists now prefer to rename the cultures in terms of ceramics. This is due to the fact that the presence of copper is very limited in the so-called Chalcolithic culture, and iron had appeared much earlier in the Chalcolithic period of eastern India. Archaeologists seem to avoid much reference to presence of metal, but are concerned about the quality and variations in design of the ceramic objects.

It is interesting to note that no copper weapon or copper agricultural implement of copper has been found in the eastern India in the Chalcolithic or BRW culture. The needle is the only craft tool made of copper in Mangalkot. Copper bangles and rings were popular in that period. The beginning of BRW in the eastern India was around 1000 BCE, and from 700 or 600 BCE, the ceramics changed to the Northern Black Polished Ware (NBPW). It is also interesting to note that there exists no archaeological evidence of the Chalcolithic or Iron Age culture in the northeastern region. Here, from the Neolithic Age to the appearance of iron, no coherent archaeological context has yet been confirmed. In eastern parts of Bangladesh, the lithic context was corroborated by stone artefacts. Metal appeared only in the NBPW context, for example, at Mahasthan.

Copper became of secondary importance after the appearance of iron. Throughout the ages, copper was used for coins of low value, utensils for religious use and in copper-based alloys.

Iron

Iron appeared in the Indian subcontinent in the later phase of the Chalcolithic culture, sometime around 1500 BCE. The earliest date for iron is from Uttar Pradesh, and the site is Raja Nal ka Tila. This site is not very far from the eastern India. It can be safely assumed that iron was introduced in eastern India some time in 1200 BCE. The well-developed iron objects were found from Hatikra dated to around 1000 BCE, from Bahiri also dated to around 1000 BCE. Perhaps the origin of iron in Chirand was in 1200 BCE, as a fragmentary piece of a heavily rusted iron blade was found from Period IIB (Verma 2007:12).

Manufacturing of iron and its impact on the society were quite evident from the iron implements. Iron in the beginning was similar to the wrought iron. It was mixed with slag, which the smiths could not get rid of completely. It was free from any carburisation. Carburisation is the addition of carbon to iron. Iron objects pick up carbon from the hearth during heating and forging. The smiths learnt this technique through hundreds of years of experience. The earliest example of carburisation has been detected in the knife of Hatikra in West Bengal, dating around *c.* 1000 BCE (Ghosh, Nag and Chattopadhyay 1987-88: 21-27). This object clearly indicates that carburisation was not accidental, because after forging, the finished product had to be heated in a furnace for further carburisation. The evidence of Widmanstatten pattern in the microstructure also supports this argument. Another important evidence of carburisation dated to *c.* 810 BCE is from Barudih of Jharkhand (Ghosh and Chattopadhyay 1982: 63-64). Use of quenching and tempering has been reported to be in practice since the third century BCE at Pandu Rajar Dhibi (De and Chattopadhyay 1989: 33-41). After a short period, a sudden development was noticed. This was due to the discovery of steel-making processes with deliberate addition of carbon to iron. This played a major role in large-scale deforestation in the middle and lower Gangetic plain in eastern India (Balasubramaniam 2007: 102-107). The technological developmentof the intentional addition of carbon to iron will be discussed in the relevant chapter. In the medieval period, development of arms and cannons were noticed. Eastern India has also contributed to the technology of wrought iron cannons. The appearance of cast iron will also be addressed briefly in the chapters related to iron.

Other Metals

Eastern India witnessed the use of gold and silver objects throughout the ages. Gold was traced mainly from the alluvial sands of Jharkhand and Assam provinces. Gold and silver ornaments have been unearthed in the excavated layers of early historic and early medieval periods. People used both ornaments and coins made of these two metals. There wil be further elaboration of this in the relevant chapters.

The people of eastern India also used minor metals like tin, zinc and lead. Amongst those elements, tin is available in Chhattisgarh, and the artisans possess the traditional knowledge of making it from its ores. These are scarce metals, and their provenance and mines in this part of the country, shal be discussed.

Often tin, zinc and lead were added to copper to make alloys. The specific information on alloying is reported from a needle from period III at Senuwar. The composition of this artefact (Accession No 1112) was analysed and it was found to contain as much as 15.162% tin (Sn), at NBPW levels. The bronze alloys were manufactured at the site itself. For example, at Tilpi (Southern Twenty four Pargana District, West Bengal), excavations revealed a furnace complex, where the direct evidence of bronze-making was established. Bronze mirrors were revealed in Chandraketugarh and Mahasthan along with utensils made of this alloy. The people of eastern India were not only satisfied with tools and tackles of his meal for their everyday use. However, they preferred to build the images of their Gods in this metal. All this will be discussed in the relevant chapters.

Brass bangles were found at late Chalcolithic to Early Historic period contexts in Senuwar and also at Kanjipani in Orissa. In the late medieval period, there was large-scale manufacturing of brass objects in Orissa, West Bengal and Assam. The subsequent beginning of metallic images was noticed in Early Historic period. All these will be dealt with in the relevant chapter.

THE SCHEME OF THE BOOK

The archaeometallurgy of eastern India and Bangladesh is a study divided into eleven chapters including the present one. Chapter 1 provides an overall introduction to the metal crafts of this region. The technological changes with the passage of time have been discussed in the historical context. The history of the region has been briefly highlighted in Chapter 2. Copper, one of the elements first known to the mankind, and its technology are dealt with in Chapter 3. This chapter also contains sections on the objects made of copper, including the copper hoards. Technologically, iron is an important material, which can lay its claim for having changed the fate of the world. Eastern India may take credit for the earliest carburisation and quenching processes. The role played by iron in the eastern India is described in the Chapter 4. Gold is available in the riverbeds of this part of the country. Gold technology, right from panning to manufacture of finished goods, like coins, has been discussed in the Chapter 5.

Since the time coins were issued, silver played an important role in the economy. Chapter 6 discusses the archaeometallurgical details of silver, with special reference to the foreign sources of silver, including the trade routes. Silver is the by product of lead ore, which some scholars consider as the first element isolated from its ore mineral. Chapter 7 has dealt with minor metals – lead, tin and zinc metallurgy. These metals are available in this part of the country. The artisans had identified usefulness of these metals in the Early Historic period.

Besides the elements discussed earlier, the artisans were also comfortable with making alloys of copper. In Chapter 8, we have discussed different alloys of copper, and the wide application of those alloys in casting images, brass cannons and for a few other metal crafts. Chapter 9 is the concluding chapter, wherein we have summarised the knowledge evolved and the further research required in this field.

2

HISTORICAL BACKGROUND OF ARCHAEOLOGICAL CULTURES IN EASTERN INDIA AND BANGLADESH

IN THIS CHAPTER, THE HISTORICAL BACKGROUND OF THE EASTERN India and Bangladesh is presented. It includes a discussion of the beginning of metal technology from the protohistoric period onwards. Metallurgy developed gradually with the need of the people, and the social support it derived from that need. Initally, the social history that determined the background for metallurgy will be delineated.

The protohistoric period is the gap between the Prehistoric and Early Historic ones. This gap comprises two well-developed phases of human culture, namely, the Chalcolithic Period and the Iron Age. In the first chapter, we have simply introduced the beginning of copper and iron metallurgy. From 1000 BCE onwards, we find an important culture in the western part of the eastern India. The Megalithic culture was related to the use of large size ('mega') stone ('lithic') monuments.

THE MEGALITHIC CULTURE

There are examples of this culture, which is evidenced to have begun around 1000 BCE, in Chhattisgarh. Some small quantities of copper and gold artefacts were also noted in an excavation at Karkabhat. The people in the regions of Chhattisgarh, Jharkhand and Orissa led a stable way of life depending on agriculture and hunting. The presence of the sickle and ploughshare is attestedto at Karkabhat in Chhattisgarh, indicating advancement in agriculture (Sharma 2000: 48-51). This advancement resulted in the discovery and mastery of manufacturing iron objects. The beginning of the Megalithic culture was older than that of the NBPW culture.

The Megalithic culture has also been reported from the northeastern part of the country. Remains of that culture, with the presence of megalithic monuments, were discovered in a number of places in Manipur and Nagaland. The ancient Kachari capital, Dimapur, is one of the important sites of this culture. The ruins at Dimapur appear to be contemporary to the Kachari civilisation, founded before the Ahom invasion in the CE 13th century. That culture continued until the pre-modern period. Archaeologists have also discovered iron objects in megalithic burials (Jamir 2006: 449-463).

BLACK-AND-RED-WARE CULTURE

The overall development in the Gangetic plains between 700-600 BCE has been much discussed by the historians. The ceramics have already been dealt with in Chaper 1. Iron was also developed first in this area. The impact of iron upon human settlement in this regon will be discussed in Chapter 4.

NORTHERN BLACK POLISHED WARE CULTURE IN THE WESTERN PART OF EASTERN INDIA

There has been earlier mention of the ceramics in the Gangetic plain. From Bihar to Bangladesh, the Northern Black Polished Ware (NBPW) Culture, flourished across the Gangetic Valley. Overall growth of this culture, including metallurgy, flourished in the eastern part of India. The inception of silver coins, gold ornaments, high tin-bronze artefacts and varieties of iron objects have been reported from this region. Iron agricultural tools had also developed considerably.

NORTHEAST INDIA

In the case of northeastern India, the context of metal is quite different. There is no evidence of Chalcolithic or early Iron Age cultures that can be equated with the NBPW culture has been found here. Metallurgy developed here at a much later period. Only in the Historic period, similar to that in the western part of India, evidence for metal craft was detected. Regarding the absence of a corresponding Chalcolithic or Iron Age, it is hoped that archaeologists will identify this gap. These Cultures have been identified in Bangladesh and neighbouring regions of Southeast Asia.

This region has seen a confluence of people from all directions, such as from the Indo-Aryan, Austro-Asiatic and Tibeto-Burman cultures. People from China, Thailand and other southeastern countries settled here. Thus, technology shifted here; apart from the local technology aready present. In Bangladesh, the absence of cultural continuation at one site, may be ascribed to the fact that people shifted to new places on account of natural disasters/heavy rains and other reasons. Therefore, the archaeological records are not very definite.

EARLY HISTORIC CULTURE IN EASTERN INDIA

In Bihar and West Bengal, around 600 BCE, cultures with the sophisticated NBPW ware flourished. Several types of iron objects were noticed. Coin manufacturing, bead-making, ivory-carving and crafting of excellent bronze objects were carried out by the people for their use. Forest clearance and dressing of stones required well developed craft tools, like axes and chisels. The people achieved this through the knowledge and skills of carburised iron making.

The historical account of Assam begins with the establishment of the kingdom of Kamarup by Pushya Varman of the Varman dynasty in the CE fourth century. This dynasty was most likely of aboriginal origin, but drew its lineage from Narakasur. The kingdom reached its zenith under Bhaskarvarman in the CE seventh century. From significant Chinese sources, it is learnt that Xuanzang (Yuan Chwang) visited the court of Bhaskarvarman (Watters 1996, II:186). After the Varmans, the kingdom was passed on to Salasthamba, who established the Mlechchha dynasty.

Assam is the only state in India, which defeated 17 successive attempts of the Sultanate and the Mughal rulers of Delhi, except for a single defeat in CE 1662, at the hands of Mir Jumla, the Mughal Viceroy of Dhaka. In that battle, Mir Jumla advanced up to the Brahmaputra River in Assam. There was widespread dissent among the Ahoms, and they could not have put up any worthwhile resistance. The Ahom capital at Gargaon was left to the invader and King Jayadhvaja Simha fled to the hills.

SOURCE OF METAL OBJECTS

Throughout the ages, people of the eastern part of the subcontinent procured metals from local sources, and also through external trade. Most of the ancient mines are defunct now. Silver is obtained from silver-bearing lead ore-argentiferous galena.

In the five maps given in this chapter, the state-wise distribution of copper, gold, iron, lead and tin and the important archaeological sites have been indicated. The map (Figure 2.1) shows the northeastern region including the states of Assam, Arunachal Pradesh, Manipur, Meghalaya, Mizoram, Nagaland and Tripura. The map (Figure 2.2)

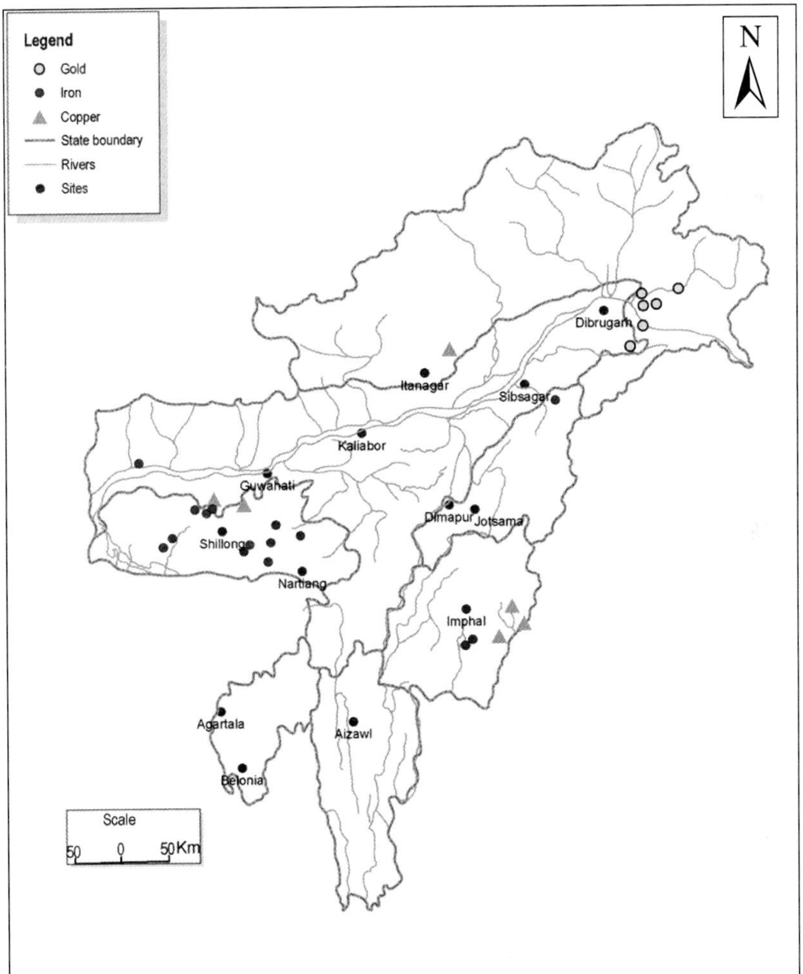

Fig. 2.1: *Map of Northeast India showing the location of ore-minerals and some important sites*

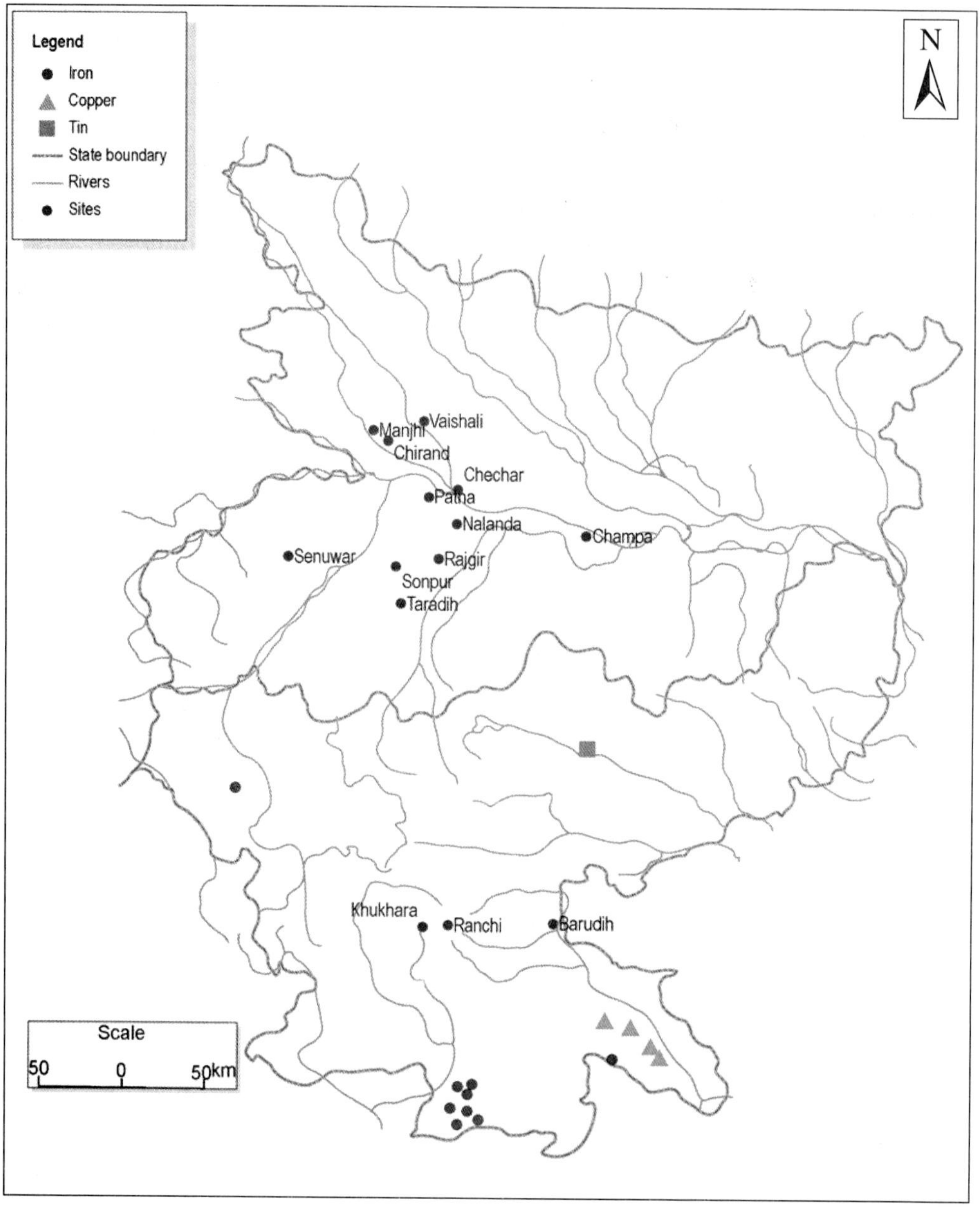

Fig. 2.2: *Map of Bihar and Jharkhand showing location of ore-minerals and some important sites*

shows Bihar and Jharkhand. Orissa is shown in the map in Figure 2.3. The map of West Bengal is shown in Figure 2.4, and in Figure 2.5, that of Bangladesh.

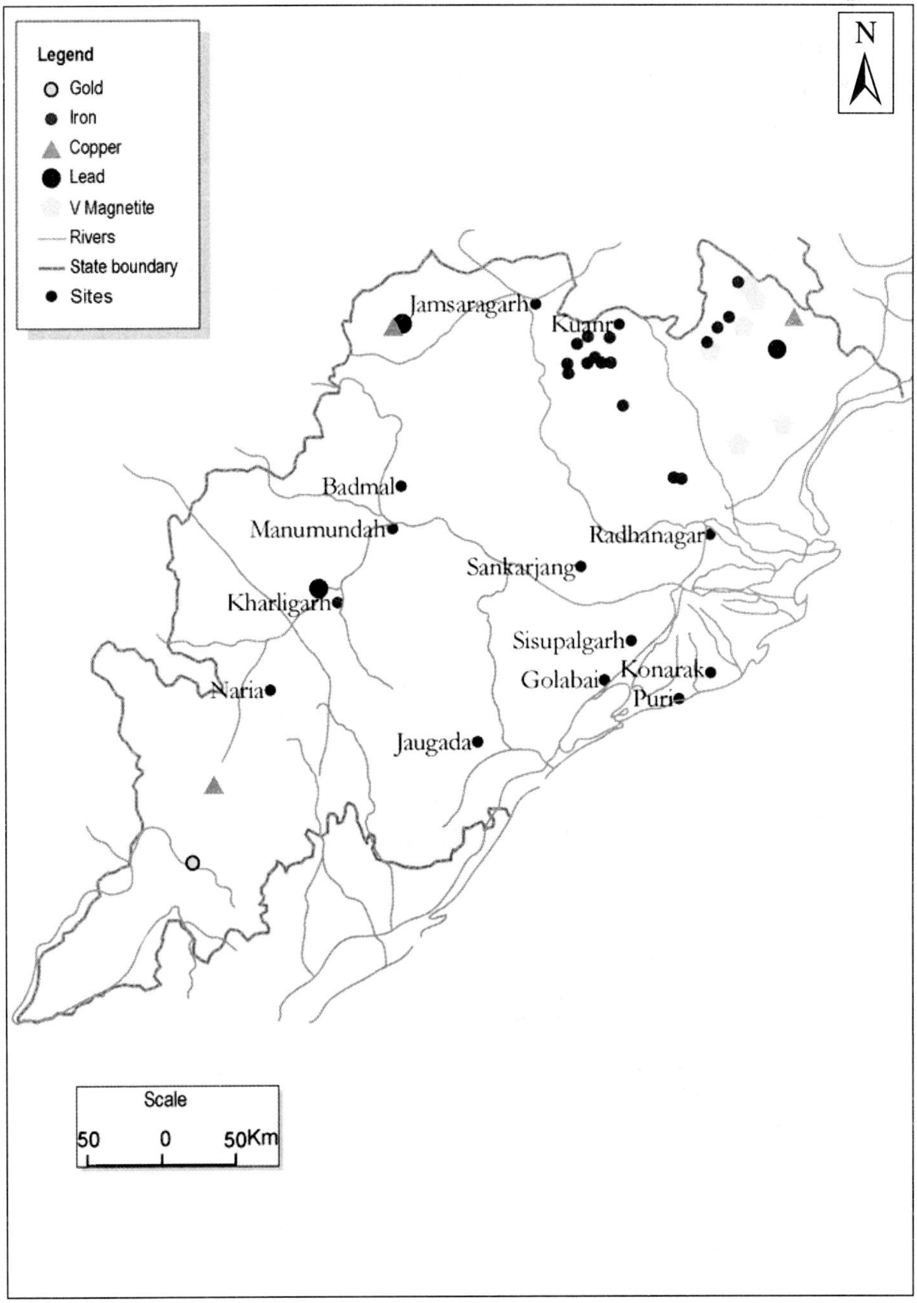

Fig. 2.3: *Map of Orissa showing the location of ore-minerals and some important sites*

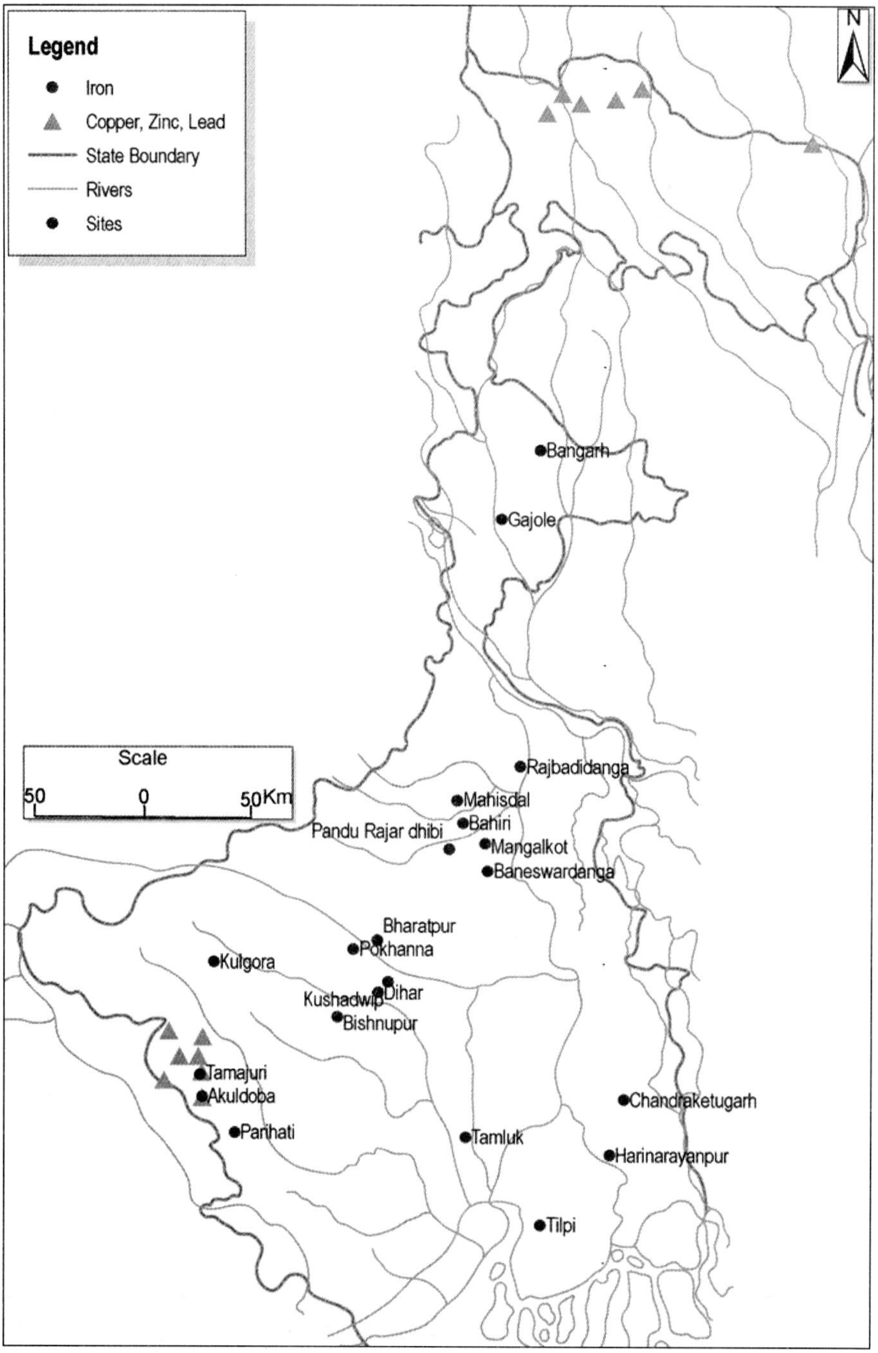

Fig. 2.4: *Map of West Bengal showing location of ore-minerals and some important sites*

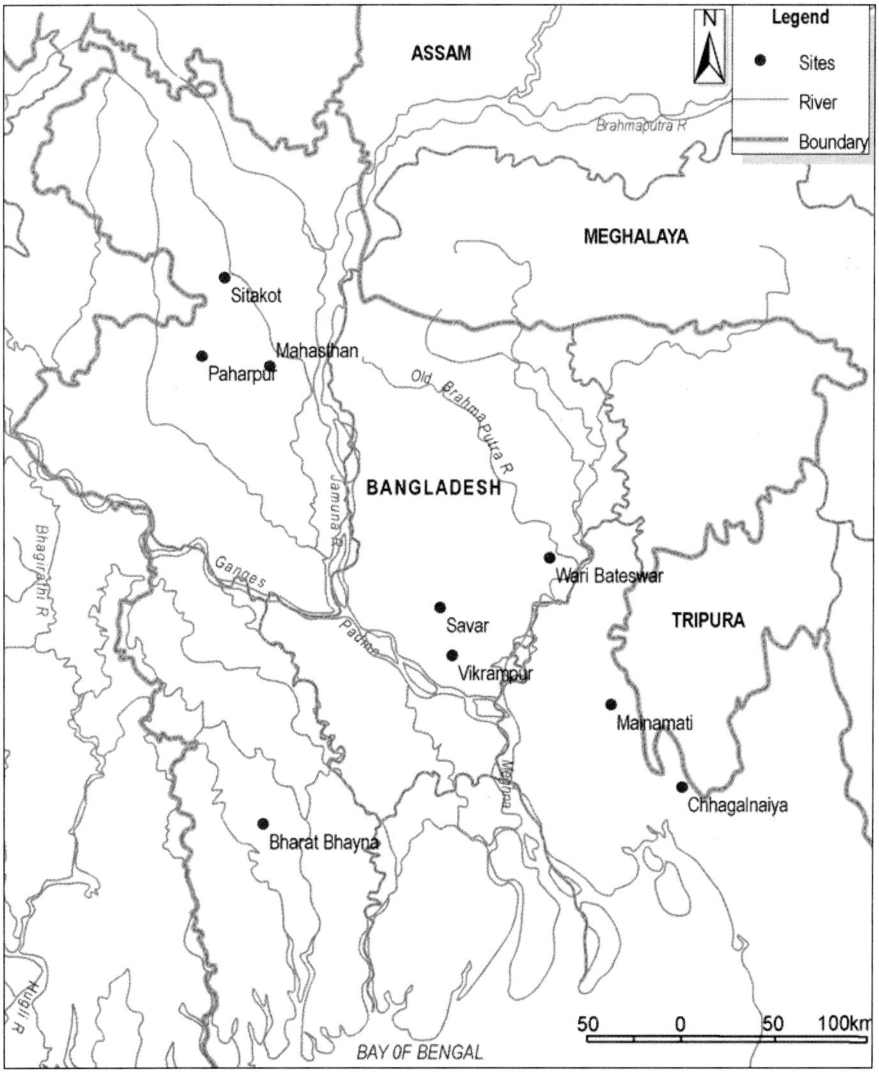

Fig. 2.5: *Map of Bangladesh showing location of ore-minerals and some important sites*

The Trade of Metal Objects

Traders were mostly responsible for the development of metallurgy. They not only supplied raw materials, but also helped sell the manufacturer's products. The trading of metal objects, which began in the early historic period and continued thereafter, was quite prevalent in the eastern India. Some remarkable studies were made by Gupta

(1991: 280-299) on metal trade. The region of Southeast Asia faced political changes from the late Chalcolithic period. The introduction of iron took place in the first millennium BCE in the Menam Valley of Vietnam.

The beginning of iron in the eastern India and this part of the subcontinent were contemporary. From the records, one can find the name *Subarnabhumi* for the Malay Peninsula and *Suvarnadwipa* for Sumatra. The western scholars quotted Ptolemy who used the term *Argyre* (the silver land) for Myanmar, and *Chryse* (the gold land) for Malay (Singer 2008: 3-7).

From around the second century BCE, eastern India was well connected with China, including Yunnan (southern China), Burma (present Myanmar), Arakan, Vietnam, Laos, Malaysia, Sumatra and Thailand. Regular trade links between Southeast Asia and India were established from the second century BCE to the sixth century CE. The earliest Chinese record, *Hansu* or the history of Han dynasty written by Ban Gu (CE 32-92) refers to the trade between China and India at the time of Emperor Wudi (CE 140-87), through the southeast Asian route (Ray 1999: 8). The voyage from China to Andhra via Vietnam and Myanmar was also known. It is also known that the king of Funam (South Vietnam) sent an ambassador to India in CE 243.

Besides sea trade, land trade also flourished between Yunnan and India through the Bhamo route. Amongst the items of trade; pearls, jade, silver, copper, silk and gold were common. Similar reference had also been cited by Bagchi (1951:17) describing the Assam-Burma route to China. This route began from Pataliputra, and subsequently moved through Pundrabardhan and Kamarup. In that route, there existed the most important post, Bhamo (24° 16' N, 97° 17' E) that was the junction of four significant routes. Those were, (1) from the Brahmaputra-Patkoi range to upper Myanmar, (2) through Manipur to Chindwin Valley, and (3) through Arakan up to the Irrawaddy Valley, and (4) Bhamo; this was further connected to Yunnan, the main city of southern province of China. The importance of Bhamo continued until the beginning of British rule, as recorded by John M'Cosh (Chakrabarti and Lahiri 1986: 123-134).

From the inscriptions and coins, it appears that the agricultural economy flourished, and farming communities had segregated into villages. In that period, there was a multi-layered composition in society. Commercial networks were established between the rural hinterland and the urban nodes, especially where geographical parameters favoured such development. The network of rivers in the lower Ganga plain was utilised for communications, as is evident from the settlement pattern. That was quite evident especially in the Radha and lower delta sub-regions. The rise in the number of sites, especially in the last two regions mentioned, in the Sunga-Kushan context and thereafter may be taken to indicate the growth-supporting links in the network of economy. The evidence points to the parallel development of farming and trade. The early initiation of metal technology and its growth into a regular utility craft is concurrent with this paradigm of the history of this region (Dasgupta and Chattopadhyay 2009:78-85).

Amongst all the metals traded, silver had the greatest demand in the internal market. India's internal production of silver was rather meagre. From other regions, traders brought silver to eastern India.

3

COPPER

THE INVENTION OF COPPER TECHNOLOGY THROUGHLY CHANGED THE face of human civilisation. Copper is one of the earliest elements to be discovered by man. The introduction of copper in eastern India took place in the later phase of Neolithic period. The discovery of copper along with stone implements in an archaeological context is defined as the chalcolithic culture.

In the Neolithic-Chalcolithic period, copper was used in its pure or native form. When it is mixed with tin, it forms an alloy, namely, bronze. When it is added to zinc, it forms another alloy, that is, brass. No alloying element was detected in copper objects from Senuwar in the beginning. In the later Chalcolithic phase, tin as the alloying element was noticed. In the earlier stages, tin was used less, around 5% to 10%, whereas in the Early Historic period, people added more tin to copper and discovered the high tin-bronze alloy, which is golden in colour. In this chapter, reference is made throughout to pure copper and that mixed with 10% tin as alloying element.

In the beginning of the Neolithic-Chalcolithic (transition from the neolithic to chalcolithic) period, copper was used in its native form. However, after a short period, the evidence of alloying was noted. It is also likely that the knowledge of alloy was an accident; the outcome of extraction, using mixed ores. For example, the mixing of a small amount of tin ore – cassiterite – along with copper ore in the extraction process probably helped the discovery of bronze alloy. Again, mixing of a small amount of zinc ore – sphalerite – along with copper ore in the extraction process resulted in brass alloy. Thet continuation of alloying demonstrates knowledge and skill of alloying that has been discussed in Chapter 8.

SOURCES OF COPPER

The beginning of copper metallurgy depends on the availability of copper ore-minerals. Copper exists in nature in three forms, as (1) pure copper, (2) oxide-hydroxide-carbonates, and (3) in the sulphide state. The common minerals are native copper [Cu] in thr first group; in the second group are included the cuprite [Cu_2O], malachite [$CuCO_3.Cu(OH)_2$] and azurite [$2CuCO_3.Cu(OH)_2$]. In the third group, chalcopyrite [$CuFeS_2$] and chalcocite [Cu_2S] are included. Often these minerals are found mixed with other minerals.

A major source of copper is known from the Singhbhum and other, neighbouring districts of Chotanagpur in the Jharkhand copper belt. These ores are found in chlorite rocks. This belt is around 128 km long, and is an over-thrust in the Dharwar schists and intrusive granite. A number of ancient copper mines of Bihar, Jharkhand, Orissa and West Bengal are well known from the exploration of GSI. The problem with these ancient mines and old workings is that they are not dated. Unfortunately, no radiocarbon or thermoluminiscence date is available for these ancient mines of eastern India. Hence, it is not possible to determine the period of their operation. The recovery of Puri-Kushan coins from the Rakha mines indicates that mining was carried out even before the second century CE.

The *Arthshastra* refers to state control over the mines during the Mauryan period. The presence of precious stone beads in the early mining regions of Singhbhum and adjoining areas, strengthens the view regarding mining activities in the Early Historic period (Murray 1940: 79-104.).

The mines with remnants of ancient copper mining have been re-explored by the European scholars and geologists of Geological Survey of India (Mallet 1874: 23-44; Ball 1880: 168; Chakrabarti 1979: 61-74; 1986: 65-72; 1988: 239-244; Chakrabarti *et al.* 1983: 121-163; Dunn 1937:37-141). For example, from the Singhbhum District alone, here is a long alphabetic list of the ancient mines. This belt has mines, where remains of old shafts, furnace remains, heaps of slag and other objects are found representing past mining practices and smelting activities.

The old mining sites of the east and west Singhbhum districts are recorded as: Astakoale (22° 25' N, 85° 29' E,), Chapri (22° 37' N, 86° 24' E), Charakmara (22° 17' N, 86° 41' E), Dhobani (22° 17' N, 86° 26' 30" E), Duarpuram (22° 46' N, 85° 34'E), Dugni (22° 46' N, 85° 58'E), Galudih (22° 47'N, 85° 44'E), Jaypur (22° 45'N, 85°

30'E), Kendadih (22° 36' N, 86° 25' 30" E), Lankesera (22° 33'N,86° 27' E), Mosaboni (22° 31' N, 86° 28' E), Purnapani (22° 34' N, 86° 26' E), Rajadih (22° 41' N, 86° 17'E), Rakhamines (22° 38' N, 86° 22' 30" E), Ramchandrapahar (22° 43' N, 86° 12' 30" E), Ruam (22° 57' N, 86° 24' E), Sidheswar (22° 37' N, 86° 24' N), Sini (22° 47'N, 85° 57'E), Surda (22° 33'N, 86° 26'E) and Tama Dungri (22° 45' N, 86° 2' E). The ancient mine at Kendadih has been revisited by Upadhyay (Figure 3.1).

Copper ore-minerals, like chalcopyrite, chalcocite and native copper are known in the Singhbhum District. The Rakha mines have yielded old copper workings, down to 50 m and extension of upto 122 m. Plenty of old workings in chloritic schist are reported at Ramchandra Pahar. At Sidheswar and Ruam, old copper-smelting remains were reported. From Mosaboni and its surroundings, ancient mines are the largest ones, with depths up to 18 m. Old rotten timbers from the mine shaft have been reported by Dunn (1937:55).

Fig. 3.1: *Ancient Mine Shaft near Kendadih, Singhbum (Photograph courtesy: Prabhakar Upadhyay)*

The surrounding districts also indicate ancient mining. From Charkipahari and Tulsitanr of the Santhal paraganas of Jharkhand, old workings and mine dumps are reported. From Baraganda (22° 43' N, 86°12' 30" E) of Hazaribagh, similar observations were noted. At Kulianpur and Rajdoha (22° 41' N, 86°17'E) of Singhbhum area, old copper mines, furnace, dwellings and slag were reported (Ball 1880: 106, 125). Ancient shafts of copper mines are known from Chapri, Sidheswar and a few other mines of the erstwhile Singhbhum District.

In West Bengal, the known occurrences of copper, lead and zinc ores are, in fact, part of the long copper belt shear zone. These zones can be traced towards the western portion of the state. Concentrations of copper are noted in the regions of Jharkhand, Orissa and West Bengal. The first one from the 'shear zone' rock formation shows mica schist, quartzite, granite and basalt with copper mineralisation. The second one is located in Bankura and Purulia regions, where copper mineralisation is noticed in quartzite, granite and mica schist. From Bankura, the sites noted are Chhedapathar (22°15' N, 86°45' E) and Tamakhum (22°53' N, 86°45' E). From Purulia only few sites are known: Beldie (23° 03' N, 86° 18' E), Biramdih (22° 05'N, 86° 12' E), Kantagora (22° 58' N, 86° 42' E), Punda (22° 59' N, 86° 40' E), Chirugora (22° 55' N, 86° 36' E) and Tamakhun (22° 59' N, 86° 36'E). From Medinipur, one ancient mine is known at Gohalbaria (22° 39' N, 86° 43' E). Copper was also known in small pockets from Darjeeling and Buxa of the Jalpaiguri District. Buxa is an extension of the copper belt in Sikkim. Ball (1881: 276) had pointed out the pre-industrial mining tradition at Buxa. Copper mines are also known in Orissa at a few sites in the Sambalpur District, Sargipalli of the Sundargarh District and Kusumbari and Kesarpur of the Mayurbhanj District. Being close to Singhbhum, a portion of the Mayurbhanj District lies on the extension of the copper belt.

There is information on the sources of copper from northeastern states. From the state of Sikkim, use of copper is known at Rangpo, Dikchu and Chikung. It is interesting to note that *Rasaratna Samuchchyay* (Vol. 44, as quoted by Neogi 1979: 61) refers to the occurrences of copper in the Nepal as also in the Himalayas in Sikkim. Copper is also known at Pancharatna, Goalpara District, Borjurid-Karbi Anglong District of Assam; Pange, Subansiri District, and Buragaon and a few other localities of the Kameng District of Arunachal Pradesh. From Manipur, copper ore is available near Ukhrul, which is being exploited since centuries. Some of the other places are Nungau, Kongal Thana and Sadangchina hill areas. Other extinct mines are reported from Sikkim by (Bose 1928: 66-72). The most important one was Pachikhani: the composition of the ore is reported to be 20.31% copper. The other mines were Rathokhani, Rhenock, Barmiak, Lingui, Ronglichu, Lindok, Bhotang, amonst others.

THE PROCESS OF COPPER EXTRACTION

In eastern India, it is known that chalcopyrite ores were mixed with cow-dung, clay and wood charcoal in a cylindrical crucible furnace to be processed. It was a three-step process (Datta and Chattopadhyay 2007: 39-55).

(1) Air was blown from the top through tuyeres, and a slag-notch was attached a the bottom to take out the slag produced. During the initial roasting with air iron sulphide in the ore was oxidised to iron oxide, the gangue was remove as the iron sulphide (FeS) at moderate temperature, and carbon an hydrocarbons were oxidised to carbon monoxide or carbon dioxide for generation of heat.

(2) In the second step, the role of silica sand (SiO_2) was important. Here an excess supply of silica separated the gangue component (iron) in the form of an immiscible light liquid slag phase from the fluid heavy metal phase of copper at the smelting temperature of around 1200° C (Biswas and Davenport 1976: 87). The application of alumina (in clay) and lime further stabilised the isolation of slag from the metal phase in two separate zones (like oil-water separation). Having separated fully, the slag floats over the liquid metal phase. The presence of silica caused them to separate into two immiscible liquid phases—a real invention of eastern copper workers, without knowledge of modern chemistry. The amount of silica as a flux is also significant—the amount should be at least 40-42%; it may be higher due to the presence of lime (CaO).

(3) The removal of slag through the slag-notch is the third step. Copper-rich (~80% copper), known as 'white metal', is collected below, and it is converted to blister copper by oxidation, avoiding contamination. The blow holes in copper lumps indicate the presence of entrapped gas during casting in the mould. In Israel, no slag-notch was used in the crucibles; the total slag and metal prills were allowed to solidify in the cavity (Rothenberg 1978: 21). The metal was then separated from the brittle slag by stone hammering.

COPPER MANUFACTURING IN SIKKIM

The observations on copper making procees in the other areas of eastern India will be examined now. The European administrators did mention it in their reports. For example,

Blanford studied the process of copper making. Percy also recorded copper manufacturing (Neogi 1979:71) in Sikkim. These descriptions are available; from the mineral dressing to copper production stages. Usually, women crushed and washed copper ore. Washing of the ore was done on small tiles, made up of six pieces of thirty cm planks fixed on edge in the ground. The women workers, who were engaged there, poured water with one hand, and washed the crushed ore with the other. The mineral used by the smelters of Sikkim was chalcopyrite mixed with quartz and hornblende along with gangue materials.

Chakraborty and Lahiri mention that Percy had observed (Chakraborty and Lahiri 1996:163) that the smelting furnaces were made of sandy clay. These were about 60 cm in depth (below the ground), and consisted of a back wall of around 45 cm height (above the ground) in the form of a truncated pyramid. The design was made in such a way that the slag was expelled in the process. The operators removed the slag from the furnace by using pincers. The front wall was around 30 cm above the furnace-bed and 15 cm above the earthen platform. The bellows, made of goatskin, were placed over this earthen platform and connected with the furnace through a nozzle or tuyère. Charcoal was used in the furnace as fuel. The report includes the process of copper manufacturing in stages. At the first stage, a few handfuls of washed and dried ore mixed with charcoal were tossed into the heated furnace.

Regarding the smelting practice in 'Sikhim' (Bose 1928: 57-73), it is known that the crushed charcoal and air was blown in alternatively with two bellows until a sufficient amount of regulus (unrefined metal) collected at the bottom of furnace, covered by the lighter slag. After raking the charcoal, the surface of the slag was cooled with whips of wet straw. Solidified cakes of slag were removed and the fluid regulus was subsequently cooled and extracted. The regulus was then pounded, mixed with equal amount of cow dung and made into balls.

After drying, those balls were spread over a layer of charcoal inside the open furnace. Those were then roasted with free access of air into the furnace. The roasted balls were then broken up on the ground and the powder sprinkled into the furnace. Thus, the copper ingots were produced by the inhabitants. The miners of Sikkim belong to the *Mangar* caste. In CE 1891, mining was performed during October to June, in which men, women and children were engaged. The miners worked in gangs. The distribution of the product was so done that one part went to the smelter (*kami*) and four parts to the miner. The whole product was sold to the *taksari*, who had the lease of mines.

ARCHEOLOGICAL EVIDENCE OF COPPER

The period from 2000 to 1300 BCE

The period between 2000 to 1300 BCE is identified as the Neolithic-Chalcolithic. Prior to the use of copper, major implements were made of bone and stone. Copper tools slowly replaced those, even though a simultaneous occurrence of both continued in this part of the country. The first use of metal is recorded from a few sites of Bihar, Orissa and West Bengal in the neolithic-chalcolithic context. Senuwar (24° 56' N, 83° 56' E) is the most important site, others are Chirand (22° 45' N, 84° 50' E), Pandu Rajar Dhibi (23° 35' N, 87° 39' E) and Golabai Sasan (20° 01' N, 83° 33' E). The earliest evidence of copper in this part of the subcontinent is known from Senuwar. That is supported by two C^{14} dates of 1770±120 BCE and 1500±110 BCE. It has been inferred that the copper smiths of Senuwar had definitely started smelting copper ores from 1950 BCE. The objects recovered are points or piercers, fishhook, wire, rod and nail. The earliest ornaments are bangles, made of copper wires and finished by light hammering. During that period, no metal object was detected in Bangladesh and other northeastern states.

However, the copper objects found at Senuwar are very few in number. The objects were mostly small pieces of wire, used as fishhooks or fine needles. The copper objects discovered in Period IB of Senuwar are point, fishhook, bangles, nail, wire, rod, and so on (Singh, B.P. 2004: 386-404). Some of the copper objects from that site of Period IA, IB and II are shown in Figure 3.2. One intact needle and intact nails were recovered from here. This indicates that both copper and lead smelting was carried out earlier in this part of the country. It has not been ascertained as to whether native copper was utilised to make the artefacts However, one may infer the probable use of malachite ore, which was available in the top layer of the copper mines.

In Orissa, the most important site is Golabai Sasan. This site is situated in the lateritic zone, on the left bank of River Mandakini (a tributary of Rive Daya), which flows into the Chilika Lake in the Khurda District. Excavations at this site were carried out by the Archaeological Survey of India (ASI) in 1991-92 and 1992-93 (Sinha 1992-93: 48-50; 2000: 322-348).

The excavation has revealed the Neolithic (Period I), then the osteo-Chalcolithic phase (Period IIA), ferro-Chalcolithic (Period IIB) and finally the early Iron Age (Period III). The earliest evidence of the copper fishhook, datable to C^{14} date of 2100 $\pm$ 100

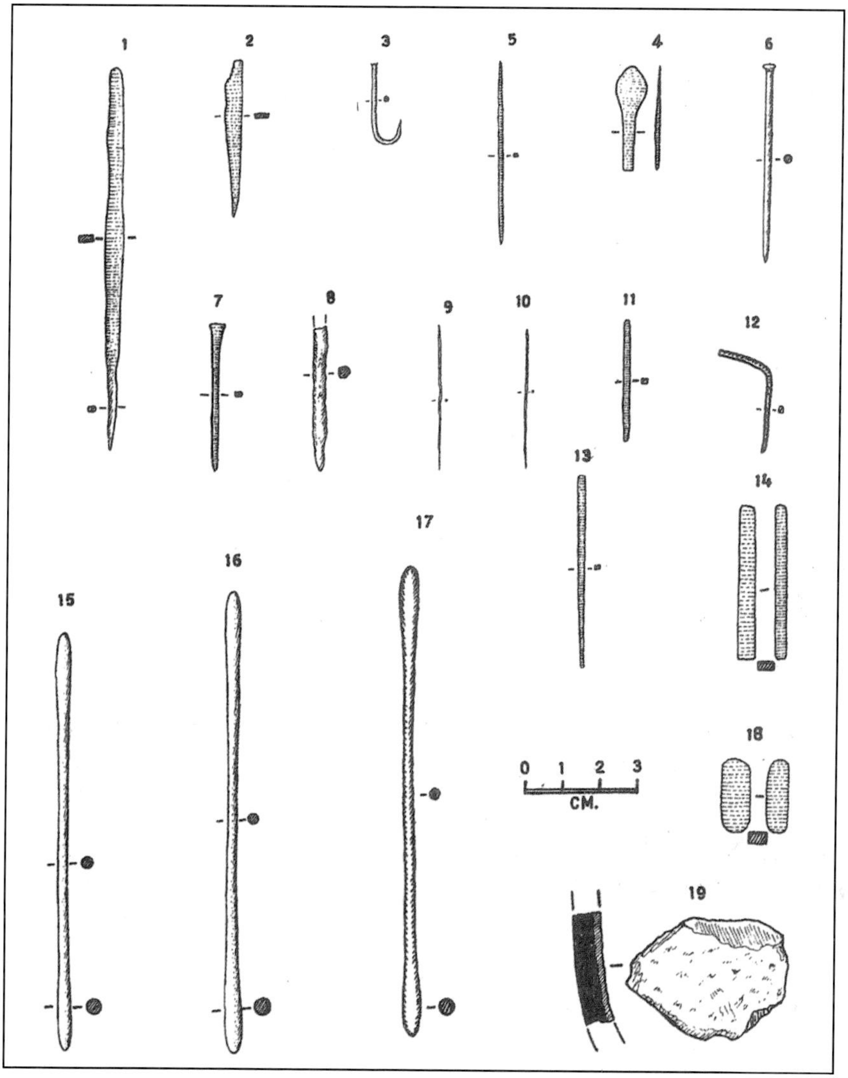

Fig. 3.2: *Copper objects of Senuwar. No 19 indicates a fragment of crucible with copper incrustation (Courtesy: Birendra Pratap Singh)*

BCE (PRL 1637) was obtained from this site. A furnace, along with a good number of long, narrow, tubular and round-bottomed crucibles, clearly identified it as a copper smelting site. The copper objects included rings, bangles, a chisel and fishhook. All these are shown in Table 3.1.

Table 3.1: Copper objects: 2000 to 1300 BCE

Place	Site	Bangle	Point	Fishhook	Wire	Ring	Crucible
Bihar	Chirand	XXX	XXX	XXX	XXX		
	Senuwar	XXX	XXX	XXX	XXX	XXX	XXX
Orissa	Golabai Sasan	XXX		XXX	XXX	XXX	XXX
West Bengal	Pandu Rajar Dhibi	XXX	XXX	XXX			

The period from 1300 to 600 BCE

The period under reference is called the Chalcolithic Period. The majority of archaeologists accept it now as the BRW culture, which is contemporary to the Chalcolithic one. This culture occurs with the Chalcolithic from the previous mentioned sites in Bihar, Orissa and West Bengal.

The first evidence of Chalcolithic sites in Orissa are recorded from Golabai Sasan, Manamunda, Bhagrapir and Khiching (possibly Chalcolithic). Sankerjang, on the other hand, was established to be a Late Neolithic or the early Chalcolithic burial site. The site of Khameswaripali (20° 46' N, 83° 50' E) Period II had the presence of copper. The excavation of 2007 yielded two ^{14}C dates. For Period IA, the date obtained is 1555 ± 60 Cal. BCE (Lab. No. IP-273) and from upper level of Period IB, it is 1065 ± 66 Cal. BCE (Lab. No. IP-307).

Golabai Sasan, Period II (1100-900 BCE), revealed the bone, stone and copper tools in association with a rich pottery industry. From the excavations at this site, a large number of pottery objects were recovered, which the excavator identified as crucibles for smelting copper (Sinha 1992-93: 48-50). An extended burial was also found, which yielded skeletal remains of a young woman, whose right wrist had a copper bangle. The other objects found in that burial were a chisel, few rings and a fishhook, all made of copper. No earlier historic phase associated with the metal objects has yet been discovered in Assam, Arunachal Pradesh or Nagaland.

To be precise, the Senuwar site is contemporary to the Harappan or late-Harappan sites. There is no doubt that trace elements found in the copper artefacts clearly indicate that their origin was neither Harappan nor made from copper ore obtained from the Aravalli of Rajasthan (Chattopadhyay and Singh 1998). On the other hand, trace elements detected in the specimens had closer similarities with that of Singhbhum copper mines. The process adopted to manufacture copper objects indicates use of casting, cold working and annealing.

A similar situation was noticed at the site of Chirand in Bihar. The Period IA of that site has been identified as metal-free, whereas period IB (2300-1600 BCE) indicated the presence of some copper objects, including points, fishhooks, rods and bangles (Verma 2007:17). That phase was marked as the Neolithic-Chalcolithic one. The Neolithic habitation at Chirand developed earlier and continued up to the middle of the third millennium BCE. No Neolithic phase has been detected at Sonpur (24° 56' 29" N, 84° 50' E) in Bihar, except a solitary piece of copper discovered in sub-period IB. However, not a single piece of metal/metallic object was found from the pre-Chalcolithic phase, namely, Period I at Maner (25° 38' N, 84° 52' E) in Bihar. On the other hand, it is interesting to note that in the Chalcolithic phase, Period II, Maner, a terracotta model of a double-axe type copper hoard was recovered. The important copper objects of that period include a fishhook, three arrowheads and three bangles. Regular metal objects were found from the NBPW phase. There are a few more sites in Bihar, in which the initial period was identified as a metal-free Neolithic one. Metal was traced there in the upper strata. The other important sites of Bihar, include Taradih (24° 42' N, 85° 0' E) and Chechar-Kutubpur in Vaisali District. In the period IB of Taradih, was first observed the presence of metal with a few fishhooks made of copper. In Period II of Taradih, copper was used for arrowheads and fishhooks.

An important site was found at Sankerjang (20° 52' N, 84° 59' E) of Orissa. Copper-bronze age of Sankerjang gives the first C^{14} date as 795 BCE (KN 3755). That and the surroundings sites yielded ring like copper hoards and ground tools, copper bangles from a number of group burials (Yule and Rath 2000: 285-321). Twenty two bangles were excavated from this site are preserved now in the Orissa State Museum, Bhubaneswar (Figure 3.3). The external diameter of those bangles ranges from 5.40 to 7.20 cm, and weigh between nine to 24 gm. Nail-parers and small copper rods have also been found. From Chandrasagar Nala, copper bangles were discovered (Figure 3.4).

From West Bengal, a number of pre-Chalcolithic sites were identified, for example, Baneswardanga Period I (23° 24' N, 87° 50' E) and Pandu Rajar Dhibi Period I (23° 35' N, 87° 39' E). Some of those specimens are preserved now in the State Archaeological Museum, West Bengal in Kolkata. None of the sites of that stage yielded any metal object. Metal was found in the subsequent Chalcolithic phase, that is, in Period II of those two sites. Pakhanna (23° 24'45"N, 87° 22'40"E), a Chalcolithic settlement at Bhairabdanga near Pakhanna yielded bangles and rings (IAR 1996-1997: 178).

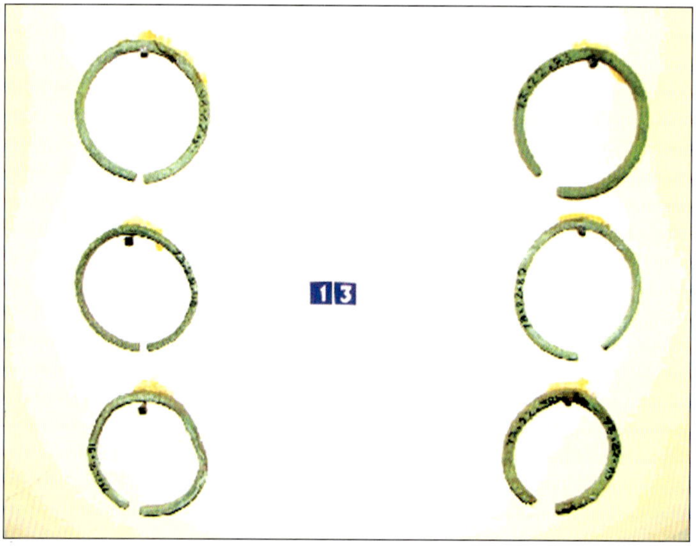

Fig. 3.3: *Bangles from Sankerjang (Courtesy: The Orissa State Museum)*

Fig. 3.4: *Bangles from Chandrasagarnala, Orissa (Courtesy: Baba Mishra)*

MANUFACTURING TECHNIQUE OF CHALCOLITHIC COPPER OBJECTS

The copper objects of the Chalcolithic period recovered from Bihar and West Bengal are points or piercers, fishhooks, wires, rods and nails. The earliest ornaments are bangles, made of copper wires and finished by light hammering. At the beginning of the Neolithic phase, copper was used in the native form, as in Senuwar. From this site, one copper object (specimen number 323) was analysed by R. N. Singh (Singh 2007: 62-74: Singh, B.P. 2004: 591-603), which indicated alloying with arsenic, of about 1.422%. In Period II – Chalcolithic at Senuwar, a copper bangle (Sp. No. 1656) indicated 5.208% of tin (analysed by R. N. Singh, Singh 1999: 593), dated 1210 ± 110 BCE (BS-915). At the same site, Senuwar (Sp. No. 1112), a needle was found with 15.162% tin in it. The specimen was recovered from the NBPW period of the seventh-sixth century BCE. The metal smiths learnt that the addition of other elements improved the strength of copper. In this manner, the knowledge of alloying might have been obtained.

In the subsequent Chalcolithic phase at Taradih, alloying of tin is evidenced, which is suggestive of significant technological development in metallurgy. Three specimens from Chirand indicated the use of pure copper. The use of casting is noted only from the beginning of the Chalcolithic period.

Specific metallurgical techniques of the Chalcolithic phase have mainly been known through the study and analysis of the remains of metal, slag and furnaces. Unfortunately, very little is known about the exact techniques used at that time. Even the analysis from other Chalcolithic sites, such as Bahiri (Period I), Pandu Rajar Dhibi (Period II), Mangalkot (Period II), Dihar (also used as Dihor) (Period I), Senuwar (Period II) and Sonpur (Periods IA, IB and II) clearly indicate that copper-based objects of these sites were made of low-tin bronze. The smiths of Senuwar were well acquainted with the technique of casting, cold working and annealing. A potsherd, perhaps a crucible or mould, recovered from Period II of Senuwar has a three mm thick copper cage (Singh 2004: 392). The potsherd has been shown in Figure 3.2, in sketch no. 19. Undoubtedly, it was connected with the melting operations.

A fragmentary crucible was discovered at Panda (or Panr) with thick incrustations of copper salts. The bottom of this crucible is oval, unlike the conical one from Senuwar. The crucible fragment obtained from Panda is 11 mm in thickness and the inside diameter of the same is 42 mm (Figure 3.5).

Very scanty information on the metallography of copper-bronze objects in West Bengal is available (Chattopadhyay 2004: 63-68). Some of it is discussed here.

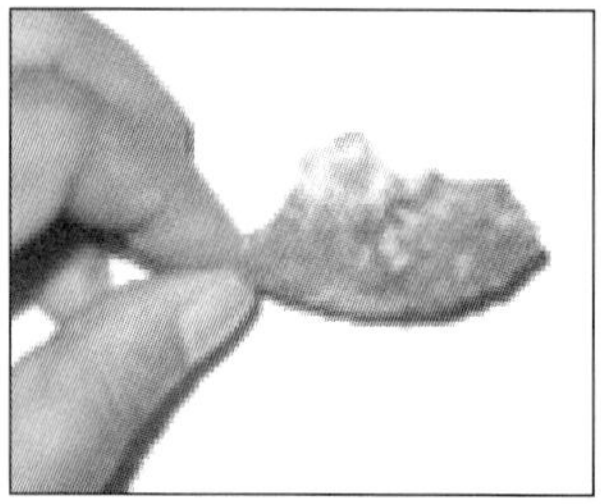

Fig. 3.5: *Fragmentary crucible, Panr (Courtesy: Bijoy Kumar Chowdhary)*

There are copper objects from the Chalcolithic period from Pandu Rajar Dhibi (Figure 3.6). It is now equated with the BRW culture. Only one specimen, an earring with a thick layer of greenish patina, from this site was analysed. Metallography revealed that the object was fully covered with inter-granular corrosion. The chemical analyses revealed it to be a bronze object with 10% tin, 0.50% lead, 0.10% bismuth; 0.10% silver; iron and arsenic are around 0.005%. A bronze fish with a three-pronged tail, with about 95.50% of copper identified as prehistoric *coelacanth* species *latemaria* was reported (Biswas *et el.* 1996: 173).

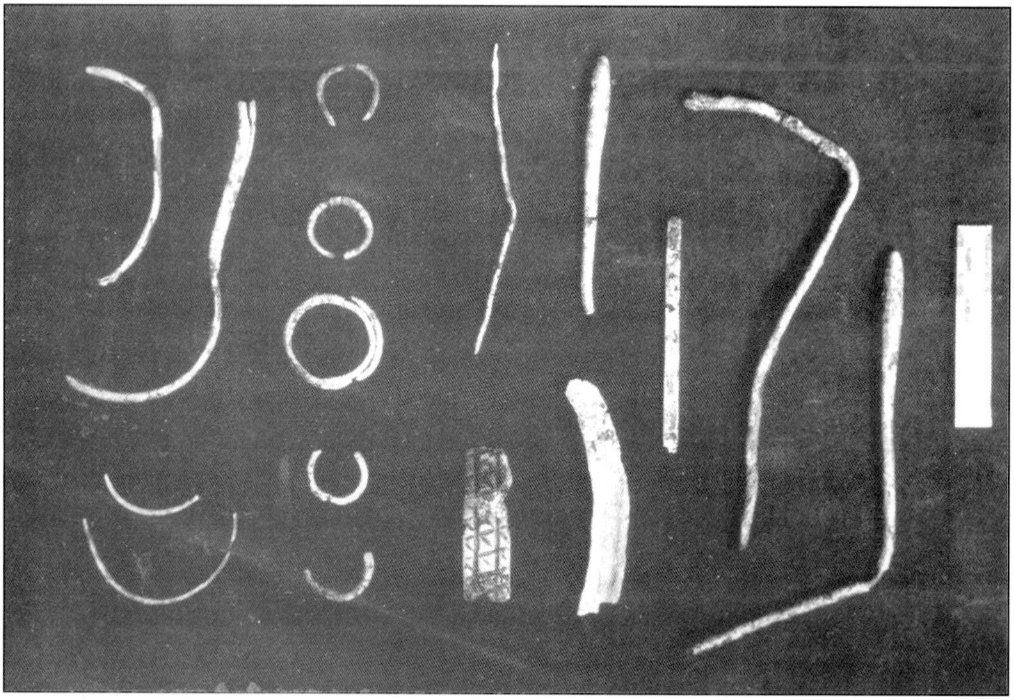

Fig. 3.6: *Copper objects of Pandu Rajar Dhibi (Coutesy: The State Archaeological Museum, Kolkata)*

From the Mangalkot excavation, one fragmentary bangle was analysed, which revealed it to be a bronze object with 10.05% tin, 0.05% lead, 0.10% antimony; with around 0.10% silver, iron and arsenic. The microstructure of this bangle is shown in Figure 3.7. From Bahiri (Chakrabarti and Hasan 1982: 111-149) one 'S'-shaped wire was analysed, which indicated 10% tin, 0.10% lead 0.10% antimony, 0.01% silver and around 0.10% arsenic (Chattopadhyay 1993-94: 159-163).

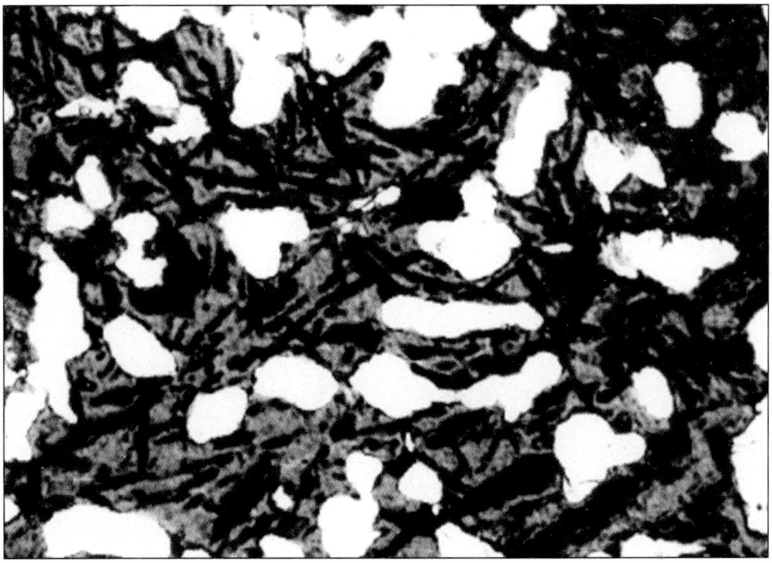

Fig. 3.7: *Microstructure of bangle from Mangalkot*

The microstructure of this specimen of Bahiri is shown in Figure 3.8. Chalcolithic copper objects from Sonpur are enigmatic; one spoon indicated alloying with 32.42% tin and the bangle contained 1.887% tin and 6.985% lead (Agrawal 1971: 169). The copper dish obtained from Chirand is shown in Figure 3.9. This is now preserved at Patna Museum.

The analysis of copper objects from these sites clearly indicates that the alloying element, mostly used, was tin. The copper-bronze wire from Bahiri had 10% tin. The bangle from Dihar was made with 9.00% tin, but the copper wire spool contained only 0.80% tin. The microstructure of the object is shown in Figure 3.10. The photomicrograph was obtained at a magnification of 800X. These percentages of tin in those sites indicate a deliberate addition for manufacturing bronze. It is likely that the

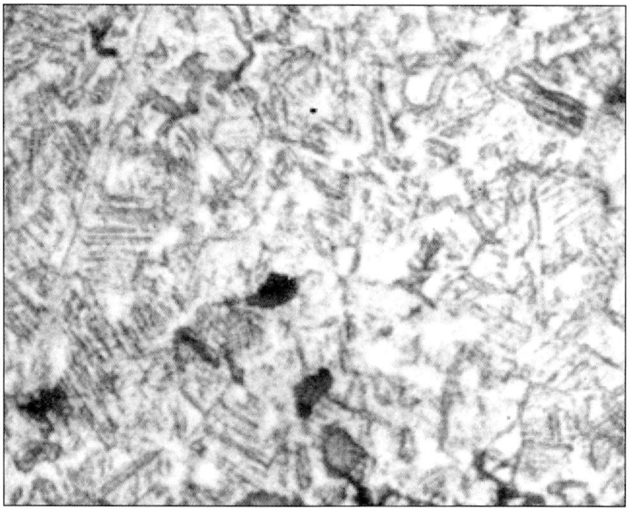

Fig. 3.8: *Microstructure of 'S' shaped wire from Bahiri showing strain bands, 800X*

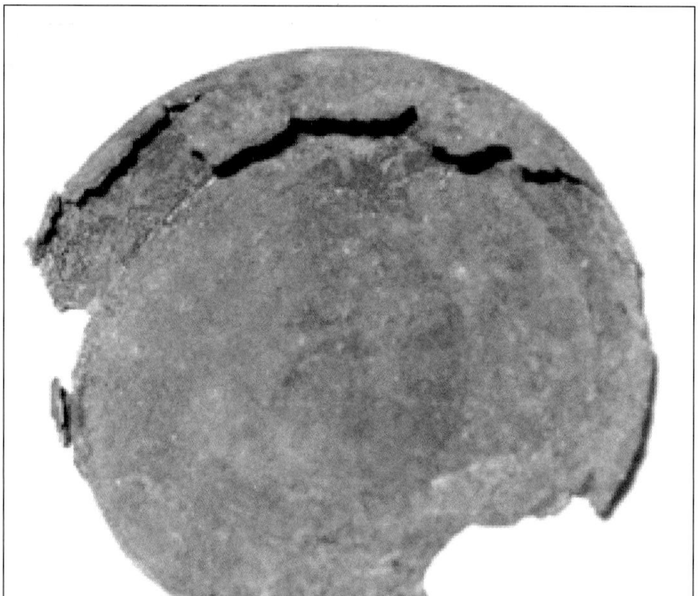

Fig. 3.9: *Dish from Chirand (Courtesy: The Patna Museum)*

smelters used cassiterite as the source for tin. There are evidences of ancient mines in the Purulia, Bankura and the West Medinipur districts; either the smelters used the ores of these areas or imported the same from the Chotanagpur plateau region.

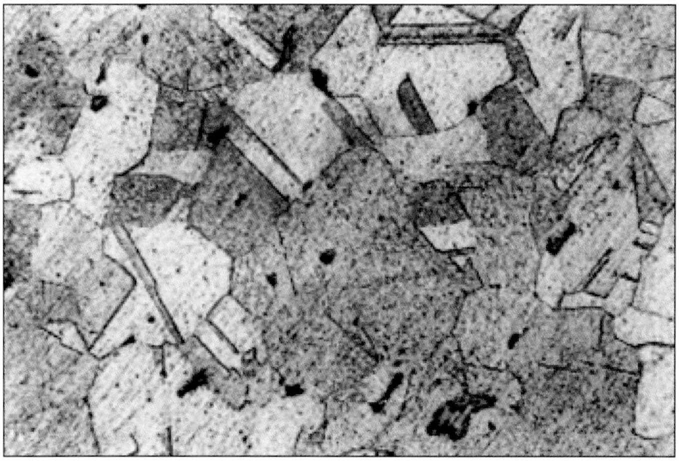

Fig. 3.10: *Microstructure of copper wire from Dihor, 500X*

In alloying copper objects, during the Chalcolithic period in this part of the country, metal smiths learnt the importance of adding tin in alloying, but their knowledge about proper composition seems inadequate. The reason might be that availability of tin was poor or that the minerals that they used contained cassiterite of different proportions. Besides, there is no evidence that the arsenic had ever been used as an alloy in eastern India, but arsenic was traced in some of the metal objects.

The slag obtained from Parihati in the West Medinipur District was taken to be from the Chalcolithic Age. If the assumed dating of Parihati is correct, it may be accepted that it was borax, which was used as a flux in the then contemporary copper smelting. In the copper hoard object from the same site, boron was barely visible in spectrographic analysis. The major copper objects are shown in Table 3.2.

The period from 600 BCE to CE 300

The period under review is known as the Early Historic period in Indian history. The beginning of writing, use of coins and all round growth in metallurgy was initiated in this period. Throughout the western part, copper objects were found in this period.

Table 3.2: Copper objects: 1300 to 600 BCE

State	Site	Bangle	Point	Fish-hooks	Wire	Ring	Needle	Arrow-heads	Crucible
Bihar	Chirand	XXX	XXX	XXX	XXX	XXX			XXX
	Maner	XXX	XXX	XXX					
	Senuwar	XXX	XXX	XXX	XXX	XXX		XXX	XXX
	Sonpur	XXX	XXX	XXX	XXX	XXX			XXX
	Taradih	XXX	XXX	XXX			XXX	XXX	
Orissa	Golabai Sasan	XXX		XXX		XXX			XXX
	Sankerjang	XXX							
West Bengal	Baneswardanga	XXX				XXX			
	Mangalkot	XXX		XXX			XXX		
	Pakhanna	XXX				XXX			
	Pandu Rajar Dhibi	XXX		XXX					

The metal crafts of Bangladesh originated in the Early Historic period.

There are the early historic copper objects from Bihar. The excavations at Kumrahar (Altekar and Misra 1959: 19) revealed antiquities from three successive periods. Period I was dated before *c.*150 BCE, Period II ranges between 150 BCE to CE 100 and the Period III from CE 100-300. A number of personal ornaments made of copper-bronze have also been found. From Pataliputra Period II, a copper spoon with a broken handle was found (Sinha and Narain 1970: 127). Period II at Sonpur (24° 57' N, 84° 56' E) was associated with the NBPW. A large number of copper implements were revealed there. Period III of Sonpur was represented by the post-NBPW level. The copper objects recovered in that level were a bangle, a spoon handle and a variety of rings. The discovery of an earthen crucible and slag specimens indicate that it was also a metal manufacturing centre (Sinha and Narain 1970: plate XLV, 128).

At Vaisali (25° 58 '20" N, 85°11' 30" E), Period II flourished between 600 BCE to 200 BCE. Period III has been assigned from 200 BCE to CE 200. For Period IV, the span is from CE 200 to CE 600. The copper objects recovered from that site are discussed below.

The site of Balirajgarh (26° 21' N, 86° 07' E) in the Madhubani District had NBPW wares in Period I. The so-called antimony rods, cast copper coins and a melting crucible were discovered there. Period IV at Chirand has been identified as the NBPW ware phase. Copper objects discovered there included small vessels, antimony rods and few other bjects. Period IV at Taradih was also of NBPW ware phase – copper bangles and rings appeared in this phase. Period II of Panr could be identified as NBPW phase (Choudhary 2005: 11, 81-86). Basically, copper was utilised for ornaments at Panr. The objects included antimony rods, bangles, earrings and finger-rings. The end of Period II is marked by the copper punch-marked coins as well as cast copper coins. The Period III of Panr represents the Shunga-Kushan phase, which is also supported by the presence of a number of copper coins of the different Kushan rulers. One unique piece of copper alloy rod was discovered at Panr. From Maner, Period II level, copper antimony rods were found (IAR 1996-1997: 6, 1995-1996: 5). Period III of Senuwar is equated with NBPW. The copper bronze objects found at that site include points, nails, bangles and finger rings. Period IV of Senuwar is contemporary to the Kushan Age. The copper-bronze objects recovered from this site were wires, rods, coils, antimony rods, bangles and bowl fragments.

The excavations at Mahasthan revealed cast copper coins, copper vessels from level VI (third to second century BCE) along with a bronze lamp. These objects are discussed further in Chapter 8.

The Chhattisgarh excavation had revealed very little information for the Early Historic period. The excavation at Sarangpur in Rajgarh District had revealed copper objects of the Mauryan period. In the case of Jharkhand, the recent excavation at Suikiapal in the East Singhbhum District revealed a continuation of cultures from the Stone Age to the Pal period. The artefacts obtained are fishhooks and copper bangles, along with arrowheads of bone and iron (*CASTEI Newsletter* 2004:12).

In Orissa, the most important site is that of Shishupalgarh (20° 13' 30" N, 85° 51' 30" E). It was excavated by B. B. Lal in 1948. Some interesting copper objects were discovered there. The important metallic objects were a miniature blowpipe, pin and the so-called antimony rods made of copper along with an ear ornament made of lead (Lal 1949). In recent years, two sessions of excavation have been undertaken by R. K. Mohanti and M. L. Smith, who discovered fishhooks and other copper-bronze and iron artefacts.

Lots of copper objects have also been recovered from the excavation and explorations in West Bengal. The excavation at Bangarh yielded a copper amulet, cast copper coins, collyrium sticks, bangles and awl. Period III of Mangalkot was regarded to be contemporary to the Maurya-Shunga period on the basis of the finds of punch-marked silver and cast copper coins. Copper was also used for ornaments like rings and lockets.

The excavation revealed copper-bronze earrings, bangles, finger rings, needles and bowls. Fragments of copper bowls were found in abundance. Copper ornaments were found at Pakhanna, Period II, dated around the first to the third century CE (IAR 1999-2000: 197). Dihar (Period II) yielded cast copper coins, both rectangular and round in shape (IAR 1993-1994: 121). All the abovementioned sites were excavated by the University of Calcutta.

Excavations in Manipur also yielded copper objects. The excavation at Sekta (24° 53' 24" N, 94° 24' E) was conducted by the State Archaeology Department. A burial site was discovered that revealed copper masks, finger-rings, bangles and armlets.

Coins

Fig. 3.11: *Cast copper coins from Mangalkot, Harinaranpur, Chandraketugarh and Tamluk*

Coins appeared in eastern India in the Mauryan period. Copper coins were of two types – cast and punch-marked. Thousands of cast copper coins have been discovered in excavations and exploration in this part of the subcontinent. For example, regular excavations and surface explorations in Bihar, West Bengal, Orissa and Bangladesh have revealed these coins. The important sites are Bangarh, Chandraketugarh, Chechar Kutubpur, Chirand, Vaisali, Dihar, Kumrahar, Maner, Manjhi, Mahasthangarh, Mangalkot, Pakhanna and Pataliputra. A few cast copper coins are shown in Figure 3.11. The punch-marked copper coins are also known from some of those sites. The important copper objects of eastern India are listed in Table 3.3.

Copper Smelting Activities in the Early Historic Period

We now have the archaeological evidences of smelting activities of the Early Historic period. Recent excavation has revealed around eight hearths at Tilpi in the South Twenty-four Pargana District (Figure 3.12). The hearths are found with charcoal, slag and small crucibles. From the trench ZE3, a bronze lump was discovered. This evidently indicates the existence of a small industry at the site.

Table 3.3: Important Copper objects: 600 BCE to CE 300

State/Country	Site	Important objects
Bangladesh	Mahasthan	Copper vessels, cast copper coins, bangles
Bihar	Chirand	Copper chain, solid armlet, antimony rod, bangles
	Maner	Antimony rod, bangles
	Panr	Antimony rod, bangles
	Rampurva	Copper bolt used in Asokan pillar
	Senuwar	Bowl fragments, ring, antimony rod, crucible, bangles
	Sonpur	Perforated pot, spoon, ring, flattened bar, wire, bangles
	Taradih	Needle, fishhook, bangles
	Vaisali	Antimony rods, rings, bowls, cast copper coin, bangles
Chattisgarh	Sarangpur	Limited objects and bangles
Jharkand	Sukiapal	Fishhook, bangles
Manipur	Sekta	Copper masks, finger rings, armlet, bangles
Orissa	Golabai Sasan	Bangles
	Sankerjang	Nail parer, small rods, bangles
	Sisupalgarh	Blowpipe, antimony rod, bangles
West Bengal	Pandu Rajar Dhibi	Earring, bead, bangles
	Mangalkot	Earring, needle, bowls, cast copper coin, bangles
	Pakhanna	Cast copper coin, bangles

Fig. 3.12: *Hearths excavated at Tilpi (Courtesy: Amal Ray)*

Crucibles were usually made by the potters of clay by hand (handmade) or on the turntable (wheel made). The crucibles were used for melting copper, bronze, brass, gold, silver or lead. Usually some slag adhered to the crucible. A crucible from the Tilpi site is shown in Figure 3.13. Analysis with EPMA (electron probe micro analyses) indicates that it was used to melt bronze.

Crucibles have been found from the Chalcolithic levels of Golabai Sasan. A number of crucibles of the Early Historic Period were recovered from Senuwar, Sonpur, Bangarh and Tilpi during excavations. The excavated crucible from Sonpur is shown in Figure 3.14. The crucible from Bangarh had a pointed bottom, it was 9.02 cm long and 6.98 cm in diameter, and was unearthed from 3.80 m below the ground. The excavator associates it with the Mauryan or early Shunga period (Goswami 1948: 33). The Senuwar excavation revealed two crucibles of a similar form from Period IV (Kushan, first to third century CE). One of them was a medium-sized crucible of 8.40 cm diameter and of 9.20 cm depth, with a pointed bottom. The other crucible was of 5 cm diameter and 5.50 cm depth, with a straight wall. The importance of those two crucibles lay in the hard bluish-green copper slag that adhered to these, revealed bronze melting. Crucibles have also been reported from the excavation at Tilpi (Datta, Chattopadhyay and Ray 2007:13-16). One of these is similar to the crucible recovered at Senuwar, which has a pointed bottom. However, since the thickness varies between 9 mm and 12 mm (not uniform), it may be guessed that the crucible was a handmade. A number of crucibles are also reported from the Chandraketugarh and Tamluk area.

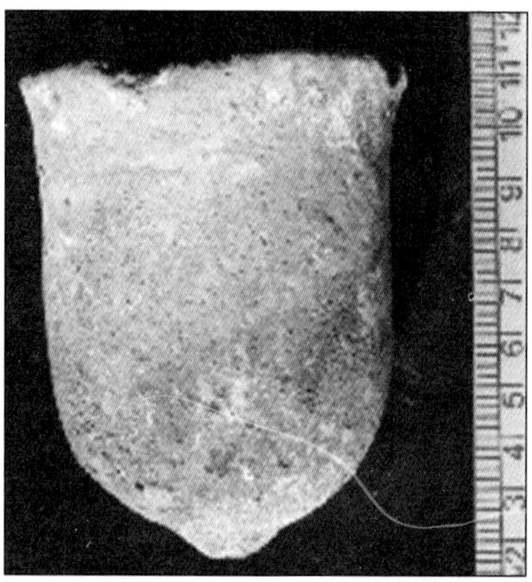

Fig. 3.13: *Crucible from Tilpi*
(Courtesy: Debishankar Middya)

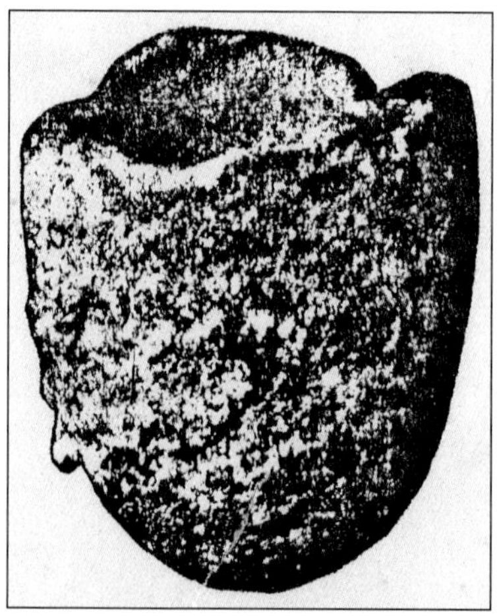

Fig. 3.14: Crucible from Sonpur
(Sinha and Verma 1977)

The manufacturing centres of copper are identified by the presence of slag, crucibles and tuyères. Analysis of slag specimens may indicate the condition of the furnace, ore-metal correlation, source of the ore and other smelting features. Chemical composition of slag is found to be different during different stages of the processing.

The analysis by M. L. Dutta revealed the use of borax in copper smelting (Dutta 1982: 487-88; 2005: 271-273; Ghosh and Chattopadhyay 1981: 262-263). Borax is a natural compound of sodium and boron. This compound is even used by gold and silver smiths of the present times as a flux, which reduces the melting temperature and helps improve slag formation.

The synthetic barium base standards in the spectrograph indicated the presence of boron in the copper slag from Parihati. As the base element in the slag was silicon; to offset the variation of the matrix, nickel oxide was added to the matrix; copper, sodium, boron and vanadium were thus detected. In the slag, sodium was found to be 0.10% and boron 0.095%. Thus, it was concluded that the borax was used as flux in copper smelting. Subsequently, a number of excavated copper specimens of eastern India indicated trace amounts of boron in them.

Ornaments of the Early Historic Period

The bangles, bracelets, *kundalas* (earrings), *anguriyas* (finger-rings), ear pendants, and other ornaments were common ornaments of the Early Historic period. Similar objects were also made of ivory, bone, glass or even terracotta, but the maximum use was made of copper-bronze for this purpose.

Most of the ornaments were made with a simple wire of a round or rectangular crosssection, with or without any external design. Sometimes, the use of crescent-shaped earrings, with one end coiled or looped, is also noted. Bangles of simple plain rounded wire were generally used, but open club-ended bangles were also made. Amulets, made of copper-bronzes, were also popular. Excavators have widely reported the presence of the so-called antimony rods in eastern as well as north Indian sites. Those objects were made of the low-tin bronze. The hairpins were of the thick varieties. The tiny ear-cleaning scoops were of the thin variety pins, and ones with slightly clubbed end were identified as the collyrium stick. Those objects are known from a number of sites, including Bangarh, Kumrahar, Vaisali and Mahasthan.

From Vaisali, more than 46 objects of different shapes have been discovered from

Periods III and IV. This site also revealed a copper *nupur* from the early level of Period IV. From the Sonpur excavation, a bangle, a rope design copper ring, an earring, a nail, and other copper objects were recovered from Period III. From the Kumrahar excavations, several coils were found from Maurya period CE 100-300 levels. One of those, about 15.00 cm in breadth and 1.27 mm in thickness, was wound on a rod in the form of a coil. It is interesting to note that it was mentioned as a low tin bronze object (analysed by B. B. Lal, referred to in Altekar and Misra 1959: 136). Perhaps this was the raw material for manufacturing ornaments or other utility objects. One may recall the presence of a spool of copper wire from Dihar from the black-and-red ware level, which was also perhaps raw material.

Domestic Objects of the Early Historic Period

A very important copper bolt was recovered at Rampurwa in the Champaran District, Bihar in CE 1880. The specimen is now preserved in the Indian Museum, Kolkata (Figure 3.15). This barrel-shaped specimen, with the tapering ends, is around 36.14 kg in weight, 62.23 cm in length and of 13.49 cm in diameter at the centre. The metal used was true copper and not bronze. The bolt was manufactured by forging from a cast product (Neogi 1979: 22; Patil 1963: 483), and further finished by hammering. This piece, probabily made during the third century BCE, was used to fix the stone capital to the pillar.

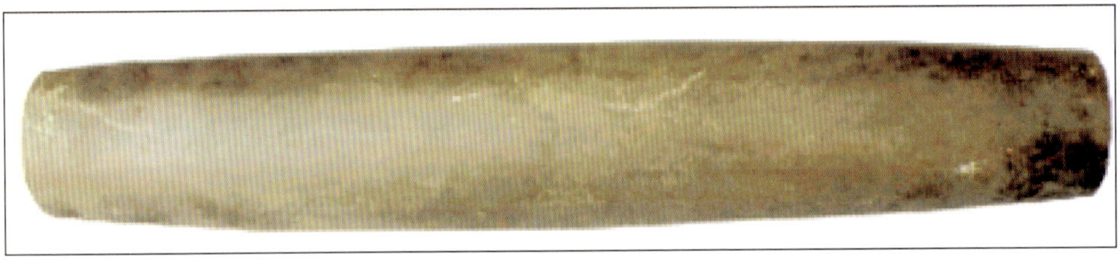

Fig. 3.15: *Copper bolt: Rampurwa Ashokan Pillar, Indian Museum*

During the Early Historic period, eastern India also witnessed the use of miniature arrowheads, nails, small *ghoongroos* (trinkets), and other objects of everyday life. One masterpiece – a bronze lamp – had been obtained from the Mahasthan excavation. A nail-parer and the copper hooks were obtained from Vaisali along with four copper bells, used as ornaments for the animals.

The use of bowls and dishes was also popular in the Early Historic period. Bowl fragments of this period, made of copper alloy, were found at Chirand, Senuwar, Mahasthan, and so on. More than four bronze bowls or containers have been discovered at Mahasthan. From Vaisali, two copper bowls of featureless rim, one thin and the other, thick, were obtained from Period III. From Sonpur, a copper spoon handle was found. From the Kumrahar excavation, 14 copper objects (in partial, broken condition), comprising antimony rods, ear cleaner and toothpicks were recovered.

Important surface explorations were conducted in the south Bengal. During those explorations, a number of copper bronze ornaments, comprising bangles and rings, along with copper and silver coins, were recovered. Some of those are preserved at Sundarban Pratna Gabeshana Kendra at Kashinagar of the South Twenty-four pargana (Figure 3.16).

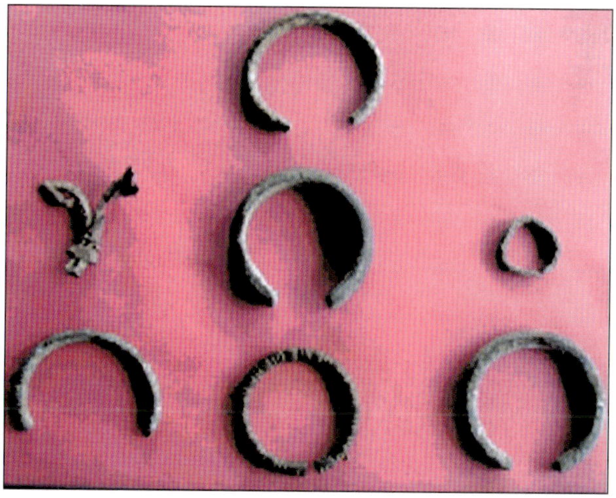

Fig. 3.16: *Copper bronze ornaments from South Bengal*
(Courtesy: Sundarban Pratna Gabeshana Kendra, Kashinagar)

The Period between CE 300 and 200

Throughout eastern India, there is evidence of copper manufacturing. The technological activities are clear from the remnants of furnaces, crucibles, slag and ingots, along with the metallic artefacts. For example, the site of Sultanganj (25°19' 20" N, 86° 48' 25" E), has yielded the famous copper image of Buddha, with lumps of copper ore in the vicinity, suggesting it might be a probable smelting and casting spot. The associated metal objects included a copper disk, hand of a large copper figure, rusty domestic copper objects, lumps of copper ore, miniature copper bell, a crucible, lumps of clay and the round hollow pieces of copper gilt, stamped with the figure of *chaitya* on each side (Mitra 1864: 360-373).

From Orissa, the ruins of the ancient city of Sampa were discovered (*IAR* 1956-1957: 31). Lots of copper beads were found at this site. A number of Early Historic sites in the Kalahandi District yielded copper objects (Mohanty and Mishra 2002: 471-492). Bangles were discovered at the Chandrasagarnala excavation of 2004 (Singh *et al.* 2006: 133-141).

Copperplates

Copperplates are the most dependable written record of the early as well as the medieval history. The records on paper or palm leaf are perishable, but the inscriptions on rocks or pillars are non-perishable, and the rulers used those for their recording and dissemination of information. In the case of copperplates, it was not only easy to carry them, but those also served as permanent records for land grants. Copper was chosen for a number of metallurgical and social factors. The metallurgical factor includes the malleability, ductility and minimum corrosion that made them survive for two thousand years. The social factor includes the style of writing and poetic excellence of the issuer. Copper was also considered sacred.

From excavations at various places, a number of copperplates have been discovered. The excavation at Paharpur has also revealed a copperplate of 19.00 x 11.30 cm, dated to 159 of the Gupta Era (CE 478-479) (*Epigraphiya Indica* XIX, p. 59). Seven copperplates discovered at Salban *vihar*, belonged to the Khadga dynasty (seventh century). Four copperplates were also found at the Charpatramura excavation. Hundreds of copperplates were discovered from Bengal. For example, a copperplate dated to CE 448 (Figure 3.17) of Kumargupta was discovered at Baigram in the District Bagura of Bangladesh.

It is now preserved in the Indian Museum. A good numbers of copperplates were recovered from Assam, Bengal and Orissa between the third century BCE and CE 12th century. The historians have studied the palaeographyand linguistic features of these finds, and correlated the same with the social and political history of Bengal. Around twenty-three copperplate inscriptions of the Gupta, Khadga, Rata, Dev and Chandra dynasties were discovered in the Mainamati and Devaparbat regions. It is interesting to note that copperplates of the Khadga dynasty were preserved in Salaban *vihar* until the eighth century during the Dev period. The copperplates of same dynasty were preserved in that *vihar* from ninth-11th century during the times of Harikela and Chandra rulers (Khan 2007: 5-36).

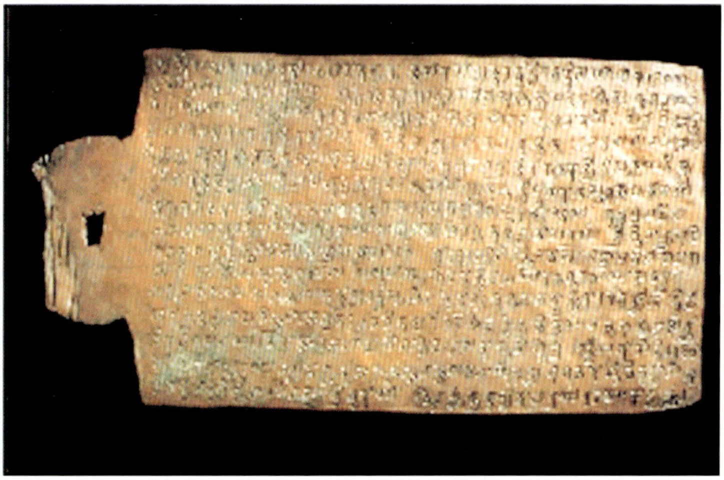

Fig. 3.17: *Copperplate of Kumargupta, CE 448, Baigram, Bangladesh (Courtesy: Indian Museum)*

In the case of Orissa, there have been little or no analytical study of this metal, its source, manufacturing technique and the tools and technique of writing or engraving the inscription/s on it. One of the copperplates in the collection of N. K. Sahoo Museum in the Sambalpur University is illustrated here (Figure 3.18). This copperplate, dated to the ninth century, belonged to Prithivi Bigraha.

Fig. 3.18: *Copperplate: Prithivi Bigraha (Courtesy: The Sambalpur University Museum)*

From Assam, a number of copperplates of Bhaskaravarman (seventh century), Sri Harisha Varmadev of Salasthambha dynasty (seventh-10th century), Harjaravarman (mid-ninth century), Balavarman III (ninth century), Dharmpal (12th century), among others have enriched the history of northeast India. Shrikumar's (eighth century) copper bell inscription is important. The pre-Ahom inscriptions are mostly written in the mixed prose and verse. There are a number of references of the *takshkar* (engraver), *svarnakar* (goldsmith), *rupykar* (silversmith), *tamrkar* (coppersmith) and *karmkar* (ironsmith). That further indicates the existence of a well developed team of workmen for manufacturing copperplates and bells in that state. Copperplate of Shri Harisa Varmadev was discovered at Dighaligaon near Kaliabor in the Nagaon District. One famous inscription of Bhaskarvarman was discovered at Nidhanpur in the Sylhet District in Bangladesh. That copperplate is made of a set of seven plates, only two of them are preserved now in Assam State Museum, Guwahati. That copperplate indicates that Bhaskarvarman's grandfather, Sri Bhutivarman offered land to two hundred Brahmins of the Mayurasalmala *agrahar* in Chandrapura Visaya. The Khonamukh copperplate of Dharmpal is in this museum (Figure 3.19). Some of the copperplates of Assam used Tai scripts.

Fig. 3.19: *Khonamukh Copperplate of Dharmpal (12th century) at the Assam State Museum, Guwahati*

The Nagari plate of Anangabhimadev III refers to the *tamrkars* (coppersmiths), who made the copperplates (Epigraphiya Indica Vol. XXVIII, 235-258). Other words in the text, such as, the *tamra shilpi* (copper artisan) and *kamsyik* (brazier) are also interesting. From the recent discovery of copperplates of Anantavarman and Indravarman, the name of the engraver, Aksasalin Padmachandra is revealed. The emblem of the couchant bull was on their rings (*CASTEI Newsletter* 2004:12-13). The Dommanpal copperplate dated CE 1196, with significant engravings, has been studied by Ghosh (1975: 29-32). The discovery of a large number of copperplates, spread in different areas, reflects that the copper smithy provided employment to a large number of artisans.

The copperplates of Tripura and West Bengal also deserve mention. In the Tripura Government Museum, three copperplates are well preserved. One of those, dated to 1689 *Saka* era (CE 1767) belongs to Krishnamanikya. The inscription is written in the Bangla script, but the language is Sanskrit. That copperplate indicates a land grant.

Basically, all the copperplates of eastern India are made of two parts, plate and knob. The larger part is the plate, on which the inscription is engraved. This portion is made into a plate by forging a copper ingot. Forging makes the plate harder, so it is annealed to soften for engraving. The knob is generally made by casting. The symbol of the king not only authenticates it, but also adds beauty to it. If the text is not finished in one plate, then additional plates are added and all the plates are joined together by metallic girder with a royal seal.

ORIGIN OF THE COPPER HOARDS

In the vast area of north and peninsular India, hoards of copper implements have been discovered. All those implements are the chance finds. No dating of those finds could be established properly. In the eastern India, a number of such implements, of different shape and even a few kilogrammes in weight were discovered. The size and weight of those artefacts often brings into question their suitability for the every day use. Some of the important sites of those finds are located in the Ranchi District of Jharkhand, the Mayurbhanj District of Orissa and the West Medinipur District of West Bengal. The artefact hoards are interesting to study.

The origin and subsequent development of those copper hoard artefacts have not been satisfactorily explained. From the records of the European scholars of GSI, one can identify the discovery of a number of such objects. From the Palamau District of Jharkhand, a copper celt roughly made by casting and then beating, was discovered. This measured of 18.50 cm long and 15.40 cm wide, with a maximum thickness of

2.30 cm. From the erstwhile Manbhum District (now the Purulia District of West Bengal and the Dhanbad District of Jharkhand), information is available for 27 such specimens. Copper hoards were also reported from Mayurbhanj of Orissa (Coggin Brown 1916: 386-387; Campbell 1916: 85-86). Perhaps the owners and manufacturers of those copper hoards were the itinerant or nomads. Nothing is known about their settlements. In the absence of any remains, one may surmise that they my have been aborigines, belonging to the proto-Australoid stock of the Gangetic basin, or the ancestors of Munda, Santhal or Ho indigenes of Jharkhand, Orissa, Chhattisgarh and West Bengal.

Major Copper Hoard Sites

From eastern India, the major state-wise distributions are summarised here. Bihar, Chhattisgarh, Jharkhand, Orissa and West Bengal are the principal locations of the copper hoards. From the present state of Bihar, Kushaya (near Chatkurum mines in the Monghyr District) is the only known site which yielded copper hoards. A lot of copper hoards are preserved at the Patna Museum. From Jharkhand, the copper hoards are reported from the erstwhile Manbhum District, Andhari (Majhgaon, Singhbhum), Basia (District Ranchi), Baragunda (24° 5' N, 86° 03' 30" E), Bartala (Basia, District Ranchi), Borodanga (22° 32' 29" N, 86° 41' 52" E), Chakulia (District Singhbhum), Chansar (24° 59' 33" N, 87° 16' 47" E), Dargama (23° 02' N, 85° 19' E), Hami (District Palamou), Hara Chowrah Darh (Khunti, District Ranchi), Kamdara (District Ranchi), Karharbari (Pachamba, District Hazaribagh), Mahuadanr (District Palamou), Pachamba (Distric Giridih), Namkom (District Ranchi) (23° 20' 45" N, 85° 21' 4" E) and Saguna (District Palamau).

In Orissa, a number of copper hoards are reported from Bhagada (22° 00' N, 87° 00' 20" E), Bhagrapir (22° 00' N, 87° 00' 20" E), Bamanghaty, Kesna (21° 53' 49" N, 85° 49' 45" E), Khiching, Ksetra and Panchpir subdivisions and Viratgarh (21° 30' 2" N, 85° 40' 49" E) in the Mayurbhanj District. Some of the hoards are preserved now at Baripada Museum. Bhagrapir is the most important site, located at Bhagada Village on the left bank of river Gulpha, under police station Sulaipada in the District Mayurbhanj. This hoard is a combination of double axes. One axe ingot was reported from Dimiria (22° 00' N, 87° 00' 20" E) or Dunria Village, under police station Pallahara in the District Dhenkanal. A copper axe ingot was collected from Ludurpada Village (22° 55 '05" N, 85° 50' 17" E), located under police station Pandapara of *tehsil*

Kanjipani in the District Keonjhor. The axe ingots from this district are in the collection of the Orissa State Museum (Fig. 3.20). A copper hoard of the bar type was recovered from Kesna.

Fig. 3.20: *Copper hoard, Keonjjhar (Courtesy: Orissa State Museum)*

From West Bengal, copper hoard specimens, including axe ingots, rings, discs and bangles are reported from Aguibani (22° 56' 15" N, 87° 22' 15" E). Other important sites of this state are Akhuldoba (22° 56' 15" N, 87° 22' 15" E), Bhaktabandh (23° 22' 30" N, 87° 03' 30" E), Chatla (23° 22' 30" N, 87° 03' 30" E), Parihati (22° 31' 20" N, 86° 51' E), Perua (23° 22' 30" N, 87° 03' 30" E), Khajraveri (22° 26' N, 87° 20' E), Kulgara (23°14' 25" N, 86° 39' 30" E), Kharagpur (five km north on the bank of Kasai), Kushadwip (23° 09' N, 87° 26' E), Mahisdal (23° 43' N, 87° 42' E) and Tamajuri (22° 42' 20" N, 86° 41' 40" E). Most of those hoards are preserved in the Indian Museum, West Bengal State Archaeological Museum and Department of Archaeology, University of Calcutta. It is noted that the hoard objects known from Parihati were actually obtained from the nearby Village Jamboni (20° 31' 40" N, 86° 50' 21" E) (Bose, S. 1987: 39-43).

The probable source of copper is the Chotanagpur plateau or its extension. Evidence of ancient mining was also noticed at Tamakhun (Bankura) and Chedapathar (West Medinipur). However, the exact location of those sources is not certain, as no provenance study has yet been carried out. The flat copper celt with convex cutting edge, reported from Mahisdal, is quite doubtful. The excavation reports (*IAR* 1963-1964: 59-60) do not clearly mention whether it was found from the trench or was a chance find. Two copper hoard objects were recovered from Akhuldoba. One object out of this was analysed (Datta and Chattopadhyay 1986: 81-87). The other specimen is shown in Figure 3.21.

Fig. 3.21: *Copper celt from Akhuldoba (Courtesy: Sudhin De)*

The copper hoards of the eastern belt of Jharkhand, Orissa and West Bengal are associated with the Black-and-Red ware complex of the Chalcolithic phase. There is no doubt that some of the copper hoard finds belonged to the Neolithic-Chalcolithic transition, as there is some resemblance with their lithic counterparts. That transition is best indicated by the fact that the neolithic tools possibly served as models for the manufacture of copper tools. This is attested to by the late paleolithic celt from Belpahari in the West Medinipur District of West Bengal, which is similar to the copper celt from Ramchandrapur near Kushadwip in the Bankura District, presently preserved in the Kushadwip Sangrahasala. The above similarities are further supported by the discovery of Neolithic celt from Laljal. B. B. Lal has also reported a lithic celt from Bon Ashuria in the Bankura District, which bears a similarity with the copper celt from Gungeria in Madhya Pradesh.

Some of the ringshaped objects from the Chalcolithic level at Senuwar resemble the rings of the copper hoards found at different sites of the eastern India. Besides, a terracotta model of the double-edged axe of the copper hoard type has been discovered from the chalcolithic level at Maner in the Patna District. From the above instances, some scholars have inferred that the origin of those could be found in the Chalcolithic period. Yule and Thiel-Horstmann (1985: 121-138) have equated the OCP and the copper hoards on the one hand, and the copper hoard and the Black-and-Red ware, on the other. A bar celt from Khunti is shown in Figure 3.22. Seven axe ingots in the shape of a zebu were discovered at Khajrabheri (Yule 2001: 117-120).

The Use and Function of the Copper Hoard Artefacts

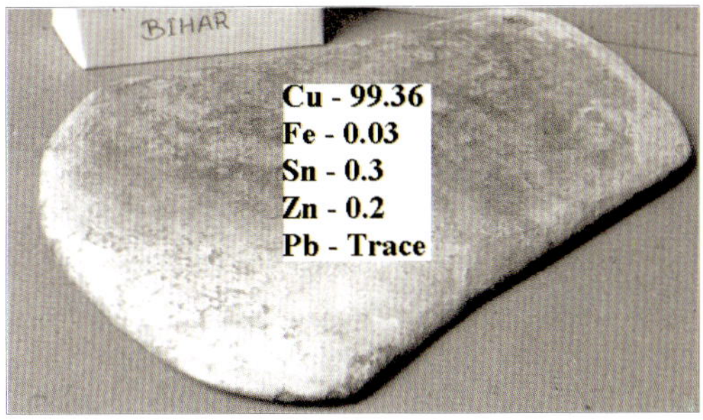

Fig. 3.22: *Double ended axe from Khunti with its composition inset (Courtesy: Prasanta Datta)*

The specific use of different tool types comprising the copper hoards has not become clear, despite scholarly research for a long time. Most of the copper hoard objects are non-utilarian (Yule 1985: 449-508). 'Shouldered celt' or 'axe ingot', and 'bar celt-ingot,' and so on are simply, quite heavy cast products. The two hoard objects from Akhuldoba, namely the 'axe ingots' have cutting edges, but the question arises: whether is it really possible to chop large pieces of wood with those? No trace of ancient wear or mechanical damage was observed in the hoard of Bhaktabandh. Those objects might have been used as ingots to meet the need of small-scale copper industry. A question may arise, why those typical shapes were used? In this regard, example may be cited of the 'ox-hide' ingots of the Mediterranean origin that resembled the shape of hide of an ox (Wheeler *et al.* 1979: 139-152).

One 'twin-headed double-axe' was found from Kharagpur (Figure 3.23). That is at present located at the Acharya Jogeshchandra Purakirti Bhawan at Bishnupur. That object cannot be gripped with one hand or even with the two with ease. Perhaps, one may imagine it to be a 'shield' of those times or possibly a trophy, given as award for excellence in sport, and so on. Perhaps, the makers of that specimen thought of a new design by placing two axes together, one upon the other and rotating the same at an angle of 30 degree. The surface of the object was not very rough, unlike the shouldered celt or axe ingots.

Fig. 3.23: *Twin headed double axe from Kharagpur (Courtesy: The Acharya Jogeshchandra Purakirti Bhawan, Bishnupur)*

An 'axe ingot' with an Oriya text was found at Garhpada estate, located about 26 km north of Balasore station in the

Mayurbhanj District of Orissa. That hoard was reported in CE 1940 in a Bengali periodical by Nirmal Kumar Bose, who informed that it was found with an ex-Brahmin converted family (Bose 2006: 28-32; Yule 1989). That hoard was originally a type I axe ingot, which was subsequently used as a land grant in CE 1483 by Raja Purushottam Deb, the king of Orissa. However, it may be that the writing might have been done during a much later period.

Querns with legs, made of stone, were quite common in ancient India. These are found in several excavations, for example, at Chandraketugarh and Tilpi. A similar object, made of copper, was obtained at Keonjhar, now preserved at the Orissa State Museum (Figure 3.24).

Fig. 3.24: *Footed copper quern, Keonjhar (Courtesy: The Orissa State Museum)*

The Archaeometallurgy of Copper Hoard Objects

The earliest evidence for the manufacturing technique used to make the copper hoard objects is known from the axe-heads of Manbhum (Campbell 1916: 85-86). The author described the running of liquid metal into a mould smaller than the finished article. The product was then beaten to the required thickness. He further discussed the reasons for variety in the shape and thickness of the cast in the mould. If the metal was beaten irregularly, it created slight difference in shape. Although hundreds of copper hoard specimens were discovered in that belt, yet only a few of those have been analysed (Agrawal *et al.* 1974: 14-18; Yule and Thiel-Horstmann 1985: 121-138; Yule, Rath and Hojgaard 1989: 107-132; 1990; Yule and Rath 2000: 285-321; Datta and Chattopadhyay 1986: 81-87). One copper hoard artefact from Parihati was analysed (Figure 3.24), the analyses indicate that it was made from malachite ore (Chattopadhyay 2004: 78).

The studies were conducted on different aspects, comprising chemical analyses, spectrography and metallography along with X-ray diffraction analyses (XRD) for material characterisation. The studies of alloying of copper celts obtained at Hami, Dhanbad and Jharkhand clearly indicated the absence of tin, and the presence of arsenic and iron in all of them, along with nickel and lead in some of them (Agrawal *et al.* 1974: 14-18). Analyses of the bangles from the burial site of Sankerjung indicated 5.70% arsenic. The alloying with arsenic at that site is certainly intriguing, for it underscores the possibilities of a rich and early metallurgical tradition.

Analyses of the trace elements in the copper hoards have established the use of borax as the flux in copper smelting (Dutta 1982: 487-88). Subsequently, trace of boron was established in the copper hoards of the Parihati and Akhuldoba. A slag analysis from Parihati copper producing centre confirms the presence of 65.10% silica (SiO_2), 10.30% alumina (Al_2O_3), 9.20% iron oxide (Fe_2O_3), 0.40% titanium oxide (TiO_2), 2.50% magnesium oxide (MgO), 9.50% calcium oxide (CaO) and 0.07% manganese oxide (MnO). It is interesting to note, that in some copper hoard objects, iron was detected in a proportion as high as 20-30%, which is a new alloy almost unknown in the old world archaeometallurgy so far (Yule and Hauptmann 1989: 193-275). Similar observation of the magnetic properties of the cast copper coins discovered at Mangalkot was noted elsewhere. Copper, with high concentration of iron, was explained in some in-depth studies (Yule *et al.* 1989; Craddock and Meeks 1987: 187-204). These alloys were deliberately produced by charging copper ore with excessive amounts of iron ore oxide, which is normally introduced as a fluxing agent. The furnaces were driven under strongly reduced conditions by means of an overly heavy charge of charcoal. The copper-iron alloy was tapped directly from the furnace.

The hoard appears to be in its initial cast condition. It might have been finished later with the non-uniform hammering, as revealed by the conspicuously visible hammering marks. In the strict sense of the term, there is hardly any cutting or working edge of appreciable sharpness anywhere, except in the four areas of intersection of outer and inner curves. The photograph of one copper hoard artefact from Parihati is shown in Figure 3.25, and the photomicrograph in Figure 3.26.

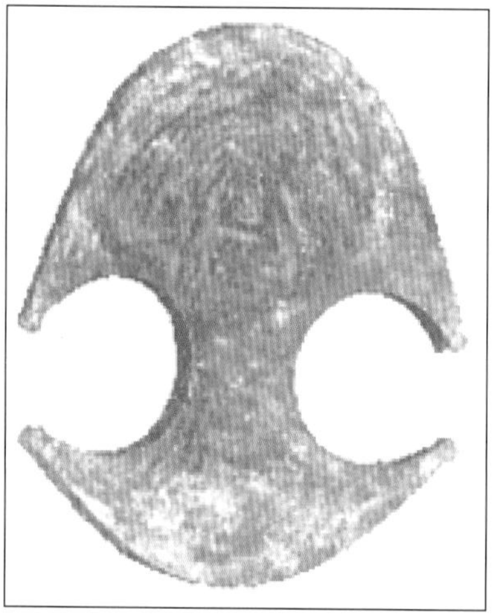

Fig. 3.25: *Copper hoard of Parihati (Courtesy: Asok K. Ghosh)*

Fig. 3.26: *Photomicrograph of copper hoard from Parihati*

Most of the hoard objects are covered with the greenish thick patina. Some of the hoard objects are found with spongy surfaces. However, it may be pointed out that all the copper hoard objects are not of the Chalcolithic phase. That tradition of the copper hoard complex probably continued to the later periods. The eastern Indian copper hoards differ both typologically and technologically from the copper hoards of the western region.

Archaeometallurgical study has revealed that the copper bronze objects from Dihar in the District Bankura bear close similarities with the copper hoard objects of Akhuldoba in the District West Medinipur (Chattopadhyay 2004: 65, 78.). Trace elements, as known through analysis, are similar in the copper objects of both the sites. This indicates that copper used in both the sites may have been obtained from the same mine. However, the ore minerals in the Dihar copper object show the presence of oxide group, namely, the malachite-azurite, while the copper hoard objects from Akhuldoba were made from the sulfide minerals, namely, chalcopyrite. Even if we presume that copper used in the objects discovered at both the sites came from the same mine, it may still be said that the Akhuldoba copper hoard objects are comparatively younger. The morphological study of the copper hoard tool types indicates that the earliest objects were thick and manufactured by the crude casting method, whereas those of the later period were comparatively thin, and these were made by the advanced forging and annealing techniques. The surfaces of those objects show uniform finishing.

Most of the previous scholars did not study the detailed characterisation of the metals. However, recent studies of copper hoards of Khuntitoli, Ranchi and also of Aguibani of West Bengal, have revealed that that these hoards are made of the pure copper casting (99%), but are full of gas holes, and so it seems that these were made in the open mould. The purity of over 99% is an excellent example of pure copper, though melting and casting techniques deserve more improvement for good casting production (Datta and Chattopadhyay, 2007:39-55). Another double-axe from the same site has also been studied. This specimen was also made of pure copper (over 99%). The metal was probably deoxidised with arsenic before pouring it in a closed mould. The beautifully cast piece was then probably hot-forged in the super plastic temperature to develop sharp edges, while the residual cast structure was allowed to remain in central section. A broken disc from a copper hoard artefact of Aguibani, with purity (over 99.5% copper) and the softness achieved in annealed condition, suggests a deep knowledge of metallurgy by the copper hoard people.

The analysis of the said copper hoard from Aguibani was observed under metallurgical microscope. That further indicates equiaxed grains with globular inclusions of $Cu-Cu_2O$ (copper and copper oxide). Analyses further indicated that the presence of eutectics or deoxidation products and low-melting constituents of insoluble lead distributed widely. The shrinkage voids indicated sound metal, revealing deoxidation techniques (by arsenic), and a good annealing treatment of the hard arsenical copper.

The sample of bar celt from Aguibani was forged form of blister copper – a copper with enough of the dissolved and residual oxygen, which exposes itself in the form of blisters over the copper surface. Later on, that type of copper was deoxidised with arsenic-bearing ore (orpiment or other) so that the material of axe was less gassy. Afterwards, the intentional degassing was made by a small amount of arsenic, which volatilised after deoxidising, but some of it remained as the residual arsenides that were found in the structure of the copper lump. The wide presence of white arsenide in the copper hoard objects confirms the intentional addition of arsenic to refine and deoxidise the metal at the ingot stage (Datta and Chattopadhyay 2007: 39-55). It is presumed that copper hoard objects of Jharkhand, Orissa and West Bengal are not of a single period.

The archaeometallurgical studies of ancient copper objects are very limited. Researches by R. N. Singh and his colleagues on Chalcolithic copper objects from Chirand, Senuwar and Taradih are the significant contributions. One microstructure obtained from Chirand and analysed by Singh is shown in Figure 3.27.

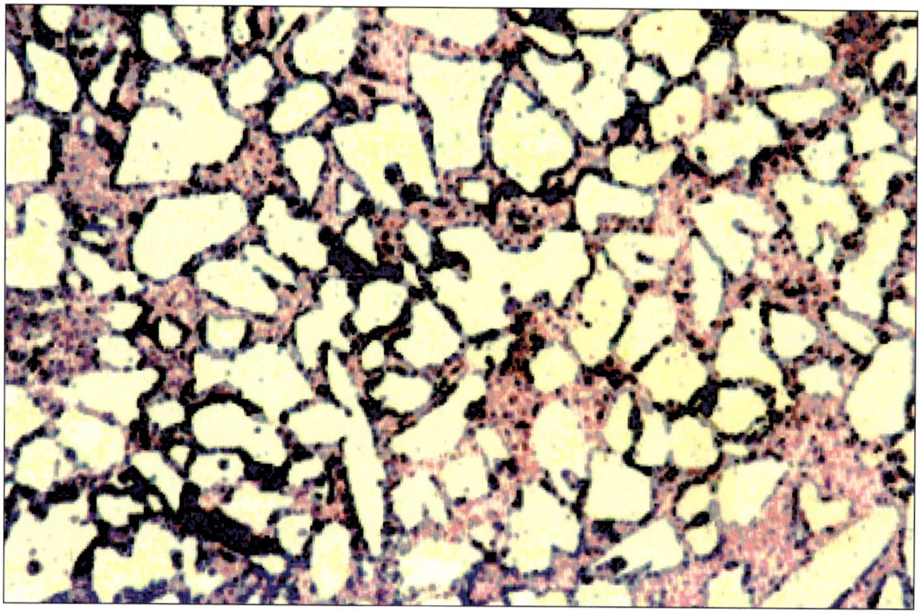

Fig. 3.27: *Photomicrograph of a copper artefact, Chirand (Courtesy: R. N. Singh)*

4

IRON

THIS CHAPTER HIGHLIGHTS SOME OF THE BASIC CONCEPTS RELATED to the metallurgy of iron. Iron came later, preceded by copper and bronze. The discovery of iron technology thoroughly changed the lifestyle of the people of eastern India. Iron is obtained throughout this region in the archaeological excavations. From wrought iron to tempered steel, all stages are noticed here. The evidence of vanadium in iron objects indicates that smiths were aware of how to increase the strength of this metal. Iron objects have been revealed in the archaeological contexts in megalithic burials and in regular excavations since 1200 BCE. An overall continuation of technology has been noticed through the traditional iron making route by the indigenes. The most important iron objects are sickles, ploughshares and different cutting objects of the early historic period. Cannons were one of the important objects of the medieval period.

The beginning of iron technology in the Indian subcontinent is an interesting topic. It is important to know that iron has not only independently originated in India, but its origin was also multi-centered. In the eastern part of this subcontinent, more than one centre has been identified. The iron technology got widely disseminated in the first half of the first millennium BCE. Excavations revealed the origin of iron around c.1000 BCE in the eastern India. Recently, excavated sites of Raja-Nal-ka-Tila and Malhar of southern Uttar Pradesh have pushed back the antiquity of iron in India, to well before 1500 BCE (Tewari *et al* 1999-2000: 69-98). The iron manufacturing in this part of the country is well evidenced by the presence of iron implements, slag and remnants of furnaces with a dated context (calibrated 5530±40 ^{14}C date PRL-2049 as 3150±90

BP). The date obtained from Malhar is about 1600 BCE (calibrated 1882-1639 BCE) BS-1623 and BS-1593 (Tewari *et al.* 2000: 69-98).

SOURCES OF IRON

Iron is obtained from iron ore. Iron ores of different varieties are abundant throughout eastern India. Iron is found in a large variety of minerals, such as oxides, hydroxides, carbonates, sulphides and silicates. The common varieties of iron ores – hematite (Fe_2O_3) and magnetite (Fe_3O_4) are the oxide type ores, siderite ($FeCO_3$) is the carbonate type ore and limonite ($2Fe_2O_3.3H_2O$) and laterite ($Fe_2O_3.3H_2O$) are the hydroxide type, whereas pyrite (FeS_2) is a sulphide ore. It is used as a source of sulphur. Laterite is a surface formation in the hot and wet tropical areas. This ore is rich in iron and aluminium, and it is formed by the intensive and long-lasting weathering of the underlying parent rock. The detail exploration for iron ores were carried by the Geological Survey of India (GSI).

Our ancestors also could differentiate between different ore-minerals. The nomenclature used by the different ethnic communities for different iron ores was *pola* for magnetite, *bichi* for hematite and *gata* for limonite/lateritic (Leuva 1963: 147). Those communities also liked the bluish iron ore particles, available with the hematite formation, which clearly indicates a developed native knowledge of identifying ore-minerals.

These iron ores are available as huge rocks as well as in the form of nodules and sand. Often these are mixed with titanium, vanadium, silica, alumina, phosphorus and other unwanted materials, known as gangue materials. Sometimes, vanadium and titanium alloying in micro levels, modifies the mineral character to a great extent.

From Assam, clay-iron stones are reported from the Lakhimpur and Sibsagar districts. Ferruginous iron sands of this area were washed and concentrated for iron making. The medieval iron industry developed at Tirupathar near Dibrugarh. From Meghalaya, iron is available in the Khasi and Jayantiya Hills area. Iron mining was also noted from the Mylliem, Nongkrem, Laitlyngkot, Nogundee and Cherrapunji areas (Syiemlieh 1988: 242-250). Yule (1842: 853-857) observed the exploration and washing of iron ores in that region for making iron. From Manipur, iron ore is available from the valley areas and the higher reaches. The iron ore, locally available behind the small streams south of Thobal, Langatal and from the shallow deposits at Kameng, was titaniferrous. In Bangladesh, low grade iron ore is available in abundance. Accumulated deposits of iron ores have been found at several locations in Madhupur Garh region, and the Wari-Bateshwar area of this region, covering an area of more than 2000 square kilometers, is full of laterite and ferruginous nodules (Khan 1991: 127).

In West Bengal, veins of limonite occur in the sandstones of the Damuda series. Until the 19th century, iron making continued at Muhammadbazar area of the Birbhum District. The people of that district utilised the local ores found in pockets and thin beds of limonite and hematite, embedded in laterite. Some of the sites include Ganpur (24° 03'N, 87° 43'E), Deocha (24° 02' N, 87° 37' E) and Mallarpur (24° 05' N, 87° 44' E). Iron stone is reported from Begunia, Chabalpur, Kulti, Sibpur, Churulia and other areas near Raniganj in the Bardhaman District.

In Jharkhand, three types of iron ore are found in the Palamou District. These are: magnetite, siderite-hematite and lateritic. Magnetite ores are also found at Daltonganj. In the East Singhbhum District of Jharkhand and its extension to Mayurbhanj, Orissa; apatite magnetite rock is closely associated with the Singhbhum copper belt. Besides the iron ores in heaps, there is a reference to the iron making from the magnetic iron sands (magnetite) obtained from the beds of rocky streams in Chotanagpur area.

From the recent explorations and excavations conducted by the Sambalpur University at a number of sites in the Mahanadi Valley of Orissa, many important iron objects were discovered. The iron objects recovered from Badmal have been studied (Behera and Chattopadhyay 2004-2005: 118-125). Those indicate that the ancient settlers of Badmal used to procure iron from two different sources – either from ores or the finished objects by trade. The presence of vanadium was noted in two out of the four analysed specimens.

The vanadiferrous magnetite deposits in Orissa have been detected in the eastern boarder of Keonjhar, few pockets in Baripada-Rairangpur belt in the Mayurbhanj District and a few localities in the Balasore District (Nayak and Das 1998: 288-297). The iron ores in Mayurbhanj are found as a continuation of the pre-Cambrian rocks of southeast Singhbhum. The titaniferous magnetites are very common in this region (Krishnan 1995: 85-92). Here, mention may be made of the typical iron ore combination, known as the banded hematite jasper rocks of Keonjhar and Bonai regions of Orissa (Krishnan 1955: 92). Jasper is an opaque, impure variety of silica; usually red, yellow or brown in colour. This mineral breaks with a smooth surface, and is used for ornamentation or as a gemstone. Early historic people of this region separated jasper, and developed a gem industry side by side with the production of iron. The use of vanadium-iron ore to give toughness to the metal was known to the smiths. A number of drill bits and other iron objects with this element were discovered at Badmal.

IRON EXTRACTION

Iron making was initiated in the eastern India in the late Chalcolithic phase, associated with the black-and-red wares in ceramic assemblages around 1000 BCE. The formation of sponge iron from lateritic or limonitic iron ore was carried out in the primitive iron smelting furnaces. No complete furnace was discovered here. However, based on the remnants of furnace and slag, it is surmised that the direct reduction method of iron extraction was practised by the ironsmiths.

The smelting furnaces of this region are commonly called the 'bloomery furnaces', as solid iron blooms are produced from iron ores. Iron-makers of the region selected ores, and removed the soils and dust by washing them in water. Then, the dried and preheated ores were charged in the furnace, placed alternately with layers of charcoal. The furnace was ignited and slowly heated to a temperature of around 1000-1200° C. The air was blown into the furnace through a nozzle or tuyère with the help of bellows. The skins of goats or other animals were used to make these bellows. The procedure reported by the English geologist V. Ball in 1880 may be seen in Figure 4.1.

The traditional process of iron making, which may be defined as the pre-industrial iron metallurgy, continued until the introduction of modern steel making practices in the 19th century.

PRE-INDUSTRIAL IRON MAKING

Iron making on a large-scale was practiced from CE 1200 onwards in India. It may be useful to have a look at that activity in this part of the subcontinent to understand the use of iron in historical perspective. The northeastern states and Bangladesh will be discussed first.

Arunachal Pradesh

Excavations in Arunachal Pradesh were carried out at East Siang in the Gomsi (Rani) District. The materials revealed an iron spearhead probably of the pre-Ahom period

(IAR 1995-1996: 3). Some other important sites are Blalukpong, Naksaparbat, Haju and Bhismanagar. Those excavations established the pre-historic use of iron. An iron spear, iron nails and other kinds of tools and implements were also found at Haju in the Lohit District. The Wanchos of Arunachal Pradesh to this day use a peculiar type of *dao* (a chopper) made of iron, with double-bladed sharp edges. This is called *changkep* (Figure 4.1).

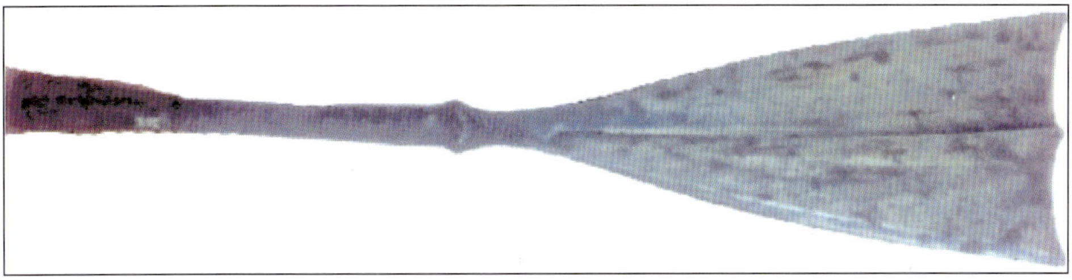

Fig. 4.1: *Changkep – double bladed dao of the Wanchos of Arunachal Pradesh (Courtesy: Dr. Tage Tada)*

Assam

Assam has a long tradition of metalwork. This tradition was highly developed during the Ahom period. One may find an unmistakable Thai influence in the metal crafts. The Assamese used iron and copper alloys, brass and bell metal. In the medieval period in Assam, iron was used for manufacturing cannons. Excellent cannons were manufactured here from the 15th century onwards.

A portion of northwest Bengal and Assam was ruled by the Koch rulers from the 16th century. The western portion was later on called Kochbihar, and the eastern portion was renamed as Koch Hajo. Excavation at Charaideo (26° 0' N, 95° 0' E) burial mounds in the Sibsagar District revealed the material remains of the Ahom kings. Excavations have revealed the presence of copper objects, fitted with the wooden hafts; iron hooks and pins, gold pendants and a few cannon balls (Jamal Hasan 2007: 16-18). The Maria communities of Assam have been known for manufacturing copper bronze vessels. In CE 1897, E. A. Gait (1897: 1-4) described in detail the tools and tackles that the Maria communities used. A variety of equipments, including anvils, hammers, chisels, crucibles, moulds, bellows and furnaces, were recorded with their local names. At Tirugaon and Hattigar, traditional iron making was still being practiced by 3,000 smiths even in the 19th century (Hannay 1856:330).

Bangladesh

This country witnessed the advanced use of iron for making boats and related accessories, with imported iron from the neighbouring region of the Khasi Hills. The iron produced by the Khasis was malleable and suitable for making these objects. The traders of Sylhet had a barter relationship with the Khasis, who exchanged iron, orange, pineapple, and so on, for rice, fish, cotton and silk cloth (Syiemlieh 1988: 242-250). That tradition continued until the early 19th century.

Meghalaya

The Khasis of Meghalaya produced iron from the local iron ores and supplied that to Bangladesh. Records are quite informative about Meghalaya, where iron-working was well-known in Khasi and Jayantiya Hills since the earlier times. Cracroft (1832: 150-151) was perhaps the first to notice iron making in this region. He has described in detail the technique of manufacturing forged iron from dressed ores. Lieutenant Yule (1842: 853-857) had also noticed iron making in the Nongkrem and Mylliem area of Khasi Hills. The flourishing iron industries of this region and the iron trade with Sylhet in Bangladesh were closed down by the British. Probably they put a stop on the indigenous production to create market for the British goods. Syiemlieh (1988: 242-250) has pointed out that the indigenous trade and industry lost to the competing traders and coercive policies of the British.

The Garos of Meghalaya used traditional iron implements in their everyday life. This community had traditional blacksmiths until 18th century. Their important iron-made agricultural implements are *ate* (*dao* or chopper) made of iron blade, *gitchi* (an iron scrapper, *attema* (a large dao used for cutting big trees) and *rua* (an axe made of solid iron for cutting big logs). By way of weapons, the *mil'am* is a two-edged and one-piece sword, made of metal, from hilt to point (Sangma 1991: 304-312).

Manipur

Although, there are few examples of excavations in the northeastern provinces, some important excavations are mentioned here. At Sekta in Manipur (24° 53' 24" N, 94° 24' E) iron spearheads and knives were excavated from the burials of the later period (*IAR*

1994-1995: 58-59). At Thoubal in the Khangabok District, the excavation revealed a wide variety of iron blades (*IAR* 1995-1996: 59).

In this state, pre-industrial metal crafts were popular until the 19th century. During iron smelting they used limestone as flux. Principal pre-industrial iron-made products of Manipur were the axes, hoes and ploughshares. Even today, iron objects are quite popular in this state. Some of those are the spear (*rung* or *bui*), harpoon (*ta*), etc. (Mao 1991: 319-355). However, *dao* is the most important iron tool that every Manipuri carries with him. The main iron implements used by the Meiteis are *langol* (plough), *thanggol* (sickle), *thangchao* (large *dao*), and so on.

Mizoram

The Mizos used iron objects like arrow, spear and dao. The *dao* was primary and essential tool. The village blacksmith was responsible for manufacturing all types of metal tools. Black-smithy was the only specialised activity in the Mizo society. The blacksmiths were a recognised category and they received a share of paddy from every household (Rengsi 1991: 313-318).

Nagaland

The metallurgy in Nagaland has been discovered from the usual neolithic and chalcolithic stages to the Iron Age, as in the southwestern part of the eastern India. People of this state are divided into a number of communities. The most important Naga communities are the Angami, Ao, Lhota, Rengma Nagas, amongst others. Black-smithy is the second most important craft particularly of the Angamis even today. The smiths produce *daos*, axes, sickles, knives, spears, and so on. Tradition has it that the Rengmas were considered the best Naga blacksmiths, who smelted iron from the iron-bearing sands.

In Nagaland, the names and shapes of the common iron objects are not the same among all the communities. The most common iron weapons are the *dao* and spears. Iron implements used by the Nagas are spearheads, daos (*zhe*), *merr* (axes) *saro-kejü* (spade-hoes), *tsukwe* (knives), *rüzhe* (chisels), sickles, *chügeh* (drill) points and awls. These objects are used for agriculture and defence.

The western Rengma and Ao Nagas used a specially made large spearhead of iron as currency. The Ao Nagas also used iron coins, called *jabili*. Two such iron coins from the Assam State Museum are shown in Figure 4.2. The eastern Rengma Nagas, on the other hand, used *daos* as currency (Mills 1982: 72). In the recent excavations at Chungliyimty in Nagaland, a *jabili* associated with kaolin ware was found. This find has been dated between the first and third centuries.

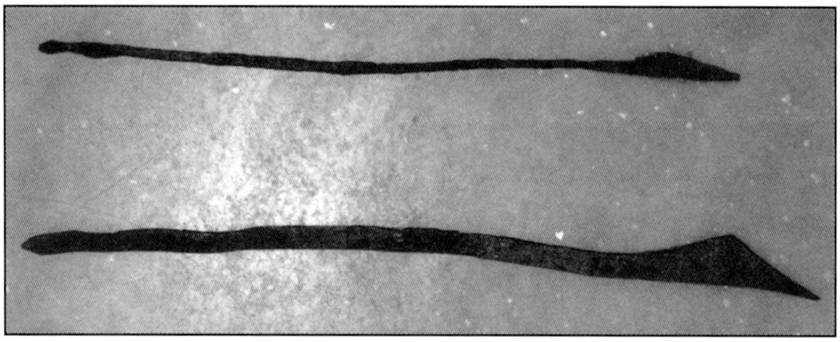

Fig. 4.2: *Jabili – used as iron currency in Nagaland (Courtesy: Assam State Museum, Guwahati)*

The Ao Nagas were not conversant with metal working before the 18th century (Mills 2003). It is known that four strangers from the plains brought iron technology that the Aos accepted. That technology further helped in manufacturing the *daos* and a few single piston bellows.

The Angami Nagas are well versed in forging iron objects. There are two or more blacksmiths in each Angami village, who cater to the basic requirements of the inhabitants. Hutton (2003 R: 63) has referred to the technology practised by the Angami Nagas. Perhaps, they did not know the iron smelting technique. They made the heating furnace with flat sandstone, with holes set upright, against which charcoal was heaped. They used to get iron from Manipur or other parts in the plains of northeast. The Lhota Nagas were also conversant with *daos* (*lepok*). The forge-shops of Naga smiths were equipped with *rekri-chi* (stone anvils), *rekri jivü* (stone hammers), *jibbeh* (pincers) made of cane, and *kuru* (bellow) made of bamboo. However, the Angami smiths possessed the knowledge of quenching and tempering. They used salt, chillies and bamboo pickles as the quenching medium. Grinding was done on the stone to sharpen the tools. Spearheads were sharpened on both sides, whereas the *daos* were sharpened on one side. After forging and shaping, the cold sickles were serrated at one side with the help of *dao.*

For the future archaeological investigations in Nagaland, the megalithic burials may be the potential source. The traditional burials are not yet dated scientifically. However, that tradition still persists and the megalithic buildings are the part of a living culture.

There is inadequate study of metal craft from the excavated metal objects of Nagaland is inadequate. Nevertheless, the excavations at the megalithic burial sites at Jotsoma (20° 40' N, 94° 03' E) and Kalogie (Figures 4.3 and 4.4) have unearthed a number of iron spearheads.

Fig. 4.3: *Iron spearhead from Megalithic Burial at Jotsoma, Nagaland (Courtesy: Tiatoshi Jamir)*

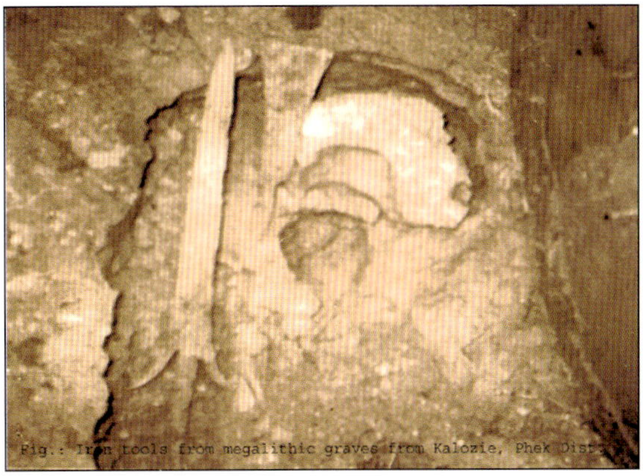

Fig. 4.4: *Iron spearhead from Megalithic Burial at Kalogie, Nagaland (Courtesy: Tiatoshi Jamir)*

The team members of Nagaland University have initiated a study of these objects (Jamir 2006: 449-463). The site of Jotsoma is dated to the 17th century. There is yet no firm radiometric date to trace the beginning of iron in the Naga Hills. According to Jamir, oral sources inform that in ancient times, metals brought from Manipur and Assam and bartered in Nagaland. For the Naga communities, being close to Myanmar, the probable accessible route for metals would have been through there.

Traditional Iron Making in the Western Part of Eastern India

Iron making was initiated by the aborigines, the ancestors of Agaria, Asur, Birgias, Birhor, Ho, Lohar, Oraons and Salui communities of Chotanagpur and its extension in Orissa and West Bengal. Until the recent past, traditional iron making was noticed in this region. Some people practiced the age-old iron manufacturing technology without any change. In the beginning, smelters used low grade iron ores, but in the course of time, they modified their furnaces to use rich ores. The European scholars of the 18th and 19th centuries have recorded the pre-industrial traditions of metal manufacturing in their works, and the Indian scholars have also taken initiative to study that tradition. Throughout the eastern and northeastern India, pre-industrial traditions are still continuing. Chakrabarti, De, Sinha, Basa and Mohanta, and others have made in depth explorations of those traditions, and they have discovered remains of pre-industrial iron smelting.

Iron smelting by the Agarias

The Agarias or Agarius of the Palamau region of Jharkhand and the Maikala Range of Chhattisgarh smelted iron under the shady trees. That process had some similarities with iron making in the modern blast furnaces. That process used to take around six to eight hours of rigorous effort. This method of iron making had been studied by Ball (1880: 668). The furnace was prepared with mud, about 0.90 m in height tapering off towards the upper end; with a diameter of about 0.60 m at the base to 0.45 m at the top; with an internal diameter of 0.15 m. The family members collected iron ore and prepared charcoal of *sal* wood (*shorea robusta*). They applied different ore dressing methods. The magnetite ores were crushed into small fragments by pounding and then powdered in millstones. Pounding was only practised for hematite ore. The hearth of the furnace was filled with a bed of charcoal. The most interesting feature of making iron was the blasting of air into the furnace, which was done with a pair of kettledrum-like bellows. The bellows were made of the wooden basins, loosely covered with leather. A valve was placed at the centre. Strings were attached to the leather covers and connected to the rude form of springs, with a slanted bamboo. A pair of hollow bamboo rods served as the conveyer of blasts to the furnace. From time to time, a mixture of ore and charcoal were thrown into the fire. The liquid slag produced in that process was tapped off through a nozzle placed a few centimetres from the top of hearth.

Before ending the process, the Agarias did not charge more ores. Air was rigorously blown into the furnace for ten minutes before finishing. The clay furnace was then broken and a hemispheric ingot – *giri* – obtained. It was made up of sponge iron, mixed with semi-molten iron slag and charcoal. Immediately, the product was forged into an ingot, hammering helped to squeeze out the slag and, thus, wrought iron was produced. The Agarias' (*Aguriah*) iron-smelting has been described by Ball (1880: 668). The photograph was taken by T. F. Peppe clearly shows that the iron making in Palamau was team work, where men and women worked together. Crushing and sizing of iron ore, blowing of air into the furnace with the help of goatskin bellows can all be seen in the photograph (Figure 4.5).

Fig. 4.5: *Iron making observed by V. Ball in 1877*

It is interesting to note that the status of the Agarias has hardly changed even after more than a century. Amitabha Sarkar of the Anthropological Survey of India conducted a survey of the Agaria iron-smelters of the Sarguja District in Chhattisgarh in 1995. He found that similar goatskin bellows, which they used earlier, in the standing posture, continues even today. They even extracted iron through indigenous techniques from the iron ore that they collected locally from the hilly areas of the forest (Figure 4.6).

In the Maikala Range in Bilaspur and Durg, the iron-smelting *bhatti* (furnaces) were of the simple conical type, about one metre high. These tapered off from the bottom upwards. The external diameter of the furnace was 1.98 m at the bottom and 1.37 m at the top. The internal diameter was 15 cm. A slanting tray, one metre in length, made of bamboo and plastered with mud, was attached to the back of the furnace. That tray was used to feed charcoal and iron-ore mixture into the furnace (Roy Chowdhury 1953: 125-137).

Fig. 4.6: *Agaria Iron smelting at Sarguja District, Chhattisgarh (Courtesy: Amitabha Sarkar)*

Iron Making by the Kols

The Kols continued to manufacture iron even until the beginning of 19th century. Watson had observed iron making in the forest near Dumka in the Santhal *pargana* of Jharkhand In 1907 (O'Malley 1999: 200-03; Watson 1907: 20-27). The Kols used to make the clay furnace under the shade of banyan trees. Its height was 86 cm; the outside diameter 66 cm at the bottom and 56 cm at the top. The inside diameter of hearth at the bottom was about 30 cm, and at the top, it was about 13 cm. On the side of furnace, there was a semicircular hole of about 30 cm. A slightly conical tuyère, 18 cm in length and 25 mm in diameter, was attached to that hole. Two bellows, made of short cylindrical pieces of wood, 40 cm diameter and 13 cm high, were hollowed out from the top to form a pillbox, with a goatskin tied to the mouth and attached to the furnace. The other ends of bellows were connected with a bamboo tube about a metre long; the distant end was connected to a nozzle, made of iron, and put into the tuyère of the furnace. The complicated blasting mechanism along with the wage of smelter has also been described by O'Malley (1999: 202). A man was engaged to work on the bellows, which alternatively sent drafts into the furnace that was kept filled with charcoal of *sal* wood.

Watson's observation is so vivid that he even noticed the ritual of putting two dabs of vermilion on the furnace wall, as a good omen. The raw hematite ore nodules were first ground to a fine powder and it, mixed with charcoal, was fed into the furnance from the top. Interestingly, Watson had, by peering into the tuyère, also observed the burning of carbon monoxide with a blue flame and white heat at the mouth of the furnace. After about half an hour of lighting the furnace, a thin stick was pushed into the moist sandy clay, and slag was tapped out. Total heating needed three to four hours, with slag tapping after 30 minutes. About 37 kg of charcoal and 18 kg of iron ore produced about six kg of crude iron, which could finally be turned into three kg of wrought iron.

The Asur-Birgia communities were practising iron manufacturing at Garha Harup Village in Netarhat near Bishunpur. Agrawal, Prasad and other members of SAIL-RDCIS, Ranchi have carried out in-depth studies on the iron manufacturing technique of that community (Agrawal, Prasad, Chauhan, Chaudhury and Aeron 1998: 218-227). Detailed social and cultural studies of that community are available now (Dasgupta 1994: 31). They are actually the inhabitants of Chotanagpur plateau, comprising the districts of Ranchi, Lohardaga, Gumla and the surrounding areas. Iron was extracted by them from the local iron ores by their own indigenous methods. The common iron implements of that community are *tangi* (axe), *rambha* (dibble) and *far* (ploughshares).

Iron-smelting was practised in the neighbourhood of Muhammadbazar area in the Birbhum District. The pre-industrial iron making was continuing in the Ganpur, Deocha and Mallarpur areas even until the 19th century. Ball (1880: 224, 345) had referred to a colony of iron-smelters at Ajudia (Ajodhya Hills, Purulia District). They used to labouriously separate the enriched magnetic sand by iron-washing.

The Keriahs were capable of iron forging. Even in the 19th century, they continued with their primitive iron making technology. They used a pair of bellows, consisting of conical caps 23 cm high, made of leaves, stitched with grass. Surprisingly, they did not use bellows, which were in general use. The ignited charcoal heaps were provided with air draft with the help of tuyères, made of bamboo. They used to forge with stone hammers on the stone anvils (Ball 1880: 91). Oldham (1852: 1-34) reported that the indigenous techniques of iron smelting in the 19th century were similar in Sambalpur and Bhagalpur, but it was different at Birbhum.

The Keriahs used a vertical shaft-type furnace and made lumps of iron ore with charcoal of *sal* wood. For blowing air, feet-operated bellows were used. At first, liquid slag was produced, which flowed to the slag pit. Sintered and lumpy sponge iron was produced in the furnace, and that was taken to a separate furnace for reheating. Iron objects were produced through very simple forging techniques.

In the Ranchi District at Chirgi near Khunti, the remains of a smelting furnace were discovered by S.P. Sinha in 1990 (Chattopadhyay 2004: 111). The furnace found was nearly cylindrical in shape and broken partly at the top and bottom. Its location was 45 cm below the surface. Iron was smelted at the iron mines of Singhbhum and Mayurbhanj. Large slagfields consisting of tuyères and other remains of smelting from the past were seen in places like Badam Pahar. No dwelling site coud be located nearby. This indicates that smiths assembled there from the nearby villages and produced iron by using the local ore and wood charcoal. In the case of Kols in Dumka area of Santhal *pargana*, description of the details of iron-smelting techniques are available in the Watson's monograph, *Iron and Steel work in the province of Bengal.* See also O'Malley (1910: 201)

In Chhattisgarh, ancient iron making in the Bastar and its surrounding districts was studied (Prakash and Igaki, 1984: 172-185; Mishra 2003: 83, 88), and it was revealed that the indigenous communities were making iron implements by using the local iron ore. Mundia and Halbi communities still manufacturing iron axes, arrowheads, sickles and other implements. Some important villages that practice metal production and metal crafts are Mokhpal, Loharpura, Koharpur, Konta, and so on.

In Orissa, there was an iron making tradition. Canons, bells and other items were produced. Around one hundred iron bells are located in the Sambaleswari temple. Those bells were manufactured 500 years ago. Iron making was reported by the Europeans, who observed this practice in Orissa. Iron anchors were manufactured by casting into moulds at Balasore (Hamilton 1708: 392). At Talcher, local laterite or magnetite ore was used for making iron (Oldham 1856: 13-16). No flux was used there, but charcoal made of *sal* wood (*shorea robusta*) was utilised. The furnaces were around one metre high and 30 cm in diameter, either cylindrical or tapering towards the top. Two bellows were attached to the furnace for air blast. Iron was obtained in a pasty condition and was repeatedly heated and forged for making it malleable.

Traditional iron making in Orissa has already drawn considerable attention. The authorities of Rourkella Steel Plant of the Steel Authority of India Limited (SAIL) took the first step in contributing marginal technological inputs to iron making process of rural Orissa (Srinivasan 1998: 228-240). There is still much left to know about the traditional techniques of iron making in this part of the country. Iron making among the indegenous communities is also known from different places of Orissa. Those communities make furnaces of clay, which are called *bhati* in the Sambalpur area and *gaana* in Koraput area. The Village Baipariguda of the Koraput District and Village Bangurkela, 20 km north of Rourkela in the Sambalpur District, have been known for their primitive method of iron smelting. In Orissa, the indigenes preferred wood of *bija sal* (*Pterocarpus marsumiam*) for making charcoal. In the Sambalpur region, they also use *sal* (*Dipterocarpus marsumiam*) (Ball 1880: 668).

A researcher, B. K. Mohanta, recently surveyed the Mayurbhanj and Keonjhor districts extensively and discovered ancient remnants of iron objects, iron-smelting furnaces, ingots, and so on (Mohanta *et al.* 2002: 81-90). The discovery of charcoal furnace (Figure 4.7) in the remote areas of Badampahar has answered many questions with regard to the ancient metallurgy in those areas, like the use of wood in iron-smelting. The nearby village, Auski at the foothill was found littered with slag and tuyère. Dilapidated furnace remains at that village were discovered by Basanta Mohanta (Figure 4.8). In the course of intensive explorations, he discovered iron blooms and finished products and subsequently did metallurgical analyses (Mohanta *et al.* 2002: 81-90).

Fig. 4.7: *Charcoal furnace on Badam Pahar (Courtesy: Basanta Mohanta)*

Fig. 4.8: *A dilapidated furnace remains at Auski, Badam Pahar (Courtesy: Basanta Mohanta)*

Iron Making: Carburisation

Iron is produced in primitive furnaces. Charcoal burns to produce heat and also carbon monoxide gas, which acts as a reducing agent. Iron ore-hematite (Fe_2O_3) first converts into magnetite (Fe_3O_4) then to iron oxide (FeO) and finally to iron (Fe). Unwanted materials, like silica (SiO_2), are changed into slag, like fayalite ($2FeO.SiO_2$) liquid form and these are allowed to flow out of the furnace. At the end of smelting, red hot iron in spongy form is obtained, which is immediately hammered into a solid mass. Entrapped slag flows out from the iron lump, though some still remains in the iron as entrapped slag particles. This iron is made of ferrite or pure iron, without carbon or other elements in it. This is similar to modern wrought iron. Repeated heating and forging to make iron objects changes the character of iron. Carbon monoxide in the charcoal furnace helps to diffuse carbon into iron, which is known as carburisation. Carburised iron is similar to steel. Carburisation is achieved by rigorous heating of iron in charcoal furnace and forging it with hammer, gripping it with tongs on an anvil.

In the beginning, iron objects were made of pure iron. Metallurgists call this stage as ferrite. The slag often found in the metal specimen as residual inclusions is called fayalite, which is a mixture of iron oxide and silica. With alternate heating and forging, the residual slag in fayalitic comes out to the surface and pours into more or less slag-free core of iron that is, ferrite, with the absorbed carbon changing into pearlite or cementite (iron carbide). That technology of carbon addition is known as carburisation. This helps to change an iron object into steel. This technique was known to the smiths of the Early Historic period. Addition of carbon or carburisation was noted in iron objects of Hatikra (*c.*1000 BCE) (Figure 4.9) and also in a secondary farming tool of Barudih (*c.*1000 BCE) (Figure 4.10). When red hot iron, having some carbon contents, is suddenly dipped in water, this process is called quenching. This increases the hardness of carburised iron. Quenching is noted in a sickle of Pandu Rajar Dhibi of the the third century BCE (De and Chattopadhyay 1989: 33-41).

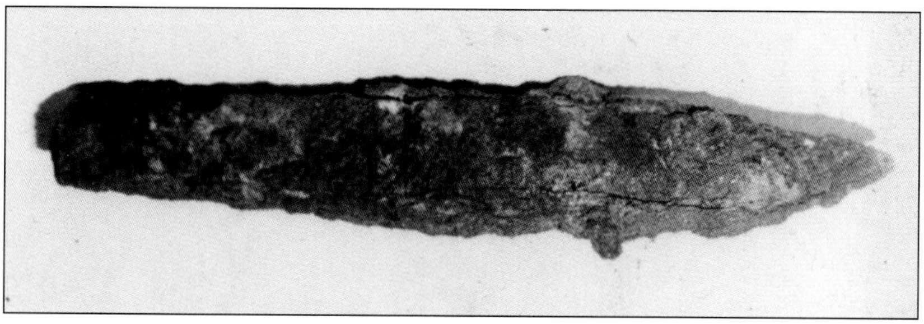

Fig. 4.9: *Iron object from Hatikra (Courtesy: Arun Nag)*

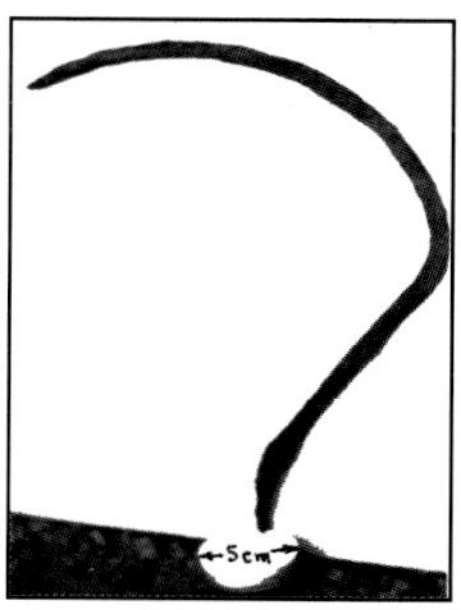

Fig. 4.10: *Secondary farming tool from Barudih (Courtesy: Asok K. Ghosh)*

By controlling the carbon contents and heat treatment, iron of different types were produced. Smiths were very efficient in producing iron objects according to their requirement. For example, iron nails were made with ferrite or low carbon by the normalisation process, namely, leaving the object exposed to air after forging. The razors and sickles need to be of very hard material. So, the smiths first increased the carbon contents (carburisation) by heating for a long time in the charcoal furnace. The heating and forging helped to absorb carbon in iron. The finished carburised object, in red hot condition, was quenched in cold water. It was hardened, and if we see a polished specimen, the martensite structure under high power microscope is visible. The hardened iron is reheated slightly. This process of heat treatment produces what is known as tempered iron.

Two basic divisions may be noted in the profession of iron making. Those, who prepare iron from the iron ore, are the smelters, and those, who forge from the prepared iron, are the forgers. In the beginning, both these trades were practised by a single group of artisans. After some time, the division of trade might have developed in the eastern India. For example, the Agarias are the smelters, who supplied only raw iron; whereas the Lohars are the forgers, who prepared the product as per the need of the villagers. In most of the regions, the Lohars are settled in each village, and they are responsible for supplying iron implements to the community.

Now let us recall the origin of iron making in this part of the country in an archaeological context.

Iron in the Archaeological Context: 1300 BCE to 600 BCE

Let us trace the occurrence of iron in regular archaeological excavations in the eastern India. Its beginning is noted in the Chalcolithic or Black-and-Red ware context at Pandu Rajar Dhibi, Hatikra and Mangalkot in West Bengal; Chirand and Senuwar (Period II) in Bihar and Golabai Sasan (Period IIb) and Badmal in Orissa. The ferro-chalcolithic level of Golabai Sasan revealed only one iron tool 7.10 cm long, 4.00 cm wide and 1.50 cm thick. That resembles polished stone celts (Sinha *et al.* 2000: 322-355).

Other important sites in Orissa are reported from theMahanadi Valley. Budhigarh had also yielded iron implements, including a spearhead, in the NBPW level. The site at Khameswaripali (Period III) revealed iron nails and a rod. Manamunda (20° 51' N, 83° 59' E) yielded iron nails, used for boat construction along with iron implements and ore nodules. We may identify from those objects that it was an iron-manufacturing area and a trade centre. Sites at Gudhel and Kharligarh, both situated in the Bolangir District, have revealed agricultural and hunting tools, such as sickles, spearheads, arrowheads, nails, knives, hilted hammers, chisels, swords and axes (Dash 1982: 53-64; Panda 2000: 202). At Kurumpadar (20° 49' 44.5" N, 84° 05' 59.6" E), definite archaeological evidences of iron-smelting were recorded (Behera 2002-2003: 87-103). In the Mahanadi Valley, another important site of Badmal (21° 06' 22" N, 84° 03' 37" E) was excavated, which yielded a number of iron objects (Behera and Chattopadhyay 2004-2005: 118-125) (Figure 4.11). The chronology of the megalithic burials of Chhattisgarh has not yet been confirmed. On the basis of typology, the iron ploughshare (Figure 4.12) of Karkabhat (20° 41'18" N, 81°19' 7" E) could be dated to the beginning of first millennium BCE (Sharma 2000:55).

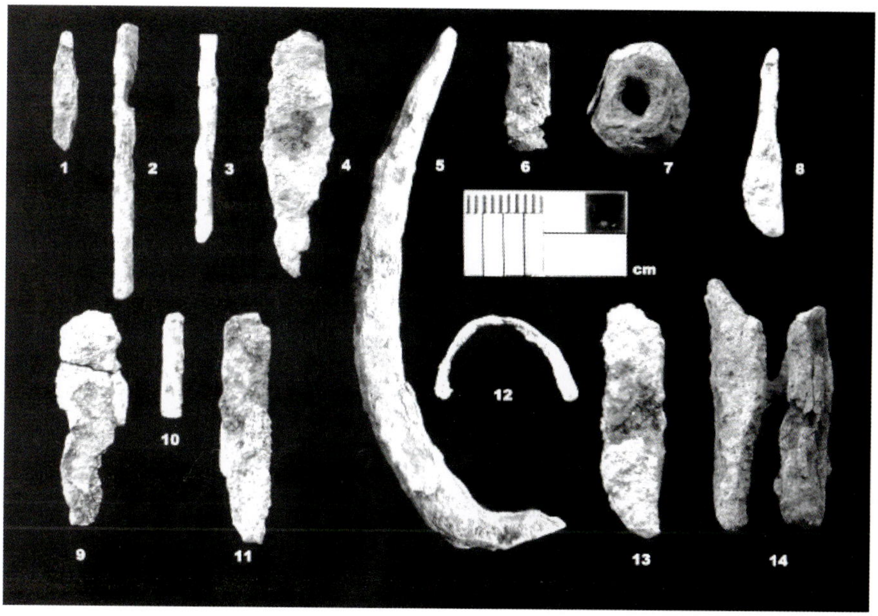

Fig. 4.11: *Iron objects of Badmal (Courtesy: Pradeep K. Behera)*

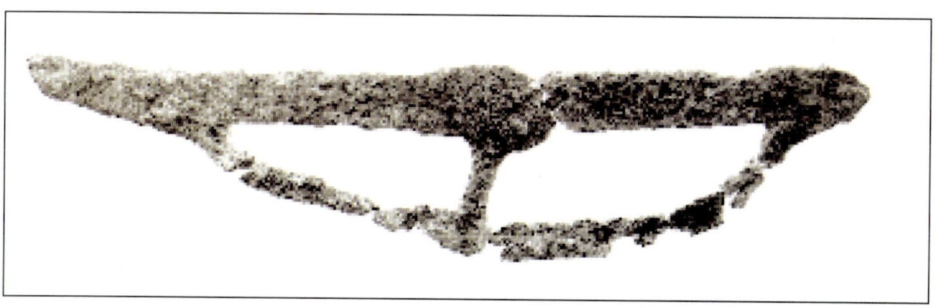

Fig. 4.12: *Ploughshare of Karkabhat (Courtesy: A. K. Sharma)*

Iron in the Archaeological Context: 600 BCE to CE 300

Most of the Early Historic sites of eastern India revealed that iron making was practised at the sites themselves.The remnants of iron making and forging were traced in Pandu Rajar Dhibi, Mangalkot, Pakhanna and Tilpi of West Bengal, which are identified as the metal-manufacturing centres. In Mangalkot, the evidence of iron-smelting is recorded in the form of a huge oven-like space, containing a large quantity of iron slag and semi-finished iron tools (Ray and Mukherjee 1992: 107-125). It is known that the residential complex for the artisans was on the border of the settlements. Their habitation has been identified at the outskirts of the site. There are also remnants of a smithy and other iron objects from Pakhanna (*CASTEI News letter* 2003: 13)

Although the maturity of iron technology is associated with the Northern Indian Black Polished ware (NBPW) culture that was well reflected in the contemporary period in Bihar. Period II of Sonpur (24° 57' N, 84° 56' E) was associated with the NBPW culture. A large number of iron and copper implements were revealed there. This may indicate considerable advancement in metallurgy. At Vaisali (25° 58' 20" N, 85° 11' 30" E), Period II flourished between 600-200 BCE. Period III has been assigned to the period between 200 BCE and CE 200. Period IV spans from CE 200 to CE 600. Dagger, sickle, lance, bell and other iron objects were recovered from Period II and Period III at Vaisali (Sinha and Roy 1969: 199-200).

The Period IV of Chirand has been identified with the NBPW phase. A profusion of iron antiquities, including spearheads, arrowheads, chisels, nails, and so on, are noted in this phase. It may be interesting to note that iron pipes were used by the people of Chirand (Figure 4.13).

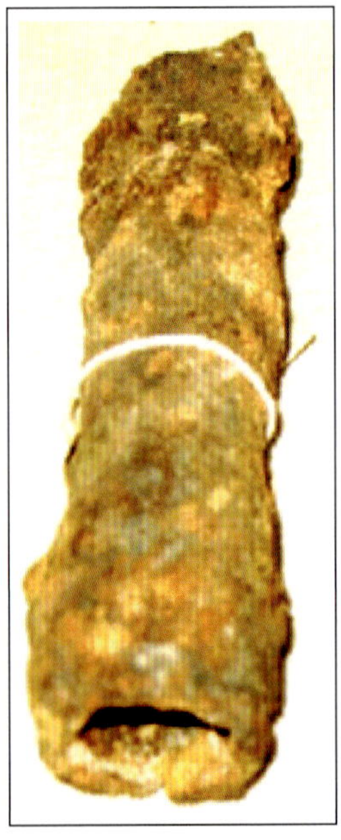

Fig. 4.13: *Iron pipe from Chirand (Courtesy: The Patna Museum)*

A variety of iron implements, along with leaf-shaped spearheads, were used in that phase at Taradih. The Period II of the earlier excavation at Panr was identified as NBPW phase (Choudhary 2005:11. 81-86). Corroded unidentified iron objects from that excavation are shown in Figure 4.14. Later excavations identified the NBPW phase as Period III. The iron objects of that phase are the nails, daggers, harpoons, hoes, hooks, knives, ploughshare, sickles, spearheads, sword-tips and other antiquities.

Fig. 4.14: *Iron objects from Panr (Courtesy: Bijoy K. Chowdhary)*

From Maner Period II, iron objects, such as the spears and nails were found (*IAR* 1996-1997:6; 1995-1996:5). An iron spearhead was also found in that assemblage, and from Period III, iron slag was reported (*IAR* 1997-1998: 17). The Vaisali excavation also revealed one *stoop*-shaped iron bell from Period IV. The Period II of Manjhi (25° 23' N, 83° 51' E) is represented by the NBPW phase, where small pieces of iron slag, several iron tools and weapons, including arrowheads, choppers, daggers, knife blades, nails, and so on were discovered. The Period III of Senuwar is equated with the NBPW period, from where from iron objects are more in number. These include a *khurpi*, a knife, a nail, rod, a sickle, arrowheads and spearheads along with iron slag. From Periods III and IV of Senuwar, the iron objects comprise agricultural and carpentry tools, household objects and weapons. Varieties of sickles (Figure 4.15) were also found at this site (Singh 2004: 394).

The Early Historic phase of Orissa is of equal interest. The ruins of the ancient city of *Samapa* have been discovered at Ganjam in the Jaugarh District (IAR 1956-1957: 31). Lots of iron implements were revealed at this site. The Sisupalgarh excavation of 1948 has revealed more than 43 iron implements. Amongst these, a caltrop, a bracelet (probably a handcuff), a latch, a staple, and so on, are worth mentioning (Lal 1949: 62-105). These implements are shown in Figure 4.16.

The excavations at a number of early historic sites in West Bengal revealed iron

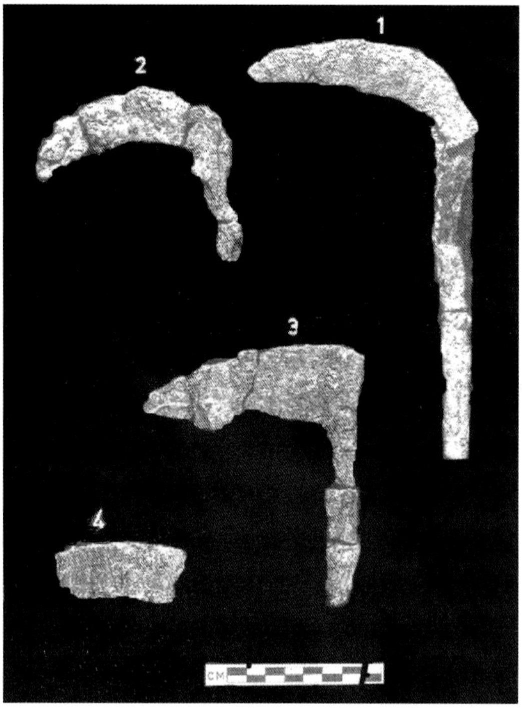

Fig. 4.15: *Sickles from Senuwar (Courtesy: Birendra Pratap Singh)*

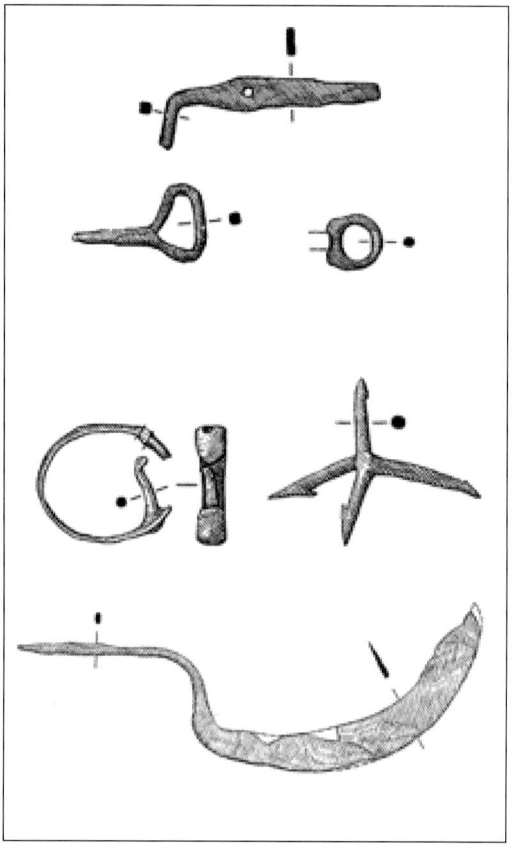

Fig. 4.16: *Selected iron objects from Sisupalgarh, Orissa (B. B. Lal 1949)*

objects. For example, Bangarh has revealed a chisel, an awl, a knife, a dagger along with the nails. The Period III of Mangalkot was contemporary of the Maurya-Shunga period. Iron objects of that period include nails, rods, sickles and daggers. Period IV of that site was contemporary to the Kushan period. Wide use of iron was confirmed by the presence of different sizes of nails, chisels, knives and clamps. From Chandraketugarh, thousands of antiquities of early historic period were recovered. The State Archaeology Museum, West Bengal, in 1999, had acquired 77 metallic objects from this site. A number of sickles (Figure 4.17), a fishhook (Figure 4.18), points, a spearhead (Figure 4.19) and a knife (Figure 4.20), made of iron have been installed. Some of these have been throughly studied (Chattopadhyay 2002: 451-61).

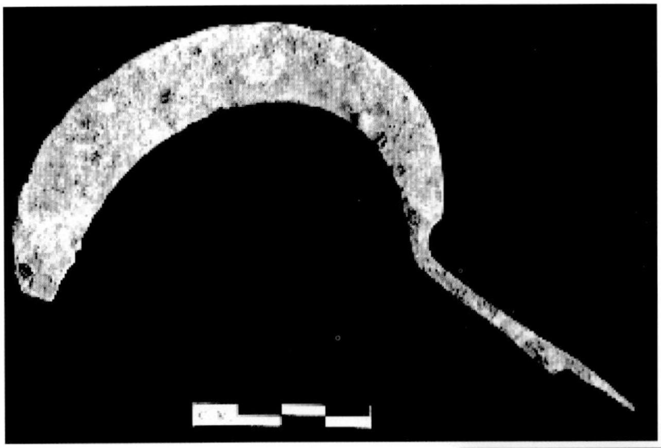

Fig. 4.17: *Sickle from Chandraketugarh (Courtesy: The State Archaeological Museum, West Bengal)*

Fig. 4.18: *Fishhook from Chandraketugarh (Courtesy: The State Archaeological Museum, West Bengal)*

Fig. 4.19: *Spearhead from Chandraketugarh (Courtesy: The State Archaeological Museum, West Bengal)*

Fig. 4.20: *Knife from Chandraketugarhat (Courtesy: The State Archaeological Museum, West Bengal)*

Excavated Smithy

Fig. 4.21: *Smithy excavated at Pakhanna, Bankura – view from the top (Courtesy: Asok Datta)*

The Department of Archaeology of the University of Calcutta has excavated the sites at Pakhanna and Dihar in the Bankura District. The Pakhanna (Period II) site revealed the iron objects (*IAR* 1993-1994: 121) and the existence of a complete smithy workplace. A hearth, an earthen pot to keep water for quenching, iron slag and burnt charcoal with iron pieces were discovered there (Figure 4.21).

This hearth may represent a village smithy/shop of the Early Historic period. All the Early Historic villages had their iron manufacturing units, which fulfilled the needs of iron artefacts that village craftsmen and farmers had, and also met the domestic needs of people. The smiths manufactured iron tools. The recent excavation (in 2009) at Dihar by R. K. Chattopadhyay has also revealed a smithy workplace. The introduction of copper and iron initiated at this site at 1300 BCE±168, supported with calibrated ^{14}C date (BS-3147).

The people of the Early Historic period of eastern India used iron extensively. Iron objects were used mostly for construction purposes and manufacturing of arms. The major iron objects excavated from Period I of Kumrahar are nails, an axe, a bar, a blade, a chisel, a chopper, a dagger, a sickle, a socket and a razor (Altekar and Mishra 1999: 140-142). Period II of Sonpur revealed lances, spearheads, arrowheads, daggers, chisels, blades and nails.

With the discovery of iron, radical changes took place in the social and economic life of people—in agriculture, urbanisation and in trade and commerce. A unique terracotta plaque (Figure 4.22) discovered in Chandraketugarh and now preserved in the State Archaeological Museum, West Bengal, shows three farmers reaping paddy in a farm with the highly developed and large iron sickles, signifying a developed agricultural practice in the Early Historic period. Besides the sickles, ploughshares, hoes, axes, chisels, and so on, were also in use.

The earliest iron objects in the archaeological context of Bangladesh are from Mahasthangarh in the Bagura District. The Franco-Bangladesh joint excavation at Mahasthan has discovered lots of antiquities. At that site, from level VII dated to 371-173 BCE, a bronze lamp, entangled with an iron axe was discovered. This has been further detailed in the chapter on copper. The trial excavation at Wari-Bateshwar yielded nails, iron slag and unidentified iron objects. That may indicate an existence of an iron smelting centre in and around that site (Haque 2001: 33). The thick layer of iron beneath the habitation affirms the existence of a source of iron at that site.

Fig. 4.22: *Terracotta plaque displaying farming scene from Chandraketugarh (Courtesy: The State Archaeological Museum, West Bengal)*

A good number of iron objects are preserved in the Mahasthan Museum, which include domestic implements, such as the head of an iron spade, spearheads, arrowheads and a ladle 20.50 cm in length. A large number of iron artefacts have been reported from Raingertek, Bateshwar and other villages neighboring Wari-Bateshwar in Bangladesh (Pathan 1989: 16). The excavation of 2000 also yielded nails and slag along with unidentified iron objects (Haque *et al.* 2000: 295). Among the collected iron artefacts, the so called 'hand-axes', spearheads, celts or digging implements and some unidentified objects are important (Fig. 4.23). The large pear-shaped iron objects look like the stone hand-axe of the prehistoric people and hence, these are called iron hand-axes. These are, on an average, 14.66 cm long, 7.50 cm

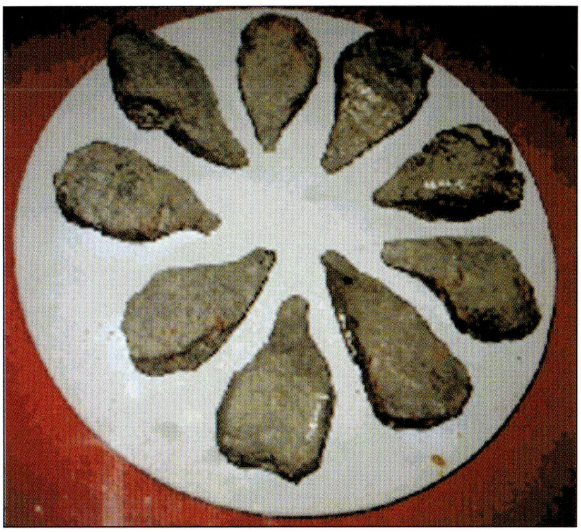

Fig. 4.23: *Iron ingots of Wari-Bateswar (Courtesy: The Bangladesh National Museum)*

broad and weigh between two and three kilogrammes. The purpose and nature of these hand-axes is not yet clear: those were perhaps used as the iron blooms or ingots (Chakrabarti 1992: 58).

About 40-50 spearheads have been collected from Wari-Bateshwar region. The handle-end of these spearheads is narrow and the working end is thin and sharp. The average length of these spearheads is 20-35 cm and these weigh 400-900 gm. Those could be used as the hunting as well as the defence implements (Ahmed 2001:35). Three celts or digging tools, also recovered from that site, are now preserved in the Bateshwar Pratna Shangrahasala (Figure 4.24). One may also mention the two massive iron objects, weighing 8-12 kg, that were probably used as anvils. Being the local source of iron, plus the presence of iron slag may definitely identify Wari-Bateshwar as an iron manufacturing and trade centre in Bangladesh. However, further investigation is necessary to identify the exact period of manufacture and use of those objects. To obtain further information about the ancient production techniques and the presence of other elements, the traditional metallographic tests, supplemented by modern technique of analysis, may be undertaken (Ahmed, Chattopadhyay and Bhuiyan 2007: 488-500).

Fig. 4.24: *Spearheads and celts of Wari-Bateswar*
(Courtesy: Habibullaha Pathan and Bulbul Ahmed)

Besides the megalithic sources in Chhattisgarh, the most important antiquity is the hanging bell of iron, 32 cm in length and 30 cm in diameter, recovered from a Buddhist temple at Sirpur in the Mahasamund District (21° 20' N, 82° 11' E). This site also revealed a large number of iron objects, including nails, dowels, door jambs, and so on. From the other parts of that temple, important iron objects, like dowels, spearheads, arrowheads, nails etc. were also recovered. Tentatively, that site is dated to between the fifth and eighth centuries (*IAR* 1999-2000: 96-99).

Iron in the Archaeological Context: CE 300 to 1200

The variety of iron objects recovered through excavation and exploration in the eastern India reveals the daily use of metal objects. These include awls, axes, adzes, flat bars, chisels, hoes, knives, nails, locks, ploughshares, razors, saws, sickles, and so on. Padlocks and keys obtained from Nalanda are unique among these finds. Among hundreds of other iron objects found in that monastery were a ladle, the tongs, a nail, a wall bracket with hook, a flat bar, a knife, a chisel, a spearhead and the daggers. From Rajbadidanga, a number of knives, one betel-nut cutter and a chisel were recovered.

From Vikramshila, a heart-shaped iron shield, bonded with iron sheets, has been recorded (Singh and Kumar 2007: 61). Besides, iron ring to hold door shutters, a rectangular pointed object with a tang and a chisel with the splayed working edge were recovered from Period IB. The Udayagiri excavation has revealed a sickle, a door bolt, a spoon and the arrow and spear heads (Bandyopadhyay 2007: 117-120). From the Lalitagiri excavation, iron sickles and spearheads were recovered. Thus, we find an overall growth of iron technology in this part of the subcontinent.

Use of Iron in Structural Components

The growth of iron technology was also manifested in the construction of stone temples. Not only the use of iron chisels for cutting of stone blocks, but also direct application of iron beams was witnessed. From the sixth to the 12th century onwards, iron beams were commonly used for the structural purposes. In Orissa, iron beams were used a great deal in construction. The magnificent Lingaraj temple of Bhubaneswar, constructed in CE 640 with beams and cornices of iron, is one of the outstanding examples in this regard. Use of iron beams was also recorded in the Konark and Jagannath temples of Puri. Iron clamps and beams were extensively used in the long-projected cornices of these temples (Neogi 2007: 39-43; Friend *et al.* 1924:313-315; Biswas *et al.* 1996: 401-03). In the Jagannath temple and its garden temple (*Gundicha Badi*), built around

12th century, there are around 239 iron beams of up to 5.18 m length of the 15 cm × 10 cm and 12.5 cm × 15 cm cross-sections.

The iron beams of Konark were manufactured between the second half of ninth century and the first half of the 13th century. Of those, around 29 beams have been measured and studied (Friend and Thorneycroft 1924: 313-315). The largest beam was 10.66 m long and about 17 cm sq in cross section, and 6000 lb or 2.72 ton in weight. There was also a reference to another beam of 7.16 m in length and 28 × 26.5 cm in cross section. The latter beam was possibly a part of the much larger one (Neogi 2007 (R) 39-44: Friend *et al.* 1924: 313-315; Biswas *et el.* 1996: 401-403). The manufacturing technique of the Konark beams has been revealed by the metallurgical studies. From the fractured surface of a beam, it was revealed that square rods of small sections were forge-welded for making the heavy beams. The closeup view of a beam is shown in Figures 4.25 and 4.25a. Similar beams are also used in the Jagannath temple, Puri (Figure 4.26).

Fig. 4.25: *Iron beams used in the superstructure of Sun Temple at Konark*

Fig. 4.25a: *Close up view of the iron beams in the super structure*

The application of welding in the laminated beams was also noticed (Ghosh 1963: 31-45). One may find rather interesting the process of heating a bundle of wrought iron bars in a lead bath. This treatment was reconstructed by Jena and associates from the traces of lead present between two pieces forged together (Prakash and Tripathy 1986: 568-79). These beams may still be found in the Konark complex. One such recent find is shown in Figure 4.27. Such beams represent the marvels of black-smithy of Orissa and have been lying in the open environment for more than thousand years without any corrosion.

WAS THERE CAST IRON IN EASTERN INDIA?

Cast iron was not used in the eastern India prior to the medieval period. In Bangladesh, cast iron was available from the eighth century onwards. One significant study is known from Bhabachandra Pat near Rangpur, where the Rangpur Sahitya Parishad had unearthed a remarkable block of cast iron from the ruins (Neogi 2007: 97-98). This is about 54.50 kg in weight. Its age in uncertain, perhaps, it was made in the later medieval

Fig. 4.26: *Iron beam (shown in deep red) used in Jagannath Temple Puri*

Fig. 4.27: *Iron beams in the Konarka complex (Photograph courtesy: Pravash Das)*

times. Cast metallic grains were visible, and the Neogi's analysis confirmed a carbon content of 2.81 percent.

HIGH CARBON STEELS OF EASTERN INDIA

The high carbon steel was known to the blacksmiths of medieval Bengal. Our information about carburisation and steeling is rather limited. Santra did some studies on the arms of late medieval Bengal (Santra 1998: 193-220). Some of those were known as *kharga* or *khadag* that were extensively used by the bodyguards of landlords. Different types of *dao* or *ramda*, preserved in temples, were widely used for animal sacrifice. Even today, these tools are corrosion-free and the decoration on them clearly visible. The hardness of those weapons indicates they were made of high carbon steel.

ARCHAEOMETALLURGY OF IRON OBJECTS OF EASTERN INDIA

In the beginning, when man discovered iron (from the iron ores), it was mixed more with slag or unwanted materials. Later, the smiths learnt to remove slag. The addition of carbon to the iron made it stronger. These stages of development may be explained as follows.

Stage I

At the introductory stage, slag was retained in the metal in large quantities. The product obtained was much similar to the modern wrought iron. No evidence of carburisation, namely, addition of carbon was found, but the excess amount of free silicon made it brittle. One of the earliest examples of this stage was the saucer-shaped object, unearthed at Pandu Rajar Dhibi of *c.* 10th century BCE (De and Chattopadhyay 1989: 33-41). The ground stone-shaped iron axe, recovered from the Period II of Golabai Sasan, Orissa (Sinha 2000: 344) is also an important find. This was a product of inefficient smelting and forging. This stage is better defined as the 'Ferrochalcolithic'. With the maturity of *Stage I*, the amount of slag became lesser than before, but no evidence of carburisation was found. It may be further mentioned that the metallographic constituents consisted of ferrite or pure iron, which is softer than bronze. In the initial stages of the iron forging technique, the repetition of heating and forging process was reflected on the formation of layers. One may find that to be true from the excavated iron objects of Senuwar and Chirand in Bihar (Singh 2007: 84-90). The best example of the layering technique (Figure 4.28) was observed in the iron objects of Badmal, Orissa (Behera and Chattopadhyay 2004-2005: 118-125).

Fig. 4.28: *Microstructure of an iron specimen of Badmal showing lamellar structure*

Stage II

The main characteristic of this stage was the process of carburisation, namely, the introduction of carbon in iron. The metal becomes harder than bronze by this process. That stage may technically be identified as the beginning of the Iron Age. The early availability of iron and its higher strength, when compared to bronze, was the foundation of the Iron Age. One of the earliest and important examples of carburisation is the dagger from Hatikra, dated around *c.* 10th century BCE (Figure 4.29). The implement clearly shows that the carburisation process was not accidental, because after forging, the finished product had been heated in a furnace for further carburisation. This has been supported by the evidence of Widmanstatten pattern (Figure 4.29) in the microstructure.

The other examples of carburisation were the sickle-shaped secondary agricultural artefacts from Barudih in Jharkhand, belonging to the ^{14}C date of 1200 BCE. Presence of ferrite and pearlite in the microstructure of those artefacts clearly indicate that after forging, the implements were left to be cooled in the open air. This process is known as normalising.

Fig. 4.29: *Microstructure of Hatikra iron implement showing Widmanstätten pattern*

From the analyses of iron objects, it was revealed that carbon contents of those objects were about 0.40 to 0.50 percent. Carburisation took place due to the diffusion at the surface of material. The available materials were found with thick corroded layers. Thus, we do not know the extent of carburisation. The inner core remained softer and the outer surface became harder due to the higher carbon contents. Carburised iron can be taken as steel.

Stage III

Before the attainment of this stage, the smiths were already conversant with the carburisation. Now, if the carburised iron is suddenly cooled (after quenching), the metal becomes very hard. When the carburised iron or steel is heated to a 'red-hot' state, the total carbon remains dissolved in iron as a solid solution of austenite. If the austenite is cooled slowly, it morphs into a pearlite structure, whereas if it is quenched in water, it transforms into the martensitic state. The martensitic structure is very hard, but at the same time it gets brittle also. This brittleness can be modified or rectified if it is further reheated. The latter operation may be called tempering. This is definitely the advanced stage in the manufacturing of iron and steel objects. However, this technique is not used for all the iron objects. This practice is used even today, for the treatment of razors, sickles and the sharp edges of axes, and so on. The earliest evidences of quenching and tempering were revealed from the tempered martensitic structure in a sickle of Period III, excavated from Pandu Rajar Dhibi, dated to the *c.* third century BCE (De and Chattopadhyay 1995: 36-39). That sickle is shown in Figure 4.30. Figure 4.31 shows the photo micrograph at 1000X and Figure 4.32, at 3000X.

It may be noted that both the stages, Stage II and Stage III, overlapped. The time difference between those may not be much.

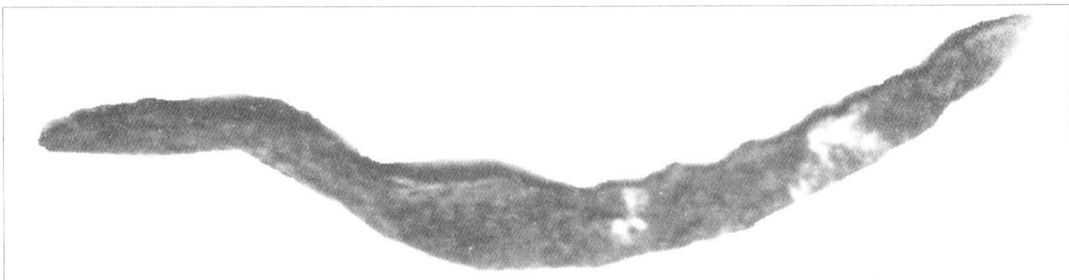

Fig. 4.30: *Sickle at Pandu Rajar Dhibi (Courtesy: The State Archaeological Museum, West Bengal)*

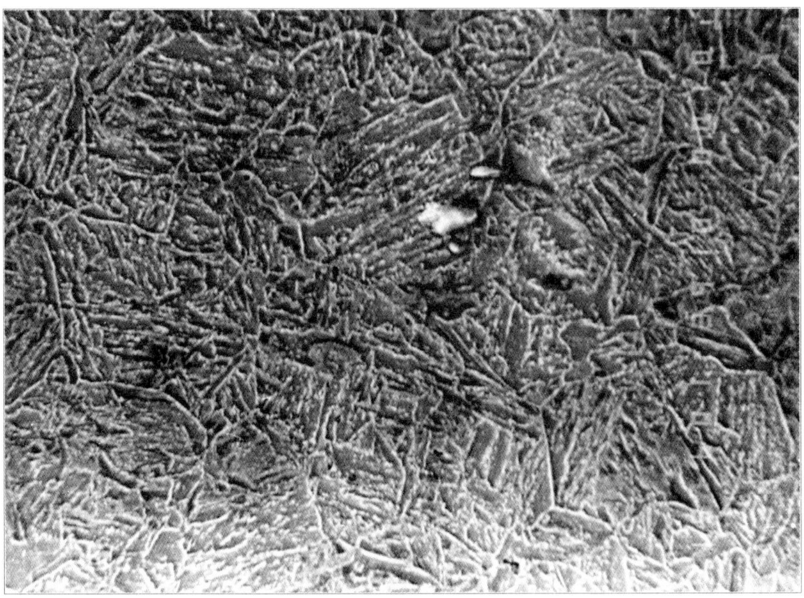

Fig. 4.31: *Microstructure showing tempered martensitic structure at 1000X*

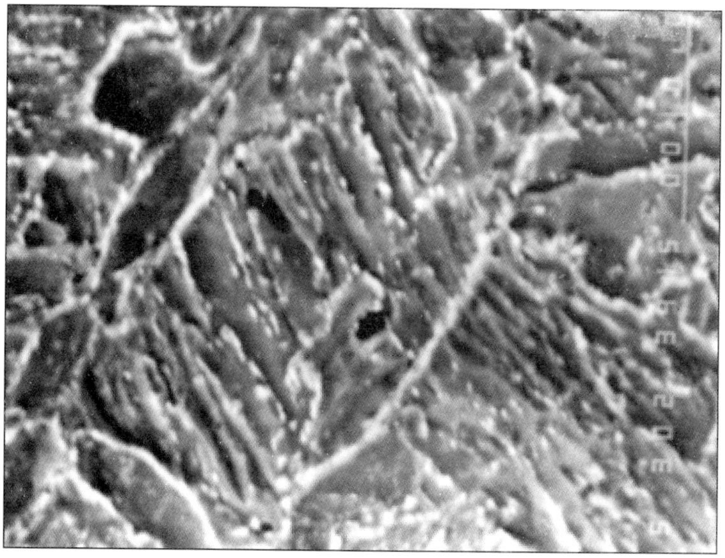

Fig. 4.32: *Microstructure showing tempered martensitic structure at 3000X*

ADVANCEMENT IN THE USE OF MICRO-ALLOY IN STEEL-MAKING

One of the recent advancements in making modern steel and alloy steels has been the use of micro-alloy. The analysis of iron objects from Badmal led to a remarkable finding (Behera and Chattopadhyay 2004-05: 118-125). This was the presence of vanadium and chromium in three of the four analysed samples. Thus, one may conclude that the smiths realised the characteristic capability of the ores was the potential of producing tough steels, with which they needed to manufacture drill bits.

CANNONS OF EASTERN INDIA

The manufacture of the cannon, the most important weapon of war in the medieval world, is quite interesting. In case of India, there is a common belief that cannons were first used during the first battle of Panipat by the Mughal invader Babur in CE 1526. The most important constituent of that technology was gunpowder, which was first brought to India from China. It may be conjectured that there were several routes for importing gunpowder to India. One of those was adopted by the Mongols under the reign of Babur.

The theory of introduction of cannons in India by Babur cannot be accepted fully.

Bhattasali (1922: 313-318) has referred to the autobiography of Babur (*the Babur-nama*) translated by A. S. Beverese, wherein it has been mentioned that on the fourth or fifth of May 1529, Babur had an encounter at Kharid with Nusrat Shah, the then Sultan of Bengal. Babur commented on the efficiency of the Bengalis in the use of cannons, but their aiming was not proper, and they used them at random. Both the facts, related to Hussein Shah and Nusrat Shah, clearly indicate that the cannons were quite popular in the eastern India in that period. In this context, a recent study made by Khan (2004: 30-31) may be cited. He has commented that the term used by Babur actually means *bans* or *howai*. Khan has further mentioned that the *ban* continued to be a favoured weapon in the military establishments of the Mughal Empire. Referring to *Ain-i-Akbari*, Datta (1986: 71-91) has commented on the *ban* as a rocket specimen. However, Babur, who possessed cannons, could not have mistaken the *ban* for the cannon with his opponents.

Classification of Cannons

The cannons, according to the type of metals used for manufacturing them, may be categorised into four types. These are indicated by how they were made, and their composition. These are the (1) forged wrought iron, (2) cast iron, (3) brass or bronze and (4) composite metal. One of the best examples of the forged wrought iron cannon is *Jahankosha* in Murshidabad. Composite cannons are made of brass or bronze and iron. One of the best examples of this type is the Tope-Zafarbaksh, located at present in the Fort Williams. There is further description of the brass, bronze and composite cannons in Chapter 8.

The cannons may also be divided into groups based on their sizes and uses. The *Ain-i Akbari* (Blochmann 1993: 119) refers to the invention of different cannons by Akbar. He made a gun (cannon), which could easily be reassembled when required. The names of cannons that appear in the text refer to the *Gajnal*, which could be easily carried by a single elephant and the *Narnal*, which could be carried by a single man.

Cannons are known from the different regions of eastern India and Bangladesh. At least, two cannons made in Shah Jahan's time and seven cannons of Sher Shah's time, still exist in different collections in West Bengal and Bangladesh.

It is rather difficult to identify cannons according to the province, because these could easily be transported and deployed at different locations. During the war, those were often captured and taken away by the conqueror. Unless a full inscription with the name of the owner and the maker are available, the source of manufacturing cannot be traced. Sometimes, the conqueror used to inscribe his name on it. Thus, inscriptions have to be studied carefully to reveal the actual history.

Some of the European cannons now available in the eastern India were made of cast iron. Some preliminary studies on those cannons have been made by Bhattasali (1922:313-318), Dutta (1986: 41-45), Miah (1991:61-90), Balasubramaniam (2005: 295-319) and Chattopadhyay (2005: 465-485).

Gunpowder is an essential adjunct of cannon. Tradition speaks of gunpowder being first discovered in Assam, and being taken from there to south China (Khan 2004: 36). However, there is insufficient proof to support that statement, though the Chinese had definite links with the Ahom kings and Bengal sultans.

Cannons of Assam

Both brass and forged welded cannons were used in medieval Assam. The best cannons came from the Teeroogong hill, located 16 km southeast of Sibsagar (Hannay 1856: 330-334). One of the largest cannons was reported to be at the Rangpur Fort. It measured 5.28 m in length and had a 19 cm bore (Krishnan 1955:73).

It is well-known that the independent rulers of Assam used cannons in wars. They had built their own cannons and also had the courage to seize cannons from Muslims. The Ahoms mostly used stone balls in their cannons, but later on they also used iron balls. The Assam State Museum has preserved hundreds of stone balls that were used as the cannon balls. One of the cannons confiscated by the Ahom rulers from the Mughals is at present in the Patna Museum. It is three metre long (of 79 rings) and is made of forge-welded iron. There is an inscription on the top of the cannon, written with braized brass letters in the Assamese script (Figure 4.33). That inscription, dated in the *Saka* Era 1540, indicates the name of its owner as Jayadhvaja Simha (CE 1648-63). The complete legend has been inscribed in a rectangle of 500 × 110 mm in two lines, with a margin of 5 mm thickness. This reads, *"Shri Shri Svarg(ga)dev Jayadhvaj Simha Maharajen Yavanam Jitva Gubaka hattvam i[da*]m yantram praptam(m) Shaka 1570"*. Perhaps, the Mughal army recaptured this cannon. The Museum obtained that subsequently from an unknown source.

It may be interesting to find a cannon in the premises of the Asiatic Society, Kolkata.

Fig. 4.33: *Cannon of Jayadvaja Simha (Courtesy: Patna Museum)*

It originally belonged to Svargadev Jayadvaj Simha, the ruler of Assam, who captured it in CE 1662 from Aurangzeb's general, Mir Jumla, the Viceroy of Dhaka. It was subsequently captured by the English and was used by them in the First Burmese War. In CE 1838, the cannon found its place at Cuttack. Still later, one Captain Petley presented the same to the Asiatic Society in CE 1891. Made of fifty-two forged rings, it is 1.9 m long (Figure 4.34).

This cannon bears a two line inscription, dated to the *Saka* Era (1)548. However, the black paint applied to protect the inscription has made it quite illegible. The legend probably reads, "*Shri Shri Svarga(ga)dev Jayadhvaj Simha Maharajen Yavanam [Jitva*] [Gu*]baka hattva i[da*]m yantram praptam(m) Shake *578*". The legends on the cannons in the Patna Museum and the Asiatic Society are identical.

Fig. 4.34: *Cannon of Jayadvaja Simha (Courtesy: The Asiatic Society, Kolkata)*

After the death of Jayadhvaj Simha, his successor Chakradhvaj Simha took the challenge to vindicate the national honour. He started making elaborate preparations for recapturing territories lost to the Mughals. The last war between the Mughals and the Ahoms, known as the Battle of Saraighat, was a notable one, for the Mughals launched a massive naval assault from the river at Saraighat. Although, the Mughals possessed hundreds of cannons and had large boats, yet they were defeated and were made to retreat from Guwahati. A large number of those cannons, especially made of brass or bronze, were definitely melted down. Some masterpieces have been preserved in the Assam State Museum, Guwahati.

While documenting the cannons of Assam, we came across five masterpieces, which were earlier lying in the Sibsagar temple complex and are now preserved in Talatalghar, Jaysagar. One of the best specimens belonged to Gadadhar Simha (1681-96) is the 3.46 metres long cannon with 10 cm bore. It is shown in Figure 4.35.

Fig. 4.35: *Cannon of Gadadhar Simha, Talatalghar, Sibsagar, Assam.*

Cannons of Bangladesh

In different museums and public places of Bangladesh, a good number of cannons are preserved. At least a dozen cannons – both the Mughal and the European – are displayed in the National Museum of Bangladesh.

It is known that the two iron cannons of the Mughal period existed in the city of Dhaka. One of those sank in the River Buriganga around CE 1780. The other cannon originally stood at Sadarghat, but later, it was shifted to the Gulisthan Natyamanch. This cannon is now in the Osmani Garden in Dhaka.There are different opinions about their names. From the published literature, several names have appeared for those cannons of Dhaka. Those are: 'Kaley Khan', 'Kalu Jham Jham' and 'Bibi Mariyam'. It is a 5.38 m long cannon, calculated from the volume of iron used, and weighed 64,814 pounds (about 30 tons) and the weight of the iron shot was 465 pound (211 kg). From its physical appearance, one can easily identify four rings attached to the clamps on the cannon's body (Figure 4.36).

Fig. 4.36: *Cannon Bibi Mariyam at Osmani Garden in Dhaka*

At the Chittagong University Museum, Chittagong, there are two iron cannons. One cannon was recently unearthed in the Village Sholekata of Chittagong. It is 2.13 m in length and weighs 740 kg. Perhaps, Subedar Sayesta Khan used it in the war of 'Chhatralla' against the Arakan and Portuguese pirates (Santra 1998: 213).

Cannons of Meghalaya

The ruins of the summer palace of the Jayantia kings at Nartiang are located on a hillock close to the well-known Nartiang temple. The palace ruins consist of several platforms and apartments, probably used as the living rooms, sacrificial rooms, entertainment halls, council chambers, and so on. According to the local tradition, the walls of that palace in its heyday were covered with the paintings and engravings. The palace appears to have been fortified with the fixed cannons, each of which pointed towards a different direction. The remains of those cannons can still be seen.

Cannons of Orissa

There are 30 cannons reported in Orissa, which are present on display in a gallery of the State Museum at Bhubaneswar. The Mughals and the Marathas had used some of those cannons. A large number of those belonged to the British. Eight big cannons were recovered from the Barabati Fort area, and two from the Lalbagh Palace in the Cuttack District. One of these cannons is shown in Figure 4.37.

Fig. 4.37: *Cannon from Barabati Fort (Courtesy Orissa State Museum, Bhubaneswar)*

Cannons of Tripura

Four cannons are preserved in the Agartala State Museum. One cannon, which Dhanyamanikya had captured from Hussain Shah, is preserved at the Kaman Chowmohani of Agartala (Figure 4.38).

Fig. 4.38: *Cannon at Kaman Chowmohani, Agartala, Tripura: Courtesy: Pratip K. Mitra*

Cannons of West Bengal

Three old cannons were located at the Kochbihar Palace. Their history and present location is not known. These cannons bear Persian inscriptions, but these are illegible on two of them, so cannot be deciphered. However, it can be inferred from the calligraphy of inscription on the third cannon that it was not made earlier than the 17th century. This cannon bears the date in the month of *Shawal* in 1022 H (CE 1613). This is a naval cannon 163 cm (5 ft 4 in) in length, with a 48.30 cm (1 ft 7 in) nozzle diameter and 4.45 cm (1.75 inches) bore diameter. It weighs around 63 kg (one maund, 28 seers and two chhataks). Perhaps it was built for the Myanmar War (Ahmed 2001: 33). The author further mentions, that the two cannons, which Raghudev Narayan (CE 1581-1603) of the eastern kingdom of Kochbihar used, are presently with the *zamindars* of Gauripur of Assam. One of these cannons, with a length of 223 cm (7 ft 4 in) and a diameter of 28 cm (11 inches), was built in 1514 *Saka* era (CE 1592), located at Hawa Mahal at Dhubri. The second one, dated to 1022 AH (CE 1613), was dodecagonal. That was 138 cm (4 ft 6 in) long, with 14 cm (5.50 inches) nozzle diameter and now missing.

The most popular cannon of West Bengal is the *Dal Mardan* or *Dal Madal*, presently located at Bishnupur in the Bankura District (Figure 4.40). That cannon has been thoroughly studied by Balasubramaniam and others (Balasubramaniam *et al.* 2005: 275-314). The research findings are well documented. However, there is neither a date on the cannon nor is there any written history to identify its manufacturer. The *Dal Mardan* was used as a defending weapon against the Maratha army under Bhaskar Pandit during the reign of the Malla King, Gopal Singh, probably sometime between CE 1600 and 1700. Originally, it was in the dilapidated fort of Bishnupur and was brought to the present location in CE 1919. The total length of *Dal Mardan* is 3.84 m and it weighs 7.90 tons (Figure 4.39). In this town, there are a number of other small cannons.

Fig. 4.39: *Dal Mardan, Bishnupur, Bankura, West Bengal*

Murshidabad

The *Jahankosha* (conqueror of the world) was located previously at the Katra Mashjid. Now, this cannon placed on a platform in the city is protected by the ASI (Archaeological Survey of India). It is bright red in colour and has a smooth finish on the exposed surface. No rust has been detected on its surface. The cannon is 533 cm in length, 160 cm in circumference, and weighs 7844 kg (Figure 4.40). It bears the largest Persian inscription. There are nine inscribed brass plates, which indicate that it was made in 1047 AH (CE 1637) by the chief mechanic, Janardan Karmakar, under the supervision of Daroga Sher Mahammad and Inspector Harabullava Das at Jahangirnagar (Dhaka). The forge-welding of the iron rings is excellently and skilfully done. It is also beautifully decorated. The forge-welding lines are almost indistinguishable. In Murshidabad, the *Bachawoli* is the other important cannon, located in front of the *Hajarduari*. This was made of the forged iron in two pieces, the chamber and the barrel (Figure 4.41).

Archaeometallurgy of Iron Cannons

The raw material for manufacturing iron cannons was sponge iron, which was further forged into iron discs. This is clearly referred to in the *Ain-i Akbari* (Blochannm 1993).

Fig. 4.40: *Jahankosha, Murshidabad, West Bengal*

Fig. 4.41: *Bachawoli, Murshidabad, West Bengal*

Rather than cutting rings out from the discs, they were were forge-welded. The discs were subsequently forge-welded and red-hot iron rings were slipped onto the joints. On cooling, the rings contracted tightly onto the joints, and the iron guns of large dimensions were made in this manner. The wrought iron cannons were mostly made by hammering and welding. The studies have revealed the presence of a higher percentage of phosphorous, which has been responsible for the corrosion-resistant property of the cannon of Bishnupur, the *Dal Mardan* (Balasubramaniam *et al.* 2005: 275-314). The in-depth chemical analyses, metallography and material characterisation are now available for a few cannons of the eastern India. One of these cannons from Bishnupur is made of the forge-welded wrought iron, with three iron rings over each other to add to the thickness of the cannon. It has 202 such rings.

ARMS OF EASTERN INDIA

Besides the cannons, people of eastern India possessed excellent arms for their defence. Different types of arms are preserved now at the Mahasthan Museum and the National Museum of Bangladesh and also at the Bhubaneswar State Museum, and the Victoria Memorial Hall. The Assamese swords and other objects are also preserved at different museums of Assam. The Tai Museum of Sibsagar, where a series of arms are displayed (Figure 4.42). Those represent a wide collection of arms, used by the people from the medieval to the pre-modern periods.

Fig. 4.42: *Arms of the Ahom period (Courtesy: The Tai Museum, Sibsagar)*

Along with cannons, matchlock muskets were also used in medieval wars. Those were known as *Tufang* and were used by the infantry (Pant 1970: 174). It is known that Babur probably brought matchlock muskets of Turkish origin and used those in the war at Panipat in CE 1526. The musket, fitted with a matchlock, when used from the ground skillfully proved to be a devastating instrument of war (Khan 2004: 144).

Babur had 1200 musketeers, but he lost the Bengal campaign. However, later on the use of muskets and the skill of using those on the horseback, did not find acceptance in the Mughal Empire.

THE WOOTZ

The different types of iron and steel objects of the eastern part of India have been described so far. In the Telengana region of south India, ancient steel-makers made wootz steel, which basically contained high carbon. This was manufactured in a specially closed crucible (Jaikishan 2009: 43-57). No such steel specimen has been found in eastern India, except for one specimen (Figure 4.43), probably made of wootz steel, discovered by Basanta Mohanta (Mohanta, Basa, Chattopadhyay and Das 2003:81-90) from Orissa.

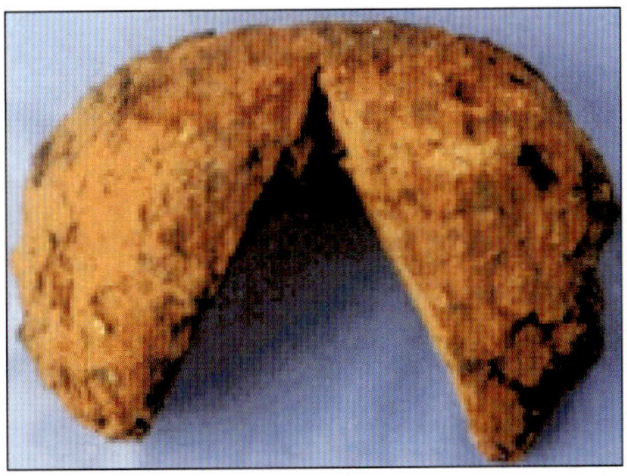

Fig. 4.43: *An ingot – probably a piece of wootz-steel ingot (Courtesy Basanta Mohanta)*

5

GOLD

ARTICLES OF GOLD WERE WELL-KNOWN IN EASTERN INDIA EVEN before the Early Historic period. The discovery of a gold coin of Kanishka I in CE 1968 may provide one of the vital proofs for the antiquity of Pandu Rajar Dhibi in West Bengal.

SOURCES OF GOLD

The earliest use of gold is known from the Neolithic period. An example is a gold ear ornament dated to 2000 BCE discovered Tekkalokota in south India (Agrawal 1982: 115). In eastern India, native gold was known to be associated with the quartz veins and also found as nuggets in the streambeds of the local rivers. In the Harappan sites, gold was well known, but sites like Lothal have revealed high amounts of silver in the metallic gold found there. That indicated the use of electrum as the source material. The gold found in Lothal was perhaps not obtained from an alluvial source.

In eastern India, alluvial gold is well known from the sand beds of rivers in the states of Jharkhand and Orissa. Many rivers, including the Subarnarekha, the Mahanadi, the Sona, the Garanadi, the Maini, the Jonk, the Kansai, the Bamni, the Tutko, the Kumari, the Ebe and the Tikaria have been yielding gold. The extensive exploration for gold was carried by GSI.

Gold flakes, mixed with sand, have been found from the upper course of Subarnarekha and other rivers. In the Sonapet Valley of Jharkhand, gold had been obtained from various streams. In the Nimdih block of Chandil area, panning for gold continues in the Subarnarekha (Chakrabarti 1993: 90). Old gold workings are known from Ankua, Anandpur-Paradih, Tamapahar, Bhalukkhad-west and Bhalukkhad-east. The alluvial sources of gold are available in the Sone, the Subarnarekha, ans so on, in the Chotanagpur plateau and its extension (Ball 1880: 123; Biswas *et al.* 1996: 309).

Some of the rivers in Assam, like the Brahmaputra and the Subarnasiri are also known for enriched alluvial gold. Panning for gold was recorded in the upper course of Brahmaputra, at the Nea-Dihing, Buri-Dihing, and also in a small stream, called the Jagle. In the Sibsagar District, a few places like Desel and Jhanzi were known for gold-bearing sand. Panning is reported from the Bhoroloi and Dikrang rivers. Maclaren (1904: 212-17) reported those gold-bearing rivers in CE 1904. Some of the rivers in Manipur also yield alluvial gold.

From West Bengal, there is information that in the Baghmundi area of the present Purulia District, gold washing is still being practised. The specks of gold found in that area are recorded to be as heavy as 0.1235 gram (Ball 1880: 118-19).

In Chhattisgarh, a number of sites are known where gold washing was carried out in the 19th century. Panning for gold is also known from the Maini, the Sonajori, the Bharari, the Indrabati and the Sangal rivers. Gold washing has also been reported from Kuncha near Dhadka in Kantagora (Ball 1880: 105).

SEPARATION OF GOLD BY THE TRADITIONAL METHOD

A wonderful traditional method was known to the indigenes of this region for separating the flakes of alluvial gold. They used to pan for gold twice a year, after the rainy season and during the winter. The washing was carried out in rectangular vats, in which gold particles were separated from other heavier minerals.

The methods of gold washing from Singhbhum in the eastern India have been well reported. In 1880, V. Ball published his memoirs on geological explorations in this region. In the Singhbhum and the erstwhile Manbhum District of Jharkhand, Ball discovered a good number of sites. One illustrations of gold washing is reproduced from Ball (1880: 123) in Figure 5.1.

The indigenous communities, Dohras or Dokras of the erstwhile Manbhum District had the practice of washing alluvial gold in the Tutko River during the rainy season. The Dohras practised that mineral-dressing technique by using a simple wooden dish for collecting sands. The wooden dish was hollow towards the centre. The dish was 90

Fig. 5.1: *Alluvial gold washing in the Tutko River (Ball 1880)*

x 60 cm in size, resembling an exceptionally broad butcher-boy's tray with an iron hook fixed to the handle. With the latter, they scraped and collected the sand and pebbles into the former, which was then placed in the water. On rubbing the contents with the hands and shaking the dish to and fro until all the large pebbles and light silt was removed, some black sand with scattered specks of gold remained in the wooden dish. Those specks were then taken out from the dish, after removing the black sand. For the separation of gold, they had no knowledge of the amalgamation process—a technique that involves dissolving gold with the help of mercury.

The Ghasis, Kols and Mundas of Singhbhum also practiced gold washing in the 19th century (Ball 1880: 81, 122, 123). The Kol and Munda women carried out gold washing during the rains.

The traditional process adopted for procuring alluvial gold in Manipur involved mineral dressing on a wooden plank, made into a tray with successive grooves that helped to separate gold particles from the mixture of gravel, sand and clay. The fine sand that remained in the grooves was then placed on a wooden trencher, polished on the inside with the black varnish of the *keoo* tree. Finally, gold particles remained in the small receptacle used by them (Kuppuram 1989: 177). A recent publication has thrown more light on gold washing in this part of the country (Upadhyaya *et al* 2006:359-366).

PURIFICATION OF GOLD

The method of purifying gold during the medieval period has been described in the *Ain-i Akbari* (Blochmann 1993: 21; Khan 1986: 71-91; Sundaram *et al.* 1999: 25). That technique was rather interesting for the separation of silver from a mixture of gold, silver, copper and other impurities. The mixture was placed beween the layers of saltpetre and brick dust inside a mound of cow-dung. As mentioned in the text, the mixture was heated or burnt 18 times, after which the gold was considered pure. The ash so produced was sprinkled on the still surface of water and the gold particles were collected at the bottom of the vessel. The remaining gold in the ash was separated with the help of mercury by the amalgam process and subsequent distillation. Further, ash was mixed with the lead powder, mild acid and saltpetre, and kneaded into balls. Those balls were further burned with charcoal and the lead was separated from gold-silver-copper (GSC) alloy.

EVIDENCE IN THE HISTORICAL RECORDS

As already stated, gold has been available from alluvial sources at a number of sites in the eastern India. The source of Assamese placer gold was very famous. This was also known to the Arabs and Persians. A 10th century text *Hudud al-Alam* refers to the numerous gold mines of Qamaroon (Kamrup) (Shanaj 2006: 78). Pliny records that some gold from the Ganga in India, even reached the Roman Empire.

During the Ahom rule in Assam, ten to twelve thousand *sonwals* (the labourers, who collected *sona* or gold) were engaged in gold washing from the sands of the Brahmaputra (Figure 5.2). That was reported by Shihabuddin Talish, who visited Assam in CE 1661-63. According to this report, it was known that the labourers had to pay one *tola* (a

Fig. 5.2: *Gold washing in Assam, showing people and equipment (Courtesy: Prabhakar Upadhyay)*

standard Indian weight equivalent to 11 grammes) of gold per head per year (Rhodes and Bose 2004: 11).

GOLD OBJECTS FOUND IN EXCAVATIONS

In Bangladesh, Mahasthan is a most important site. From that site, the France-Bangladesh joint excavation of 1999 had discovered a complete gold pendant and tiny fragments of gold rings along with jewelry stone mould (Alam and Salles 2001: 121, 159-160). The pendant, discovered from the level VIII, is accessioned as MAH. 99. 223. The period of that level was established as 19-46 BCE. From level VI of that site, gold leaves were discovered. In the 1997 excavation, a rectangular sheet of gold (accessioned as MAH. 97.705.7) was recovered from level IX (dated 19-46 BCE). It was 14.22 cm in length and 3.12 cm in breadth, indicating that the site was also an important manufacturing centre, where gold ornaments were made. From Itakhola Mura of Mainamati, three round pellets of solid gold of around 210 grams in weight were recovered along with a copperplate.

From Bihar, a gold repousse figure was recovered from a burial mound of Lauria Nandangarh, dated around the sixth century BCE. That was image of Prithivi (ASI Annual Report 1906-07: 122). The repousse is the technique of shaping or ornamenting the metal by hammering from the reverse side. At Vaisali, gold pieces along with other artefacts placed in a miniature pot were recovered from the excavation at Period III in the Garh area (Sinha and Roy 1969: 195). These objects consisted of two ear ornaments filled with copper in its interior, two earrings of solid gold, with their ends tied with the very thin gold wire, two objects, decorated with the kneeling humped bulls, a standing human figure and a hair clip or armlet. Besides, a fragmentary gold necklace, made of double pronged and double holed gold leaves, and a gold ring with thin gold wire, were also found. The metal objects discovered at Nalanda (25° 08' N, 85° 27' E) also included gold ones (Misra 1998: 272-75). Excavation at Chirand revealed gold wire rings, beads and a thin disc (Verma 2007: 151).

Sekta (24° 53' 24" N, 94° 24' E) is an important excavated site in Manipur. It was a burial place. The burials included skulls with or without metal masks. However, the most important discovery was the unique gold mask (Sharma 1994: 3) shown in Figure 5.3.

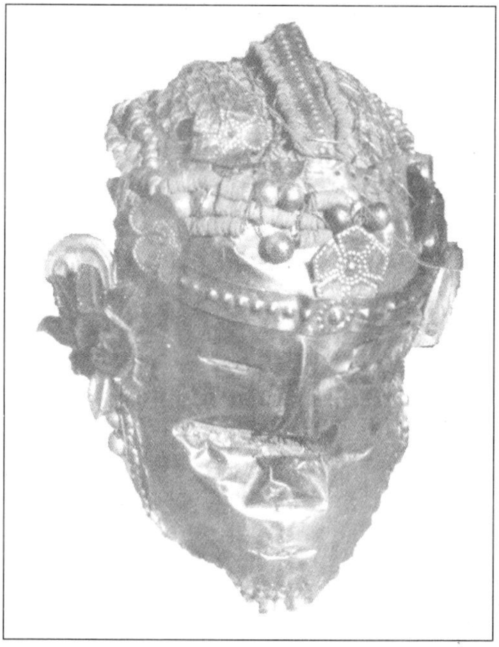

Fig. 5.3: *Gold mask recovered from Sekta, Manipur (Courtesy A, K. Sharma 1994)*

From Orissa, the excavation at Lalitagiri revealed a gold foil. The excavator has suggested that probably a Mauryan *stoop* existed somewhere in the vicinity of the site (Bandyopadhyay 2004: 2). From the mound III in Chandrasagar Nala at Medinipur Village, two pieces of gold wire were recovered from Period I (Singh *et al.* 2006: 133-141). Some interesting specimens of gold have also been recovered during excavation at that site, which include a gold leaf with floral design, beads and coins. From Udaigiri in Jajpur District of Orissa, a circular gold pendant was unearthed (Nigam 2000: 495-506; *IAR* 1961-1962: 36-37).

The excavations in West Bengal also revealed gold objects. For example, Period III of Pandu Rajar Dhibi, excavated in 1963-1964, had revealed gold pellets and a broken pin of gold. So far, that was one of the earliest examples of the discovery of the gold objects in that area. The findings appeared to be of the period earlier than the sixth century BCE (Mukherjee 1992: 8).

From Bangarh (ancient *Kotivarsha*), one inscribed gold amulet in two parts and a gold pendant were found (Goswami 1948: 12, 16). The pendant had the design of a chain bordered by beads. This relic represented the excellence that the goldsmiths of the Sunga period (from the second to the first century BCE) had achieved. The excavator opined that gold and silver ornaments were manufactured at the site itself.

GOLDPLATING

Goldplating is known from the Early Historic period in this part of the subcontinent. It was mostly done to decorate copper and brass images. Goldplating on a copper rod was identified in Period III (post-NBPW level) of Sonpur. A goldplated bronze image of Bodhisattva Manjushri (*c*. sixth century), recovered from Balaidhap and preserved in the Varendra Research Institute, is a unique art (see Figure 8.21) object (Majumder 1926: 426-428). This is the earliest known goldplated image reorted from eastern India (Saraswati 1962: 30). The date indicates that goldplating technology was developed in the eastern part of this country before it developed in Thailand. One may also mention the Deulbadi Sarvani image, discovered at Deulbadi in the Comilla District of Bangladesh in this context. That is one of the few sculptures with an inscription (Bhattasali 2001: 204; Sengupta 1989: 269-273) of the end of the seventh century. This sculpture was earlier preserved in the then Dhaka Museum.

Perhaps two different technologies were prevalent for goldplating—one used mercury amalgam with chemical deposition of gold (this is, perhaps, doubtful); the other involved wrapping with a thin sheet of gold on bronze or other material.

GOLD COINS

In eastern India, the use of gold for making coins was introduced by the Kushan rulers. Excavations and surface finds at many early historic sites in Bangladesh, Bihar, Orissa and West Bengal have yielded a number of gold coins of the Kushan period. Those coins were known as the *dinar.* A gold coin bearing a legend *Dharmdamadhar*, similar to the standing Kushan king on the obverse and a Roman bust on the reverse, was found atop the third layer from the excavation at Sisupalgarh (20°13' 30" N, 85° 51' 30" E). At that site, a Kushan gold coin was recovered from Period III, (Lal 1948: 100). This coin was a cast imitation of the original or an ornament (Tripathy 1986: 37). Some original Kushan gold coins were also traced at that site, which might have reached there by way of trade. Excavations at Chirand revealed a gold coin of Sri Gangeyadev of the Kalachuri dynasty.

Pre-Gupta Gold Coins from Bangladesh

A number of pre-Gupta gold coins (about 46 in number) were discovered at Nasirabad in Gaibandha District in Bangladesh. One of those masterpieces is known to be in the collection of Murtaja Baseer. That coin shows a figure and it weighs 4.10 grams, is 27.30 mm in diameter and 0.06 mm in thickness (Figure 5.4). The coin is similar to the Harikela coins, and punched on one side only. At the centre, there is a lotus symbol with the four petals. On the outer side of the coin, there are four symbols of the crescent moon, four solar symbols and two symbols with the proto-Bengali letter '*ka*'.

Fig. 5.4: *Pre-Gupta gold coin discovered at Nasirabad (Courtesy: Murtaja Baseer)*

Gold Coins of the Gupta Period

The next important coins of eastern India belonged to the Gupta dynasty, which ruled over the major parts of the region from the fourth century. Those coins were also known as *dinar.* A marvellous series of gold coins was issued by Samudragupta, Chandragupta II and Kumargupta. As recorded in Damodarpur Copperplate, the last Gupta ruler was Vishnugupta. The post-Gupta coins of Bengal were in circulation from CE 550 to 700. The eastern Indian numismatic art reflects the quality of contemporary sculptural style. Gold coins continued to be in use in the Samatata region of Bangladesh, but the gold content in those coins were heavily reduced. Those coins are known as the later Gupta coins and were in circulation until the seventh century. From Orissa, gold coins of Chandragupta II Vikramaditya were discovered in Lalitagiri and Cuttack, and in the Mayurbhanj District.

Technology of the Gupta Gold Coins

The coins of Gupta and post-Gupta period were manufactured by the 'die striking technique'. The major element was gold, to which copper and other elements were added to make an alloy. Molten alloy was cast into sheet. The sheet was then shaped into pieces of required size and thickness and turned into blanks. Two negative metal dies, one fixed on the anvil, and the other attached to a punch and struck with a hammer, were used. Thus, both sides of the blank received the positive impressions and turned into a coin. R. Balasubramaniam discovered that while striking a gold coin, three blows of the hammer were given (Balasubramaniam and Mahajan 2003: 331-349).

Post-Gupta Gold Coins

A variety of tiny gold coins, known as the *Ganga fanam* from Orissa may be mentioned here. Those coins were issued by the rulers of Kalinganagar between the seventh and the 11th centuries. Those coins were recently discovered from Nandigram in the East Medinipur District of West Bengal. The abundant discoveries of *Ganga fanam* in several hoards in Orissa, as well as in the gold necklaces suggest that gold coins were used both as currency and also as ornaments (Tripathy 1986: 187).

Gold coins of Samatata

A number of gold coins have been discovered from the geographical region of Tripura and the Comilla District of Bangladesh. The coins made of debased gold are of the Gupta prototype. In the western part of Bengal and Orissa, gold coins of Shashanka (CE 600-635) are known. From this area, similar prototype coins have been recovered. However, some scholars say that the Samatata coins also include those issued by the Khadga and Dev dynasties.

Gold coins of Assam

The earliest coins of Assam are known to have been issued by Bhaskarvarman sometime around CE 600-650. He was a contemporary of Harshavardhan of Kanauj and Shashanka of Gaud (Bengal). Gold coins bearing the name of *Shri Kumar* probably belonged to King Bhaskarvarman's time. On paleographic grounds, the legends appear to be of the seventh century.

Gold Coins of the Bengal Sultans

The gold coins of Bengal sultans are rare. Bakhtiyar Khilji, who captured Bengal, had issued a horseman-type gold coin, bearing the legend *Gaud Vijaye* and the date, which records capturing of Gaud, the capital of Bengal by the Islamic rulers. Gold coins are also known to be issued by Bengal sultans—details have been discussed by M. R. Tarafddar (Tarafdar 1995: 31-56).

6

SILVER

THE USE OF SILVER FOR ORNAMENTS AND COINS HAS BEEN VERY popular through the ages in India. It was used widely for ornaments in Eastern India. It may be astonishing to know that even the poor villagers of Bihar continued to use silver ornaments, about a kilogramme in weight, until the middle of the 20th century. A similar situation existed in the northeast. For example, the indigenous communities of Arunachal Pradesh, Manipur and Tripura preferred to use heavy ornaments made of this metal. Silver dust or *choornnee* was known to be used as medium of exchange in some parts of the eastern India.

THE SOURCE OF SILVER

There are two basic sources of silver. One is from electrum – a natural alloy of gold and silver, and the other is from argentiferous galena. The Latin name of silver is argentinum, so the ore is called argentiferous galena. Galena is basically lead sulphide (PbS), with traces of silver in it. There is some information on the different sources of these two elements in the eastern India, but it is not known if electrum was ever used for making silver ornaments. Nevertheless, electrum has been identified in a pendant from Lothal, which was made of 66.55% silver and the remaining was gold. The results perhaps indicate that gold used in Lothal was not obtained from an alluvial source. Like gold, silver also exists in its native form. The availability of silver in different parts of the eastern region of the subcontinent will be reviewed now. The explorations for silver in lead ores were carried by the geologists of GSI and other university Geology departments.

In Orissa, a number of mines have argentiferous galena, for example at Jhunanm in Sambalpur District. The silver obtained from the galena concentrate at this mine was 12 ounces/ton of galena concentrate. In Sargipalli mine of the Sundargarh District, silver is found associated with the lead, copper and zinc. The silver contents at this mine are 500-600 grams/ton of galena concentrate.

In West Bengal, galena is known to occur at Purulia near Dhadka in the erstwhile Manbhum District (22° 48' N, 86° 30' E) and at Beldih (23° 03' N, 86° 18' E). The ore at those two sites also contains silver. At Dhadka, evidence of old workings of galena were noticed (Ball 1880: 104; Hunday and Banerjee 1967: 293-294). Silver contents in the ore of this region are about 76.34 to 119 ounces per ton (1 ounce = 28 grams).

In Bihar, argentiferous lead ores are known from the Kharakpur hills of the Munghyr District. The silver has been reported from the argentiferous galena of the Chandi Dongri shear zone near Bemetara in Chhattisgarh, which yielded nine ounces of silver per ton of ore.

From Meghalaya, one form of silver was known as the *Rupamati*. Perhaps this was native silver. It was a mixture of silver particles and earth and other minerals (Dasgupta 1998: 261). In the medieval Assam, silver was extracted from this mixture.

In Jharkhand, both silver and gold were detected at Pahardiha (22° 30' N, 85° 12' E) of the West Singhbhum District. At Sonthalia (24° 24' N, 86° 23' E) in the Giridih District, a mixture of copper, zinc, lead and silver minerals was recovered.

Evidence in the Historical Records

In the *Arthshastra*, silver purification is clearly mentioned (Kangle 1997: Pt II. 112-115). However, that scanty text is not enough to interpret it. Sen Sarma (2001: 42-56.) studied the *Arthshastra* from the point of view of geology, mining and metallurgy. Kautilya has covered the prospecting of ore minerals to purification of precious metals in his classic work. Moreover, the technique of alloying has also been referred to in the original *sutras* (2.12.24 etc.), which elaborate upon the minting of silver punch-marked coins and their standard alloying pattern. The percentage of silver standardised in those coins was 68.75, copper being 25 and the rest 6.25 comprised iron, lead and so on.

The *Arthshastra* in *sutra 2.13.49* further tells that to purify silver, it was heated in a series of crucibles. First, it was burnt four times in a crucible with bones, four times in a crucible with an equal amount of lead, four times in a dry crucible, three times in a potsherd and twice with cow dung. Thus, the purification went through the seventeen sets of crucibles. At the end of processing, silver was made bright (polished) with the *multani mitti* (Indus earth).

Purification of silver as well as of gold during the medieval period has been described in the *Ain-i Akbari* (Blochmann 1993: 23; Khan 1986: 71-91; Sundaram *et al.* 1999: 25). The technique is rather interesting for separation of silver from the mixture of gold, silver and copper and other impurities. The complex process required that after the separation of gold, impurities were blown as oxides. That alloy was treated with charcoal of *babul* wood. On heating thrice with sulphur and thrice with copper and then allowing it to cool, silver turned into a white ash, which was purified further in a crucible with bone-ash.

Separation of Silver from Lead by the Traditional Method

For obtaining silver from its ore, the ore material was washed in water, dried and crushed. It was then placed in a crucible and fired in the furnace, to be oxidised. This meant converting lead into litharge or lead oxide. Thus, the litharge was removed. The raw silver thus produced was contaminated with lead. By employing the process of cupellation, that is, heating the molten metal with bone ash in small crucibles, the remnants of lead were removed. Ordinarily, a small amount of lead (less than one percent) still remained in the silver.

Identification of the Source of Silver

Most of the nonferrous lead isotope ratios in the silver objects serve as a clue for identification of the mine. Lead isotopes have been used for correlating metal artefacts with the ores they have been derived from. So far, the lead isotope study in India is quite inadequate, and from the eastern part, nothing is known, except from Amjhor in Bihar (Balasubrahmanian and Chandi 1976: 141-148).

Silver Objects found from Excavations

Silver objects were unknown in the proto-historic Bengal, but those were well-known during the Early Historic period in the eastern India. For example, silver is known from the excavation at Bangarh. Besides the punch-marked silver coins, a silver rod was discovered at Bangarh (Goswami 1948: 17). The excavator suggested that from the silver rods, ornaments were manufactured at the site itself.

The excavation at Mahasthan in the Bagura District in Bangladesh revealed a hoard of 93 punch-marked silver coins and a number of silver ornaments (Alam and Salles 2001: 244-264). A silver bracelet or a bangle (accessioned as MAH.95.727.10) was discovered in the 1995 excavation near the location of the said coin hoard (Alam and Salles 2001: 239). All excavated specimens indicate MAH for Mahasthan, followed with two digits indicating year, then serial number). The external diameter of that bangle was 5.59 cm, internal diameter 5.17 cm and its thickness was 0.32 cm. The cross section of this bangle was circular, with both the ends coil-shaped. The 1994 excavation also revealed a blackish bangle (MAH.94.2043) probably made of silver. It had a plain hoop with an undecorated convex surface and plano-convex cross-section. A small silver bell was recovered from the excavation at Paharpur. Several silver ingots, silver bell and bangle pieces were also recovered from the monastery cells of Salban *Vihar* in Mainamati (Khan 2002: 73-76).

Excavations at Vaisali in Bihar revealed a miniature pot, which was found with a debased silver amulet (Sinha and Roy 1969: 195). Metal objects discovered at Nalanda (25° 08' N, 85° 27' E) also included gold and silver specimens (Misra 1998: 272-275). The objects of silver comprised fragments of a thin, silver pipe, silver ring and silver coins.

From the site at Lalitagiri (20° 35' N, 86°15' E) in Orissa, 200 grams of silver slag was recovered during the excavation (Chauley 2000: 450). Thus, this site is identified as a silver manufacturing centre. The excavation also revealed silver rings and other objects along with many iron artefacts. Moreover, the discovery of Buddhist relics in a fourfold casket of gold, silver, steatite and khondalite was a significant discovery at that site (Chauley 2000: 441-455). From Udayagiri (20° 38' N, 86° 16' E), a silver finger ring and other ornaments were discovered (Bandyopadhyay 2007: 117).

The punch-marked silver coins were also obtained from the excavations, at Chandraketugarh, West Bengal. During the excavation of 1965-66, a stone inlaid silver ornament was discovered (Haque 2001: 25, 47). Banerjee (1911: 16-17) had catalogued the fragmentary silver vessels and a few other objects from Chandraketugarh during exploration. Those relics are now housed in the Bangiya Sahitya Parishad, Kolkata.

Sources of Silver for Coins and other Objects

We have plenty of evidences to establish the antiquity of silver coins and artefacts in eastern India, where the manufacture of silver ornaments and their use was very common. Whether all the silver objects were made from the Indian sources is questionable. Most scholars do not accept that silver was made from the local ores. Silver was definitely imported on a mass scale from external sources.

One pioneer scholar studied the contents of the punch-marked silver coins and correlated the sources of silver with the ores of the Bawdwin mines (Bhardwaj 1987: 134-39). Another study indicates that the silver, marketed down the Brahmaputra, contained higher contents of gold than that of the Irrawadi route (Mitchiner and Pollard 1990: 224-27). An in-depth study with lead isotopes and other intensive trace element ratios can alone pinpoint the origin of silver in this part of the continent.

External sources of Silver

Our present knowledge about the sources of silver in our country is rather limited. The important western sources are the Panjhir mines of Afghanistan. This mine was located on the River Panjhir in the valley of Hindu Kush, just south of the Khavak Pass. It was known that the Indo-Greeks first explored the Panjhir mine to manufacture coins, and subsequently the Hindu Shahis of Kabul area of the eighth and ninth centuries used the silver from that mine (Cowell and Lowick 1988: 65-74).

From Southeast Asia, two important sources of silver are known. One is located at Nan-Chao in Yunnan (Coggin Brown 1923: 149). The second one is situated at Bawdwin mines (23° 6' E, 97°18' N) in the Shan state of Myanmar (Coggin Brown 1918: 124; Calhoun 1922: 113, 12). The word 'Bawdwin' was derived from *Bawdwingyi*, which means 'the great silver mine'. This mine was perhaps started in the 10th century. The site is full of smelting remains, outcrops of galena, settlements of metal workers, and so on. Here, the lead-zinc-silver ore body occupies a prominent fault. The ore is mainly a finegrained mixture of argentiferous galena and sphalerite, with some chalcopyrite. The Bengal Sultan used silver from the Nan-Chao and Bawdwin mines to manufacturing coins with (Deyell 1983: 207-227). It also referred to the existence of argentiferous galena in the neighbourhood of Martaban and Moulmein. Tarafdar (1995: 31-56) has also mentioned that the sources of silver for the coins of the Bengal Sultans were located in south China, upper Myanmar and Pegu. Bengal and Yunnan were well connected through trade not only of silver but also of *cowry* shells through Sylhet, now in Bangladesh (Kuroda 2009: 253-34).

Trade Routes for Silver

From Southeast Asia, silver was imported to Pundranagar (present day Mahasthan) during the Gupta period. Amongst several routes, two routes were most important—the Patkai Pass leading to the Bhamo Valley, and the other through Manipur. Both the routes crossed the Irrawaddy River of Myanmar. During the later periods, when the Samatata kingdom flourished in Bengal, silver was imported through Arakan, as well as by sea, through the Gulf of Martaban and the Arakan coastal area in the Bay of Bengal. The detailed map indicating the silver trade routes is shown in Figure 6.1.

SILVER COINS

In the Indian subcontinent, the silver coins appeared first sometime during the fifth and sixth centuries BCE and continued until 1939. The earliest of these are known as the punch-marked coins, as symbols were punched on them. Silver punch-marked coins were standardised with a weight of 3.732 grams, known as *karshapan*. An example of those coins from Chandraketugarh is shown in Figure 6.2 and another from Mahasthan in Figure 6.3. As those are the earliest coins of the subcontinent, these will be discussed in detail.

Punch-marked coins

Three types of metals—silver, copper and their alloy bullion (theoretically 50% silver and 50% copper) were used for manufacturing the punch-marked coins. Until and unless those are analysed thoroughly, their metallic composition cannot be established. A certain amount of copper, lead and gold detected in such coins might have come from the ore itself. If the lead could not be driven out thoroughly from silver by the cupellation process, it would have been difficult to determine whether the alloying was natural or intentional. The guidelines provided by Kautilya in the *Arthshastra* indicate the composition of the coin as 75% silver (Ag) and 25% copper (Cu). The *sutra* 2.12.24 of the *Arthshastra* indicates that the mint master (*laksanadhyaksh*) should be

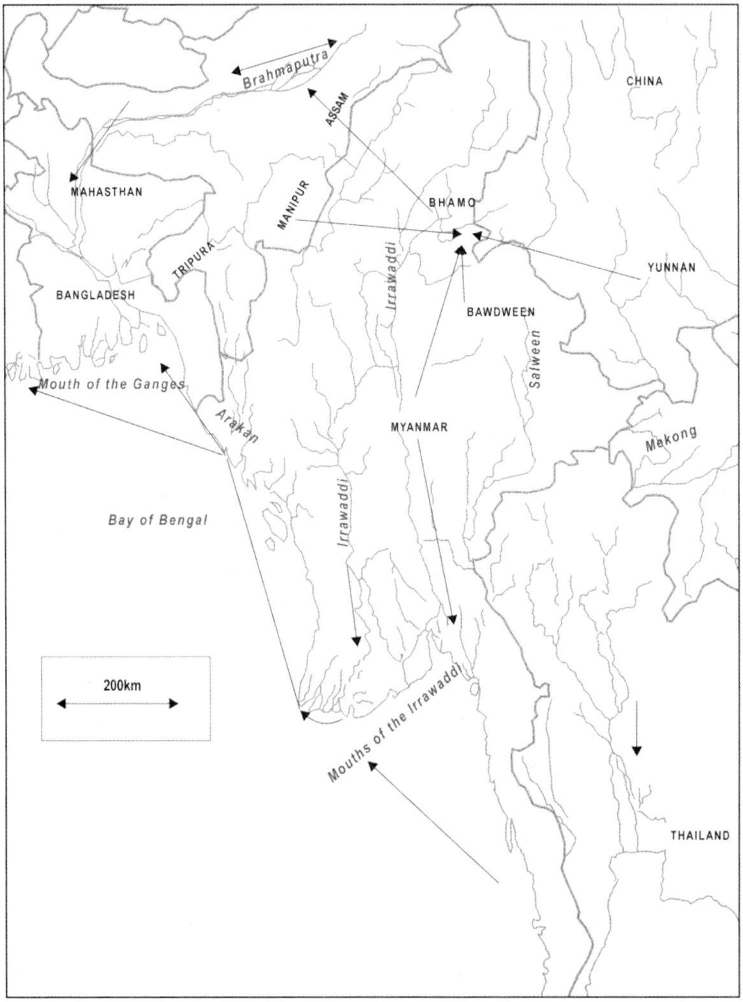

Fig. 6.1: *Map of Bangladesh and portion of South-east Asia (The silver trade route is shown with red arrows)*

Fig. 6.2: *Punched-marked coin from Chandraketugarh*

Fig. 6.3: *Punched-marked coin from Mahasthan*

responsible for minting silver coins with one-fourth part of copper and the hardening alloy of one *masa* (in weight) of one of the metals, as iron (Fe), tin (Sn), lead (Pb) and antimony (Sb) of the denominations of one *pana* (Kangle 1997: II.108; Sen Sarma 2001:202).

One may wonder what could be the metallurgical reason for standardising the composition. The composition for punch-marked silver coins perhaps developed with the experience of smelters, with an aim of overcoming the shortage of silver. Standardisation can now be studied by the characterisation of silver copper alloys. Without the knowledge of material sciences, the smiths achieved that standardisation by trial and error.

One may discuss the wage-structure in terms of the punch-marked coins. Sixty pieces of *panas* were the minimum wages paid per annum per labour in the Mauryan period. That was equivalent to five *panas*, weighing 17.50 grams of silver, per month. It may be interesting to note that the British East India Company paid exactly the same amount to the lowest Indian labour in the early 18th century (Kosambi 1977: 153). Kosambi had rightly pointed out that many samples of every group of punch-marked coins are needed for a correct chemical analysis. The previously quoted references from the *Arthshastra* are applicable to the coins of the second half of the Mauryan period only. The composition of those coins, obtained from the analysis, indicates an average use of 74.79% silver and 25.24% copper (Prasad *et al.* 1995:135-144). This composition approximately coincides with the guidelines of *Arthshastra*. The alloying elements in the composition of punch-marked coins, like iron, zinc, tin, lead and gold are also to be noted. Prasad and Ahmad (1995: 135-144) have also studied some coins of unknown places in Uttar Pradesh. They made both, the specific gravity and metallographic observations. The study revealed the composition of silver and copper only in close approximation to the specific gravity and alloy phases in microstructure. The contents in trace elements were totally avoided. In this context, one may refer to the analysis of silver punch-marked coins excavated at Narhan in Uttar Pradesh, which revealed the percentage of the principal alloying elements—copper 3.19%, lead 0.65%, tin 0.88%, with the 94.75% silver. The analyses were performed at the National Research Laboratory for Conservation of Cultural Property (NRLC) Lucknow, with the help of X-ray Diffraction and Atomic Absorption Spectroscopy and it was also the most authentic one (Agrawal, Narain and Prakash 1994: 234-245).

The primitive inflation and stress upon the currency in the Mauryan silver coins were noted after Chandragupta. That was indicated by the sudden increase of the copper contents (Kosambi 1992: 158) in the Mauryan silver coins. Recently, important studies on the archaeometallurgy have been made by scanning with the electron microscope by Mahajan and Balasubramaniam (1997-1998: 153-167). The compositional analyses, manufacturing technique and associated corrosion products were also studied in a punch-marked coin discovered from Mathura in Uttar Pradesh.

Manufacturing of punch-marked coins

The punch-marked coins of eastern India were manufactured from ingots of silver with appropriate alloying. The ingots were first forged into flat sheets (Mukherjee 1997: 175-187; Bhardwaj 2000: 100). From the flat sheets, strips were cut into small rectangular pieces. The pieces were subsequently clipped at the edge to standardise its weight to make coin-blanks. The circular or oval coins were made from the leftover metal, re-melted in a crucible and reused.

Analysis of the punch-marked coins of Orissa

Hundreds of punch-marked coins were discovered in Orissa. Some 'local' type punch-marked coins were circulated in the western part of Orissa and Chhattisgarh, which was a part of Kosal *Janapad.* The discovery of terracotta coin moulds from Sisupalgarh in the fourth century level indicated that there was deviation from the original also. The earliest varieties of punch-marked coins found in the state have been analysed and the results are incorporated here.

There are compositional analyses of the punch-marked silver coins of Orissa (Vijan *et al.* 2005: 168-171). Analyses were made with the proton induced X-ray emission (PIXE) technique directly applied on seven coins. Elements, such as copper, silver, titanium, chromium, manganese, iron, nickel, arsenic, lead and gold were identified. The analysed coins were about three grams in weight. The major element, silver was present from 66.92 to 76.65 percent. Other elements were copper (3.77 to 19.28%), gold (0.65 to 9.28%) and lead (3.80 to 9.78%). The analyses also revealed the presence of trace elements, like titanium, chromium, manganese, iron, nickel and arsenic with varying percentages. This result more or less followed the guidelines given in the *Arthshastra.*

Analyses of the punch-marked coins of Bengal

Analysis of silver coins of Bengal, including Bangladesh, is very limited. Manowar Jahan had initiated some studies. Recently an attempt was made to analyse eight silver punch-marked coins from the eastern India (Chattopadhyay, Datta, Vijayan and Rautray 2010: 91-103). Coins were found in exploration at Mahanad (23° 0' 3"N, 88° 16' E) in Hughly District, Chandraketugarh (22° 42' N, 88° 41' E) in North Twenty-four Pargana District of West Bengal; and one of Wari-Bateshwar (24° 05' 46" N, 90° 49'42" E) in Narsinghdi District of Bangladesh.

Analyses of those eight coins were conducted using PIXE (Proton Induced X-ray Emission) at the Institute of Physics, Bhubaneswar. The result is yet to be published. The two coins from Wari-Bateshwar and Chandraketugarh revealed gold percentage between 0.42 and 0.32, whereas the other six coins revealed total absence of gold. Silver constituents were between 92.08 to 78.78% (av. 88.87%), copper 1.77 to 14.12% (av. 5.11%), iron 0.02 to 1.79% (av. 0.40%) and lead 0.34 to 0.80% (av. 0.48%). Those coins have some similarities with or are slightly above the *Arthshastra* standard.

Analysis of silver coins of the Gupta period

During the Gupta period, silver coins were also used in this part of the country. One silver coin of Kumargupta (CE 415-455) from Chandraketugarh is shown in Figure 6.4. The average composition is silver 64.30%, copper 12.40%, iron 10.00%, nickel 0.80% and lead 12.00%.

Fig. 6.4: *Two sides of silver coin of Kumaragupta from Chandraketugarh*

Plating on Punch-marked coins

A number of coins made of copper with silverplating have been unearthed in excavations at various places. Initially, before cleaning, the coins appeared to be made of silver. However, cleaning identified them as the copper coins. Similar coins were discovered from the excavations at Champa, Sonpur (three coins), Kumrahar (eight coins) and Vaisali. One similar specimen was discovered from the surface exploration at Chechar Kutubpur. In the beginning, no one thought those specimens to be faked, but on cleaning with tamarind and acetone, silvery appearance was lost and the reddish glow of copper appeared. Such a thin layer could not be due to the enrichment of silver on the copper blanks. Thus, we may conclude that technology of gold and silver plating on copper began in the Early Historic period. Perhaps the import of silver stopped or aggression by the enemies made silver and gold scarce, and the rulers were forced to use copper currency with silverplating.

Harikela Coins

During the Pal-Sen period, no coins are known from the western part of Bengal. Between the ninth and 12th centuries, Harikela coins are found from a number of places from Bangladesh and Tripura. The first known site is in Sylhet in Bangladesh. The next important sites are the *vihars* or monasteries of Mynamati. At Jobra Village, under Hathajhari *upazila* of Chittagong, 28 Harikela coins were found.

In the excavation by the Archaeology Survey of India (ASI) in 2004 at Baksanagar in Tripura, one Harikela coin was recovered. From a hoard of Belonia of the south Tripura, most of the thin coins or bracteates were recovered. Beside Belonia, there are other find spots in Sylhet and Mainamati. At the Salban *Vihar* of Mainamati, 400 gold and silver coins were recovered. Some of the analysed coins of the series are shown in Figure 6.5.

The portrait on the obverse of the coin represents a recumbent bull to the left, with or without a bell or garland around its neck. On the reverse, the coin displays a *trisul* (trident), with garlands hanging from it. The symbols of the sun and the moon are also included. On both the sides, the portrait is within a circular border of dots. The legend on the obverse reads *Harikela*.

The chemical analysis and metallography of Harikela coins are available elsewhere (Chattopadhyay 2001: 127-137). The studies revealed the use of pure silver with a

Fig. 6.5: *Coins of Harikela*

little addition of copper to improve its strength. The trace amounts of other elements revealed its natural contamination. The composition and metallographic analyses are now available (Chattopadhyay 2001: 127-137). The Electron probe micro analyses (EPMA) results, in percentage composition indicated that silver 95.13, lead 0.38, iron 0.04, copper 3.62, gold 0.59, zinc 0.02, cobalt 0.01, bismuth 0.15, sulphur 0.01, arsenic 0.04 and nickel 0.01. The results clearly indicate that silver used in manufacturing the Harikela coins is superior to the punch-marked coins.

SILVER COINS OF THE MEDIEVAL PERIOD

Silver coins of Assam

In the beginning, the Ahom rulers used to strike coins only to commemorate their coronation ceremony. Thus, the coins played a very limited role. Later on, regular coins were issued in Assam. Those are mostly octagonal silver coins and the occasional gold coins. The silver coins of Assam were of high purity, between 94.10 to 98%, with the weight standard of 11.30 grams.

Coins of Tripura

It seems that the state of Tripura began issuing silver coins from the 15th century onwards. Ratna Manikya was the first ruler to issue coins by bringing in Muslim metal workers of Bengal for this purpose. He introduced the symbol of the 'lion' on his coins. This symbol continued on the coins of his successors. Perhaps the rulers of Tripura obtained silver from the Arakan sources.

Coin-making during the Medieval period

Silver coins of the medieval period were made by the die-striking technique. In Assam, the mints were known as the *rajshal* and the mint master was called *sonari bardolai* (Rhodes and Bose 2004: 57). The task of goldsmiths was to prepare *chakli* (plain sheets) of silver or gold to the required size. Two types of smiths were engaged there: one, who held the anvil and the other, who struck the hammer on the die, holding the plain metal blank between the obverse and reverse dies.

Use of Silver in making Images

Brass and bronze images were popular throughout eastern India. Side by side, silver was occasionally used for making images. An outstanding example of the silver image is the image of Vishnu, which was obtained from Sonarang near Vikrampur, Dhaka District in Bangladesh. This image dated to the 12th century, is now preserved in the Indian Museum, Kolkata (Acc. No. 12880). This well executed specimen shows Vishnu standing on the *samapad* position on a double-petalled lotus. On the right side of the image, stands Shri Devi, and Pushti is on the left side (Figure 6.6).

Use of Silver in the pre-modern period

In the 18th and 19th centuries, in eastern India and Bangladesh, decorative metalwares were widely used for domestic purposes. For example, the *atardan* (perfume pot), *phuldan*

Fig. 6.6: *Silver image of Vishnu, Sonarang, Bangladesh (Courtesy: The Indian Museum)*

(flower vase), *pandan* (betel box), *besandan* (soap case), *pikdan* (spitoon), *kalamdan* (pen-case), *surahi* (high necked pot), hookah bowl, were common items of daily use. These wares, made of silver, brass and allied alloys, bore excellent decorations.

Pre-modern use of silver in Arunachal Pradesh

The people of the northeastern states are very fond of silver ornaments. In Arunachal

Pradesh, there is extensive use of traditional silver ornaments. The silversmiths of Arunachal are averse to using non-traditional and sophisticated designs.

The *cire perdue* process is widely known throughout the eastern India for making images. A similar technique was widely used by the silversmith in Arunachal Pradesh. They used wax threads and wooden moulds. The practice was similar to the Dhokra process (described later in Chapter 8). After the first stage of the mould preparation, clay and *takam* (charcoal dust) is used. The mould is first filled with *takam* and then a small lump of wax is fixed on it. For pouring molten silver into the mould, a funnel is made of banana leaf. The *takam* is then used to wrap the mould and the funnel is also attached. The entire set is then dried by heating. The mould and the funnel are finally covered with charcoal dust to smoothen them. These are allowed to dry near the fire. After sometime, the banana funnel is removed and the empty place is filled with the pieces of silver.

The mouth of mould is covered with a potsherd and sealed with the charcoal dust. It is allowed to dry again. A hole is made almost at the centre of the funnel and the earthen container is ready for the next operation of burning. The earthen container, with its mouth downwards, is supported on the hearth-stones. It is then covered with firewood of the *taja* tree and set to fire. After about twenty minutes, the state of metal is tested by inserting an iron rod in the hole. When the silver turns into liquid and discharges a turquoise flame, the earthen mould is removed with the help of two pairs of strong bamboo tongs and slowly turned upside down. The wax in the mould is burnt off by then and when the plug disappears, there is a passage for the molten metal to pass into the mould. The molten metal fills the empty space created by the wax mould and takes the shape of an ornament.

Filigree silvercraft

The most important traditional and ornamental use of silver in Orissa is known as *tarakasi* (filigree). This craft continues today in the Cuttack area of Orissa. The process consists of drawing silver through a series of consecutively smaller holes to produce fine strands of wires. These wires are then made into various shapes by deft hands of the craftsperson, by bending them into different designs and soldering them with pincer and scissors. Almost pure silver is used for this purpose.

7

MINOR METALS

BESIDES THE MAJOR METALS LIKE COPPER, IRON, GOLD AND SILVER, noted in the forgoing chapters, the minor metals, like lead, zinc and tin also play an important role in metallurgy. In this chapter, the sources and uses of these minor metals have been discussed.

SOURCES OF LEAD

Lead is extracted from the mineral, galena, called argentiferrous galena, which is basically lead sulphide in chemical composition. Some of the lead mines also yield silver. The explorations for silver in lead ores were carried by the geologists of GSI and other university departmentsof geology.

In Orissa, minor sources of lead are found in small pockets in the Sundargarh, Bolangir, Kalahandi, Sambalpur and Mayurbhanj districts. In this state, a number of lead mines with trace amounts of silver are known. In this regard, an example may be cited of the Jhunanm mines in Sambalpur District where silver is found associated with lead, copper and zinc ore-minerals in the Sargipalli mine (Sundargarh District). Galena has also been traced at Padampur (21° 45' E, 83° 34' N), Thuntikatabarga (21° 42' E, 84° 00' N), Junai (21° 32' E, 83° 51' N) and Talpatia (21° 57' E, 84° 01' N) in the Sambalpur District.

In West Bengal, galena is known to occur at Purulia, near Dhadka (22° 48' E, 86° 30' N) and Beldih (23° 03' E, 86° 18' N), where the evidence of old workings were noticed (Ball 1880: 104; Hunday and Banerjee 1967: 293-294). In Bihar, several locations in the

Bhagalpur District are at Phaga, Baghmari, Bhorsar, Khajuria and Karda. From the Hazaribagh District, examples may be cited of Golgo and a few other minor sites. Phaga is most important among those mines, which is locally known as *'Sheesha khad'* (lead mine). Sikkim also possesses lead mines at Rangpo and Pakhyang. In Chhattisgarh, lead is available at Chandidungri of the Durg District, and at Bhelai-Dhorpur and Kundartola-Belangi of the Surguja District. Lead has now been reported at the Chandi Dongri shear zone near Bemetara, which yielded nine ounce of silver per ton of ore.

In Jharkhand, galena is known to exist at Karaikela (22° 42' N, 85° 32' E), Sili (22° 42' N, 85° 32' E), Hisatu (24° 00' N, 85° 01' E), Baragunda (24° 05' N, 86° 04' E), Phaga (24° 46' N, 86° 56' E), Dudhijarna (24° 53' N, 86° 45' E), and Golgo (24° 24' N, 86° 22' E). At Pahardiha (22° 30' N, 85° 12' E) in the West Singhbhum District, both gold and silver were detected. Sonthalia (24° 24' N, 86° 23' E) in the Giridih District is also known for the mixed copper, zinc, lead and silver minerals.

LEAD OBJECTS FOUND IN EXCAVATIONS

The earliest evidence of lead was noticed in the excavation at Senuwar IB (supported with a ^{14}C date; BS-755 – 150 BCE) (Singh 1999: 509-529). From this site, a lead rod of rectangular cross section was discovered from the Neolithic-Chalcolithic transition phase. This lead object indicates the earliest smelting of galena into metallic lead and subsequent finishing by the forging process. The chemical analyses of that object clearly revealed lead as base, with 0.20% silver, 0.01% iron, 0.10% silicon, 0.10% Mg, 0.20% copper and 0.02% tin (Chattopadhyay and Singh 1998: 17-19). From the same site, a folded thin sheet (Period III) and a coil (Period IV) of lead were discovered. The lead rod and folded thin sheet can be seen in Figure 7.1.

The lead coil obtained from Chandraketugarh has been preserved in the Indian Museum (Datta and Datta 2008: 53,141). The authors have visually compared that specimen with a similar type from Thailand and suggested that both of them had a common source.

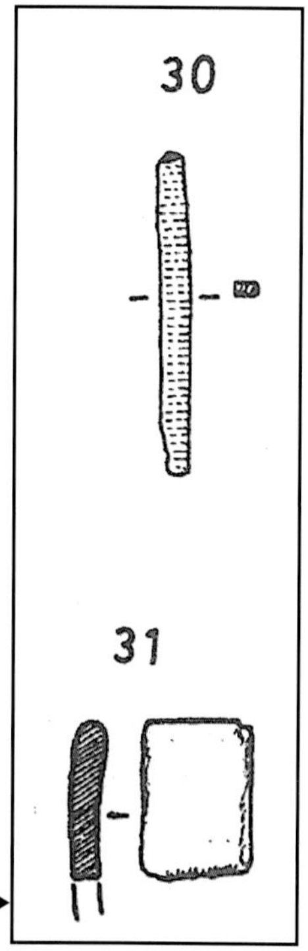

Fig. 7.1: *Lead objects from Senuwar – lead rod (30) and folded thin sheet (31)* ►
(Courtesy: B. P. Singh)

APPLICATION OF LEAD

In the chapter on iron (Chapter 4), we have mentioned about the presence of lead between the beams, which indicates that while processing, the material was heated in lead bath during structural fabrication (Prakash and Tripathy 1986: 576). This may indicates a major use of lead in the iron industry.

Lead coins

Satvahan kings issued lead coins in the central India. In eastern India, lead coins were only known from the excavations at Sisupalgarh and Chirand. The 1948 excavation revealed 14 lead coins attributed to the later Satavahan period. These coins are small round pieces, about 15 mm in diameter, with traces of Ujjain symbols. These lead coins indicate cultural and commercial contacts between the Satavahan Empire and Kaling between the second and third centuries. The Mahasthan excavations also revealed lead coins (accessioned as MAH 95/1060; Alam and Salles 2001: 236). Lead coins are also found in excavation at Bangarh, West Bengal from level of Gupta Period by ASI (*CASTEI Newsletter* 2010:19).

It may be rather difficult to identify the source of lead for these coins, because no detailed analysis is available. However, it may be surmised that the probable source of lead was in eastern India.

SOURCE OF TIN

The most important source of tin is cassiterite. This is basically tin oxide (SnO_2), often found in association with the tungsten minerals. In high temperature, the cassiterite forms veins that are usually related to igneous rocks, such as granite and rhyolite. When rocks containing cassiterite are decomposed by the action of surface waters and oxidation, the cassiterite tends to remain intact. It is eventually concentrated in streams to form 'placer' deposits, which is also known as 'stream tin'. Ancient people of our country recovered cassiterite from streams by panning. Most probably, this was the major source of tin in the eastern India in the proximity of the hilly areas of Chotanagpur. Even today, panning is practised in Chhattisgarh from the alluvial deposits.

Since the Early Historic periods, the people had learnt that the tin, when mixed with copper, changes its physical properties and improves the colour and hardness of the newly formed alloy, namely, the bronze. Bronze is widely used for making mirrors, utensils and images. The element, tin, is known in Sanskrit literature as *ranga, vanga* and *trapu.*

Tin mines of Eastern India

The sources of tin are scanty in eastern India. The use of tin bracelets by a villager belonging to the Gond community of Bastar (Chhattisgarh) has been reported by Ball. He had also reported that the village named as *Papamu* means 'tin' (Chakrabarti 1979: 63-64). The villagers here used bracelets made from black sand (cassiterite). The Gond community of Bastar was extracting tin from cassiterite and using it to make ornaments.

The tin mines in the Bastar (Chattisgarh) and Malkangiri (Orissa) districts are located on the pegmatite belt of central India. Those form perhaps the most productive tin mines in India (Pal *et al.* 2007: 30-55).

In Jharkhand, the localities of cassiterite-bearing ore were noted at Pihra (24° 39' N, 85° 49' E), Chappatand (24° 40' N, 86° 57' E), Nurungo (24° 10' N, 86° 06' E), Purgo (24° 10' N, 86° 08' E), and so on, in Hazaribagh District. Paharsingh in the Ranchi District, with its cassiterite sources in the trenches and pits, exhibits the past exploitation. It is known that at Nurungo, the pre-industrial tin smelting was being carried out in the local iron furnaces until 1849 (Mallet 1874: 23-44; Dunn 1941: 234).

An in-depth study has been made in the Govindpal area (18° 40' E, 82° 00' N), where cassiterite was found in the pegmatite rocks. The cassiterite of this belt contains around 90% tin oxide, 7.84% tantalum oxide, 0.53% niobium oxide, 0.59% iron oxide and 0.58% manganese oxide. Digging and panning of cassiterite is reported at Katekalyan, Botapara and the surrounding areas of Bastar (Upadhyay 2007: 250).

In Orissa, small pockets of tin are known from Mayurbhanj (Mallet 1874: 23-44); Chakrabarti 1979: 61-74). In West Bengal, cassiterite is reported from the pegmatite rocks of the Belamu hills (23° 27' 08" N, 86° 00' 33" E) area (Sinha 1999:88). In Bihar, tin is known to exist in the Gaya District.

There is enough evidence of the continual extraction and use of tin in India throughout the ages. Nevertheless, the scarcity of the sources of tin clearly indicates that it could not satisfy the needs of the domestic market. Therefore, it is presumed that the tin, like silver, was also imported to eastern India from Southeast Asia, including

Malaysia (Biswas *et al.* 1996: 328) with the establishment of trade connections at the juncture when most of the domestic mines were exhausted. Copper was exported from Tamluk to Malaysia and other southeastern Asian countries in exchange for bronze. There is enough scope for reevaluation of the old mines in eastern India.

Extraction of Tin

Extraction of tin from its ore is a simple process using the indigenous furnace, which is similar to the iron smelting furnace. The ore is also reduced, when heated in a crucible together with charcoal and a flux, like sand. The indigenous communities knew the technique of extracting tin by just putting the powdered ore, mixed with charcoal and sand, in an earthen crucible and placing it in an oven. Air was blown into the oven to increase the temperature. Just by removing the slag from the top of the crucible, they got liquid tin at the bottom of the crucible. This metal was used mostly for making bronze and soldering metal objects.

SOURCE OF ZINC

The common ore of zinc is sphalerite, which is sulphide of zinc (ZnS) in its chemical composition. More often, the zinc ores are found mixed with the copper, tin or the lead ore minerals. In Orissa, Jharkhand and West Bengal, the known occurrences of zinc are in the long copper belt shear zone. Examples may be cited of Amjhor and Golgo in Jharkhand. In West Bengal, zinc is reported from Gorubathan in the Darjeeling District and Gohalbaria in the West Medinipur District. In Chhattisgarh, lead is available at Chandidungri in the Durg District, and Bhelai-Dhorpur and Kundartola-Belangi in the Surguja District. A small amount of zinc is also known to occur at Potin and Rub in the Ranga Valley of Arunachal Pradesh. Meghalaya also yielded zinc at Umpyrtha and Barapani. Perhaps those places supplied zinc to Bangladesh.

Use of Zinc alloy

The people of eastern India had the knowledge of metallurgy of zinc since the Early Historic period. They knew that the zinc, when added to copper in certain proportion, changes its physical properties, and improved the colour of the newly formed alloy, the brass. The brass has been widely used for manufacturing, utensils and images through the ages.

The brass artefacts of Taxila prove that the earliest evidence of the use of zinc in the world lies in the manufacture of brass. The artefacts excavated at Bhir Mound, dated to the fourth century BCE contained 34.34% zinc. The archaeological context, chronology and composition of the artefacts are interesting in the context of Kanjipani area, where the earliest evidence of brass in Orissa was found. The composition of these materials is discussed in Chapter 8.

The people of Rajasthan were more concerned with zinc because of the presence of its ore in the region. Thousands of zinc retorts have been discovered there. Eastern India was quite familiar with zinc. However, the supply of zinc was not adequate there. The earliest evidence of brass from Orissa was reported in the Kanjipani area of the Keonjhor District (21° 30' N, 83° 28' E). The material obtained by the Anthropology Department of Calcutta University from this site was analysed (Ray *et al.* 2000: 365). The analysis indicated a copper based alloy with 54% copper, 33% zinc, 8.5% tin, 1% lead and 2.5% iron. This further indicates that it was an early brass specimen made from mixed ore-minerals.

Brass was produced in the ancient Europe by the cementation process by mixing zinc oxide with finely divided copper metal in a sealed crucible, in which a reducing atmosphere was maintained and the temperature kept within 950° and 1083 °C (Biswas *et al.* 1996: 351-53). The maximum content of zinc (Zn) in the cementation process was less than 28 percent.

Bidri-ware

In eastern India, an alloy of copper and zinc in the proportion of 1:16 has been known as *bidri*-ware. The name *bidri* is self-explanatory to indicate that this alloy originated from Bidar in Karnatak during the Bahamani rule in *c.*14th century. The technology of casting vessels of this alloy and finishing/decorating them with stylus became popular in eastern India. Small production centres of the *bidri*-ware were established at Village Belori, near Purnia in Bihar and Murshidabad in West Bengal in the 17th century (Mukherjee 1885: 40-44). The art objects made of this alloy are typically black in colour.

8

ALLOYS OF COPPER

THE ALLOYS OF COPPER WERE DEVELOPED IN EASTERN INDIA, AT THE latest, by the fifth century BCE. From literary sources, there is some information on the alloys of copper and the smiths, who manufactured alloys. The excavations conducted in the country have also revealed plaques, depicting different musical instruments made of copper alloys. In the beginning, the people of eastern India used pure copper. However, later they learnt the technique of alloying with the small amounts of tin. They also practiced alloying with arsenic. Subsquently they used higher percentages of tin for alloying. They also learnt the technique of making brass, which technique was further developed to manufacture gunmetal. Brass is an alloy of copper and zinc, whereas the gunmetal is an alloy of copper, tin, zinc and lead. These alloys were used for making the domestic utensils and images, as also, the cannons.

LITERARY EVIDENCE OF COPPER ALLOYING

Interesting information is available from Kuruspal in Chhattisgarh. The undated Kuruspal stone inscription of the Nagavamshi King Somesvar includes a word *kansaravado* (Mahajan 2000: 144, 193). The scholar has rightly pointed out that the word '*kansaravado*' refers to the hamlet inhabited by the artisans, who worked on the copper, bell metal or the brass. That place was perhaps located near Kuruspal. Another name, *Tamanaladesa*, of the same period pertaining to this region is also known (Mahajan 2000: 193). This name may be suggestive of the place where copper and bell metal workers lived.

The Chinese traveller Fa-hsien visited Bengal sometime in the fifth century. He states that he observed many musical instruments in this country and called it the land of music and dance. A highly developed musical culture prevailed in Bengal. Through the excavations at Paharpur, Mainamati, Jagjibanpur, and so on, we learn that the music was an integral part of the Bengali culture. From the ancient period, the metal craftsmen of Bengal have been manufacturing various types of musical instruments, such as *kartal* (a small cymbals), *jhanjar* (large cymbals), *kansar*, *mandira*, and so on, from *kansa* (high tin-bronze or bell metal or *pital* (brass). The name of an instrument, *kansar*, indicates that it is made of high tin-bronze. The *kartal* and *jhanjar* are made of the brass or bronze.

The most authentic evidence of the popularity of bronze comes form the early medieval literature that tells us about the *Kangsakara* caste. The *kangsa* or *kansa* is bronze and the generic name *Kangsakara,* namely, the copper-bronze worker, given to an occupational guild may indicate the popularity that it enjoyed. That also brings to us an important aspect of the human input in metal technology in the given context. The *Brahmavaivart Puran* and the *Brhaddharm Puran*, the Bengal-specific compositions of the 10th to 11th century tell us that the copper-bronze producing class was bracketed with the *Shudra* caste. The text mentions that the *Karmakar* (iron smith) and the *Kangsakar* belonged to the highest category of the *Shudra* (Dasgupta and Chattopadhyay 2009: 78-85). These references in the *Puran* actually indicate expansion of the fourfold caste-based society by bringing the non-caste occupational or artisan communities into the caste system as *Shudras*. Although, the term *kansa* for bronze was already known from the early literary sources of the Middle Ganga Valley, yet the *Kangsakar* occupational group is first mentioned in the *Puran* of the 10th-11th century, in the context of lower Ganga plain.

Bronze and its varieties

We now know that bronze is an alloy of copper with tin, and that the copper-bronze objects, bangles, beads, earrings, finger rings, fishhooks, and so on, found since the chalcolithic period indicate, less than 10% tin. In fact, the simple alloys of copper and tin may be classified in three categories according to the percentage of tin in copper. In the first category, the percentage of tin is less than ten. Metallurgists call it 'alpha bronze'. In the second category, the percentage of tin is around 10 to 20 (beta bronze). In the third category, tin is above 20 percent. The last category is called the high tin-bronze or bell metal. In the beginning, people found that casting with pure copper was difficult, because of its high melting point (1084°C). Adding tin to copper reduceds the melting temperature. Moreover, a better cast product is obtained. Increasing the percentage of tin added to copper not only improves casting, but at the same time its colour also changes. However, any further increase in the tin contents makes the product golden in hue, but brittle.

In the middle of the Early Historic period, the smiths found that by increasing the contents of tin, the copper alloy became golden in colour. Its colour and mechanical properties improve, when it has around 22 to 25% tin. The *kansa* or bell metal has been a very popular alloy in the Indian subcontinent. The metallurgists often classify bronze on the basis of its tin contents.

If the bronze alloy is observed through the microscope, different metallurgical structures can be identified. The metallurgists can easily make out whether the object was made by simple casting or by other techniques, like forging and other types of heat treatment. Depending on the desired use, the artisans have been applying different techniques for different objects.

For example, to make a bell produce a loud sound, the cast product was forged and quenched in water. The smiths learned that technique through their experience with iron and steel, while making swords, razors and sickles. For bronze objects, like bowls, the people might have preferred a hard and golden surface; but during forging operations, these bowls and such other objects often developed cracks. In order to avoid these cracks, the smiths resorted to the technique of quenching at an intermediate stage and, thus, they turned out a finished product that was intact. An improved sound property was required for bells. For that, casting alone was not enough, but producing the martensite structures was necessary. The metal craftsmen perfected that technique skilfully.

In metallurgical terminology, the low tin-bronzes are made of a kind of structure, known as 'alpha grains'. The tin contents enrich those grains. In case of high tin-bronze, the cast structure is found to be a mixture of alpha and beta grains. Looking through a microscope, we can easily identify those grains. The beta grains are formed with a high concentration of tin. With an electron microscope, one can observe that the beta grains are similar to martensite. The smiths of early historic Bengal utilised that technique for making thin objects like eating plates.

The high tin-bronze alloy was known in eastern India since the sixth century BCE. The use of this alloy continues to this day.

The use of some interesting bronze objects

Mirrors made of the copper-bronze alloy are known from different parts of the Prehistoric and the Early Historic world. This popular household object was known to the people of Indus Civilisation, Kulli culture of Baluchistan and also to the Han dynasties of China. For manufacturing bronze mirrors, 20-30% tin was used and simple casting was practised. That high tin alloy was selected for manufacturing the polished surface, so that the surface appeared almost similar to reflecting glass mirrors. However, the smiths at Lothal made mirrors with low tin-bronze.

Examples from the Eastern part of the Subcontinent

Jharkhand

The first evidence of this alloy in an archaeological context was reported by Caldwell (1920: 409-411) from an Asura burial in Jharkhand. At Khuntitoli (23° 04' N, 85° 17' E) in the Ranchi District, a Megalithic post-cremation burial site was excavated by S. C. Roy (*IAR* 1965-1966: 10). The site revealed copper-bronze objects, including a bangle, placed in a central urn with a lid.

Assam

A number of interesting bell metal objects are known from this state. The Assam State Museum has many inscribed bells in its collection. The well-known examples are the inscribed bells of the ninth and 10th centuries from Odalbakra. It is also noteworthy that the bell metal coins were also manufactured in Assam and Manipur during the later periods. The copper-bronze coins of Harjaravarman (CE *c.* 829) from the Tulip hoard (Rhodes and Bose 2003: 34-35) are the example in this regard.

Bangladesh

From Bangladesh, the excavation of Mahasthan, a bronze lamp entangled with an iron axe, bronze earrings and a bronze mirror, dated to 371-173 BCE, were discovered at level VII. This bronze mirror was 18.50 cm in diameter. It had a 6.40 cm long and 2.00 cm wide (at the fastening end) tang for handle. The reflecting surface of that mirror was flat (Salles 1999: 25-32). Previously, two mirrors were discovered at that site. Those are now preserved in the Mahasthan Museum. At level VIII, bronze jewellery and earrings, dated to the 197-46 BCE, were found.

Bronze bangles of the Early Historic period were recovered from Pubertek Village (24° 5' 34" N, 90° 49' 48" E), located in the suburbs of Wari-Bateshwar. An interesting knobbed vessel was also recovered from Wari-Bateshwar (Figure 8.1). The analysis of this object indicated that it was made of tin.

Fig. 8.1: *Knobbed vessel from Wari Bateswar (Courtesy: Shanaj Husne Jahan and Muhammad Habibullah Pathan)*

The massive bronze bell of Rupban Kanya Mura of Mainamati in Bangladesh is the most important one. Perhaps it is made of bell metal, but there is no further information. We do not know whether any analysis of this relic has so far been done or not. This bell was made during the Chandra period, CE 10th to 11th century. The bell weighs about 500 kg. It is 100 cm in height and 220 cm in circumference (Harunur Rashid 1997: 190).

Manipur

High tin-bronzes alloys from the state of Manipur are well-known. Bell metal production has been popular here since the Early Historic period. At Khangabok in the Thoubal District, the excavation revealed bronze rings and thin bronze plates (*IAR* 1995-1996: 59). Here, this alloy is known as *senjeng,* and is used for manufacturing utensils and other objects. The traditional bell metal-based products of Manipur are *chaisal*, *tukana* (drinking pot), *khujai* (drinking tumbler), *korphu, korphan* and *tekana* (cooking pot), *senga* (lidded container), *shanpal* (small plates), and so on (Figure 8.2).

Fig. 8.2: *Cooking pots from Manipur (Korphu, Korphan and Tekana – from left to right) (Courtesy: P. Binodini Devi)*

West Bengal

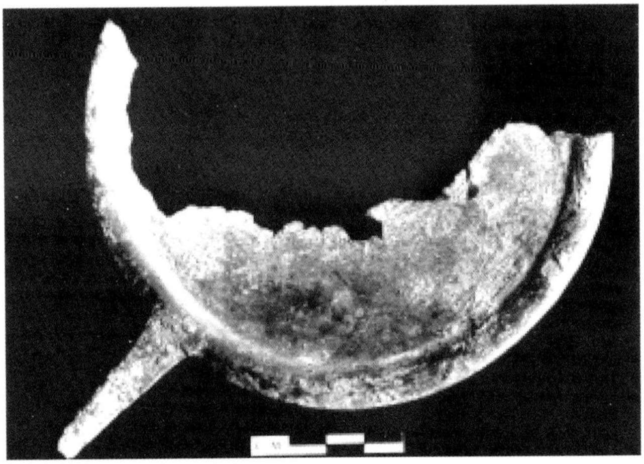

Fig. 8.3: *Bronze mirror from Chandraketugar*
(Courtesy: The State Archaeological Museum, West Bengal)

A bronze lump and a crucible were discovered at the recent excavations at Tilpi. This may indicate that high tin-bronze objects were produced at the site. The discovery of a high tin-bronze mirror from Chandraketugarh, now preserved in the State Archaeological Museum, highlights the stages of metal craft in the Early Historic period (Figure 8.3). From the Bangarh excavation, a plumb bob was recovered from the trench 5 at a depth of 3.96 m. According to the excavator, it was made of bell metal and it had a ring at one end (Goswami 1948: 33).

Orissa

From Orissa, high tin-bronze is known from Jamgadapadar. Baba Mishra has analysed two high tin-bronze objects from that site. One of the specimens, a perforated plate, was analysed to contain 68.969% copper, 30.439% tin, 0.343% iron, 0.066% lead and 0.184% arsenic. Zinc was not detected. The other specimen, a small bell, revealed a composition of 76.946% copper, 22.567% tin, 0.208% iron, 0.117% zinc, 0.043% lead and 0.119% arsenic.

A bronze ornamental lid, with its tip portion designed as a pointed knob, was recovered from the Udayagiri excavation (Bandyopadhyay 2007: 117-18). The alloying composition of this artefact is not known.

Metallurgy of high tin-bronze

In the case of high tin-bronzes/beta-bronze of around 22.5% tin; this is produced between temperatures of 586° and 755°C. However, the 22.5% tin, when mixed with copper at slow cooling, forms an inter-metallic brittle compound of copper and tin

($Cu_{31}Sn_8$). When metal at that phase is heated, to between 586-798°C, the alloy changes to varying degrees of alpha and beta phases, which are workable only in a hot condition. The high tin-bronze vessels were made by casting in the *cire perdue* or the lost wax process, followed by quenching and polishing. Some of them were finished with the bands of fine incised decorations.

Studies on Thermo-mechanical Treatments

For manufacturing high tin-bronze utensils in the eastern India, an interesting set of processes were undertaken (Chattopadhyay and Datta 2004-2005: 315-326). In the initial stage, the copper-bronze alloyed objects were manufactured by the casting process. Then, application of forging was undertaken for manufacturing vessels.

The forging of thin articles of the high tin-bronze was rather a complicated process. In most of the cases, the metal cracked because of the high tin contents that increased brittleness and decreased ductility. That alloy became hard and brittle on slow cooling. Those problems were overcome by the eastern Indian artisans by identifying the correct temperature range, which maintained proper ductility and malleability during processing. For that, the artisans used their experience of iron metallurgy.

After the in-depth studies of bronze objects from Wari-Bateshwar, Tilpi, Agiabir, and other sites, the researchers did ethno-archaeological studies at Khagra and tried to understand the ancient technique of bronze making in this part of the subcontinent. In the initial stage, the ingot was cast with a mixture of alpha and beta bronze, where tin contents were above 20 percent. On further heating the ingot to around 650°C it became beta bronze. At this temperature, the primary drop forging started. Heavy reduction of the cast ingots was made by using an open blocking die to obtain a rough contour of the object. Subsequently, soaking was done in a charcoal furnace at around 650°C. Repetition of the primary and finishing of drop forgings was done until the bar or handle portion could be made by using open dies.

Forging was done two to three times as per the need of cold finishing, and the heat treatment was done to smoothen out the rims after the specimen has been quenched in water. Heating to 650°C with salt and clay coating, and quenching in water was repeated to relieve the internal strains, developed during forging. We have analysed one excavated high tin-bronze object of the 12th century from Gajole in the Maldah District of West Bengal (Figure 8.4). Different processes, such as Scanning Electron Microscope (SEM) analysis (Figure 8.5), Neutron Diffraction (Figure 8.6) and Transmission Electron

Fig. 8.4: *High tin bronze bowl from Gajole, Maldah, West Bengal (Courtesy: Prasanta K. Datta)*

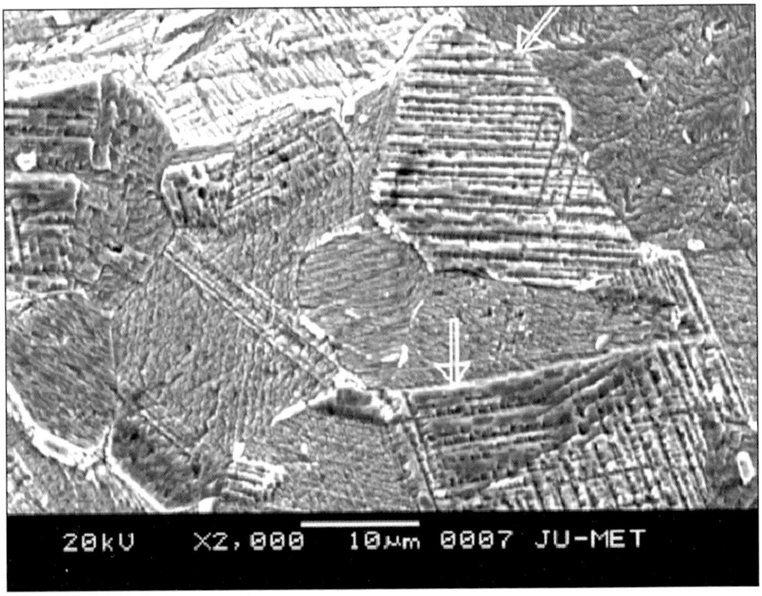

Fig. 8.5: *SEM analysis of the Gajole specimen at 2000X (Courtesy: Jadavpur University)*
The deformation slip bands (marked by arrow) of β′-phase can be seen within the grains. Similar, fine slip bands in the β-region also surround the β′-phase.

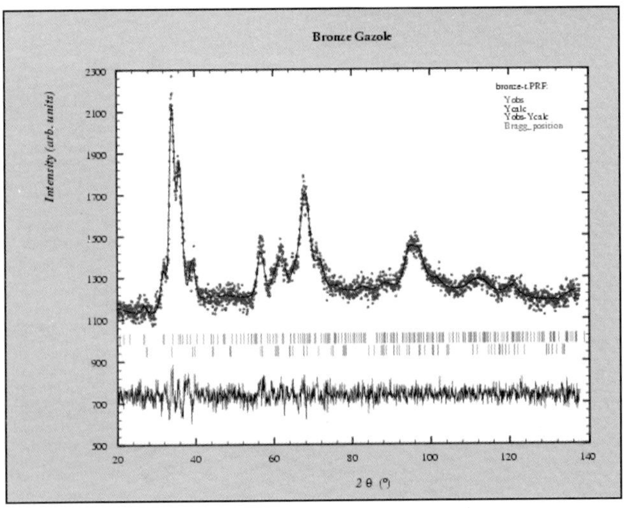

Fig. 8.6: *Neutron Diffraction Pattern of the specimen (Courtesy: Bhaba Atomic Research Centre)*

Microscope (TEM) analysis, were undertaken to analyse the object. Micrographs of the object clearly indicated the formations of martensite on magnifications of 12000X (Figure 8.7). Following the aforementioned steps, the artisans of eastern India could perform cold finishing and buffing for obtaining a bright and shiny surface.

Fig. 8.7: *TEM micrograph - specimen from Gajole showing martensite at 12000X (Courtesy: Prof. S. Das, The Indian Institute of Technoloy, Kharagpur)*

The artisans followed the abovementioned procedure to make the articles fracture-safe; the hot-forged bronze was soaked and quenched in water so that the further development of a brittle phase was inhibited. The production and use of the high tin-copper alloys developed in eastern India and Bangladesh before the beginning of the Common Era. The development of the technique of making high tin-bronze was also not accidental, but incidental. The people might have had the knowledge of the sponginess and high melting point of the low-tin bronzes. Otherwise, they would not allow such a generous addition of costly tin in copper to shorten the liquidus-solidus gap (in copper-tin alloy diagram) and to lower the melting temperature of the bronzes. All the findings point out towards an intelligent, industrialised population that existed in this region. People had a highly efficient and innovative approach to the material problems and they ran well organised business and trade.

Gunmetal

Gunmetal is an alloy of copper, tin, zinc and lead. According to the applications, there are lots of variations in its composition defined by the BS (British Standard) specifications, as G1, G3, LG1, LG3 and LG4 according to the percentage ranges of major elements, as tin (2-10%), zinc (2-10%), lead (0-6%), nickel up to 6% and rest, copper.

This alloy was popularised in the late medieval Europe for making guns and cannons. Since metallurgical analyses of copper-bronze objects in the eastern region were not adequate, one could not know that the smiths of this region also knew making of gunmetal and its uses. However, one object: a metallic artefact of the Gupta Period, fourth to fifth century, was recovered from Mahasthan by the Joint France-Bangladesh excavation in 2005 (sample number MZ.05.2841.1). The analysed specimen was 69 mm long and 5.50 mm in diameter. The specimen was found to be a combination of two phases, with a dendritic surface, indicating a cast structure. The specimen was thoroughly analysed, using scanning electron microscope with energy dispersive x-ray facilities (SEM-EDX) and X-Ray Diffraction (XRD). That observation indicated an alloy, similar to the modern gunmetal composed of copper, tin, zinc and lead. The detailed analyses with microstructure have been published elsewhere (Datta and Chattopadhyay 2007: 39-55). A few images made of this alloy have also been reported. One thing is clear that the artisans of this part of the subcontinent made such alloys much before the Europeans did.

Brass

The earliest evidence of brass in the form of a bangle was reported by the Anthropology Department of the University of Calcutta (Figure 8.8) from the Kanjipani area of Keonjhor District (21° 30' N, 83° 28' E) in Orissa (Ray *et al.* 2000: 356-67). The analyses of this specimen may be doubtful for the lack of clear archaeological context, but the analyses of bangles of Senuwar made of brass (copper 64.32% and zinc 35.52%), dated to to the Kushan period, clearly indicate that the smiths of this region knew the manufacturing of brass. Three pieces of heavy brass bangle and a solid copper armlet were also discovered at Chirand in CE 700-1200 level (Verma 2007: 226).

Fig. 8.8: *Earliest evidence of brass bangles from Kanjipani (Courtesy: Ranjana Ray)*

During the later Chalcolithic period, perhaps tin was identified as an alloying element. The people used local ore-minerals for alloying. The copper ore was mixed with the ores of tin as cassiterite, zinc as sphalerite or lead as galena. Knowingly or unknowingly, they used those ores and prepared bronze or brass alloys. The earliest evidence of the excavated brass was detected at Senuwar (Singh 2004: 591-601). The so-called antimony rod and a bangle from Kushan period at Senuwar revealed that those were made of brass, using 36% zinc in copper.

Metal industry was well established during the medieval period in the northeastern part of the subcontinent. From Arunachal Pradesh, there is an image of a mythical lion from Ita Forte, Itanagar, probably belonging to the 17th century (Figure 8.9). The indigenous communities of this area are fond of brass ornaments, like the *beyop*, a brass waistband used by the Adis (Figure 8.10).

In Assam, utensils of domestic use have been quite different from the rest of the country. Some influence of Southeast Asia is reflected in those items. In fact, the emigrants of Thailand or the cultural diffusion from Thailand may be responsible for this influence. The main difference has been that each plate or bowl has a little stand at the bottom (Dasgupta 1998: 251-262).The utensils of medieval Assam were made of the brass and bronze. The brass utensils were mostly made from sheets, whereas bronzes were mostly made by casting. One of the major utensils is the *ban-bati* – a bowl with stand similar to the Tibetan butter lamps lit in the monasteries. The lamp-stand in this

Fig. 8.9: *Bronze mythical lion of c. 17th century, Ita Fort, Arunachal Pradesh (Courtesy: Tage Tada)*

Fig. 8.10: *Beyop, a brass waist band used by the Adi's (Courtesy: Tage Tada)*

region is known as the *gacha*. This lamp-stand has a similar name and shape as in Bangladesh. In this part of the subcontinent, such lamp-stands are made of the cast brass or bronze, placed on the bold lotus pedestal held by a single, deeply chiselled figure of a *garud* or the rampant Ahom lion, and so on. In Bangladesh and West Bengal, the variety of lamps was so large that it was one of the major lamp producing centres of the subcontinent (Sarma 1975: 145-152). The lamps of Bengal may be found in eight or more varieties, such as the *deep lakshmi*, *arati deep*, *garud deep*, *nag deep*, *gaj deep*, *nandi deep*, *simha deep* and the *gacha*, and so on. The *deep lakshmi* type is the most important one for its bold style.

Brass chariot

Chariots have been popular in eastern India. Originally, these were made of wood and exhibited the artistry of the carpenters. However, during the 19th century, wood was replaced partially with the brass sheets and the cast brass images. The brass chariots are still used in ifferent parts regions of West Bengal. The earliest of these were reported from the Village Bankati, near Kanksha in the Bardhaman District. However, the largest one is reported from the Village Ramgarh near Binpur in the West Medinipur District (it is 9.10 m in height). The *repousse* technique is used on the brass sheets to decorate the chariots with the images of religious and social characters (Santra 1996: 433-55). One of the brass chariots resembles the nine-faceted Bengal temple, at present located at Birnagar in the Nadia District (Figure 8.11).

Fig. 8.11: *Brass Chariot at Birnagar, Nadia*

Manufacturing the Copper Alloys

In Bengal, old copper was collected to make brass and bronze, but that was never used directly for manufacturing vessels (Mukherjee 1885: 40-44). In the northeastern region, raw material was obtained from the broken or unserviceable bell metal articles. Thus, manufactured objects, mostly utensils and vessels, were morphologically diverse. These are produced even today.

For manufacturing utensils, the artisans use a set of implements, which include a wooden hammer, a polisher, a presser, some small brass pins and a wooden plank. The wooden hammer is used for pounding clay, with which the models were made. The polisher is a semicircular piece of wood having a highly polished surface. It is used to polish the bell metal objects. A presser is basically a wood and brass mechanism, used for making wax wires. Brass pins are fixed at different points on the surface of the wax model. These help to get uniform space between the core and outer covering of the clay on removing the wax. Wooden planks are used to roll bangles (Chattopadhyay and Dasgupta 2005: 1.103-105). Among the *Thetari Ranas* of Mayurbhanj, the use of wooden chisels, wooden borer and wooden hammers for kneading clay was also seen. The metal smiths made all those tools themselves (Reeves 1962: 20-40).

Image-making

Art historians usually use the term 'bronzes' for all types of metal images. Thus, this term may refer to all types of the images, whether made of copper alloys, silver and even gold. The images of the Buddhist, Jain and Brahmanical gods and goddesses have been manufactured here right from the sixth century BCE, and that activity reached its zenith during ninth and 10th centuries.

The Centres of Metal Casting

Most of the Buddhist *vihars* of eastern India were not only centres for learning, but as the existence of brass and bronze foundries in some of those *vihars* indicate, they were also the training and production centres of making images. However, we do not have sufficient corroborative evidence of that activity, except at Nalanda.

At Nalanda monastery (25° 08' N, 85° 27' E) in Bihar, the activity of metal casting is known from the second century. I-Tsing has described the collective worship of images by the students as a distinctive feature of that establishment (Biswas *et al* 1996: 444). Lama Taranath mentions that a new school of Pal art was founded during the reigns of Dharmpal (CE 783-818) and Devpal (CE 818-858). The existence of a brick oven, which might have been a brick kiln or smelting furnace, was recorded near Temple 13 of Nalanda (Ghosh 1989, II: 305-306). This had four chambers within a square area, divided by low walls. Each of the chambers was provided with two flues, one for fire to burn in, and the other for air to pass through. The reported finds, which include burnt metal pieces, slag and other objects, identify the place as a casting site (Ghosh 1989, II: 305-306). The excavation at Ratnagiri (20° 38' N, 86° 20' E) revealed copper ingots, copper bars, crucibles in front of cell 17, double oven with burnt earth, slag and copper bits, which clearly indicate that it was also a metal casting site (Mitra 1983: 283, 353).

Lama Taranath further mentions the activities of Dhiman and his son Bitopal of Varendra, who lived during the reign of Dharmpal and Devpal. Both the father and son were skilled in painting, sculpting and bronze casting. Bitopal, who reigned in Bengal, was regarded as the head of the eastern school of bronze casting (Majumdar 1943: 534). With the bronze ingots discovered during the excavation at the Rupban Kanya *Vihar* at Mainamati, that site was clearly identified as a *vihara*. It was possibly a production centre of bronze images as well. The craftsmen of the contemporary period were masters in the lost wax technology.

The Important Metal Castings

Metal objects made of copper, brass and bronze were extremely popular in the eastern India. Copper was widely used for issuing charters during the Gupta period. The metal lamps, though rare, were also made and used in the eastern India. One of the best specimens of those was found in the excavation at Mahasthan. Though a detailed metallic analysis of that object is under progress, one can tentatively take it to be a bronze piece.

Religious objects

The *dharmchakra* has been the most important religious object of the Buddhists that was worshipped independently. This was made by the casting process. The excavation of Rajbadidanga has revealed one such specimen of seventh to eighth centuries (Das 1971: 47; 1968:42). This specimen, 4.40 cm in diameter and weighing 148 grams, is made of cast bronze. It has exterior knobs radiating from the central knob, and a tang below (Figure 8.12). A similar specimen, a miniature bronze *chaitya,* was found in the antechamber in the excavation at Paharpur, along with a miniature copper bell, a small broken copper jar and a copper inkpot. A votive bronze *stoop* or *chaitya*, was discovered at Ashrafpur in Bangladesh (Figure 8.13).

Fig. 8.12: *Dharmachakra, Rajbadidanga, Department of Archaeology, Calcutta University (S. R. Das 1971)*

Fig. 8.13: *Bronze votive stoop from Ashrafpur, Bangladesh (Courtesy: The Indian Museum)* ▶

Some inscribed copper vases are important to the history of Bengal. One of the vases, of 38 cm height and with a maximum circumference of 70 cm, is preserved in the National Museum of Bangladesh (Bhattacharya 1996b: 237-247.). This vase carries a Sanskrit inscription written in the Siddhamatrika script (a type of the eastern Indian script of the eighth century). That is a Buddhist relic, probably of the Harikela region. The inscription records the land transaction from the share of goldsmiths (the *suvarnakars*).

Mention may be made of the typical medallion-like bronze objects of around 17 to 21 cm in diameter, hung on the walls in houses at Narakasur Hill and Kahilipara in Assam (Figure 8.14 and 8.15). These objects, dated around 10th-11th century are now preserved in the Assam State Museum. Generally, most of those artefacts were obtained from the sites located outside the Brahmaputra Valley.

Fig. 8.14: *Bronze medallion, Kahilipara (Courtesy: The Assam State Museum, Guwahati)*

Fig. 8.15: *Bronze medallion, Kahilipara (Courtesy: The Assam State Museum, Guwahati)*

Some Important Images

The site at Sultanganj (25° 19' 20" N, 86° 48' 25" E) in Bihar in Bhagalpur District, yielded the famous copper image of Buddha, now preserved in the Birmingham Museum (Figure 8.16). The image was discovered in the ruins of an old Buddhist monastery together with a coin of the last *satrap* of Saurastra and a coin of Chandragupta II Vikramaditya. That image, dated to the fifth century, is 2.28 m in height (minus the base, it is 2 m) and weighs nearly a ton (Mitra 1864: 360-373). From Mainamati in the Comilla District of Bangladesh, a massive Vajrasattva image of the ninth and 10th centuries was recovered. This image is 1.30 m in height. It is the largest seated and best preserved image found in eastern India (Figure 8.17). In the Tripura State Museum, we have studied a number of interesting ancient bronze

Fig. 8.16: *Sultanganj Buddha (Photograph © Birmingham Museum & Art Gallery)*

images. One of them, of Avalokiteshvar, dated to the ninth-10th century, is shown in Figure 8.18. From the Salban Vihar, amongst a number of images, an earlier image of Avalokiteshvar was also discovered. This is now preserved in the Chittagong University Museum (Figure 8.19).

Fig. 8.17: *Vajrasattva image, Mainamati (Courtesy: Vincent Lefevre and Department of Archaeology, Government of Bangladesh)*

Fig. 8.18: *Avalokiteœvara 9th-10th century (Courtesy: The Tripura Government Museum)*

Fig. 8.19: *Avalokitesvara, Salban Vihara, Chittagong University Museum (Courtesy: Shamsul Hussain)*

Alloying Composition of Images

Some information on the icons made of copper and its alloys is available from eastern India. The famous Buddha image of Sultanganj, described earlier, was made of pure copper by the *cire perdue* process (Biswas 1996: 190). The founders of Nalanda used copper, brass and tin for manufacturing images. Apart from pure copper (97.85%), high tin-bronzes (16.19-23.68% tin), brass (from 7.54-16% zinc) were used for making images, at Nalanda (Lal 1956: 53-57). On the other hand, the specimens from Chausa were undoubtedly identified as bronze, with high amount of tin. The metallurgical composition of *ashtdhatu* is similar to that of brass.

It is interesting to note that in the south India, the alloy used for making the Chola bronzes is known as '*panchloha*'; an alloy of five elements, copper, gold, silver, lead and brass. Copper, brass and lead are used in the ratio of 29:2:1, whereas brass is used as the master alloy.

Manufacturing Techniques of Bronze Images

Bronze images are technically classified into three types: (1) hollow, (2) solid and (3) apparently solid, with a clay core inside. Sometimes, images are made half hollow and half solid. Controlling the thickness of an image is a highly sophisticated process. The medieval artisans often used metal armature, chaplets and moulds of clay with wax, along with two other components—the runner and the riser. The runner is a channel through which the molten metal is carried from the sprue to the gate. The riser is column of metal placed in the mould to fill the casting as it shrinkes and solidifies. The chaplet is often an iron wire, which fixes the clay core in the mould. After casting, the major task left to the artisan is giving an overall finish to the image. Sometimes, the pre-planned holes appear in the casting. These are closed with soldering, and in some cases, jewels are fixed in those holes.

At times, the hollow image was partially filled with the molten lead to make it heavy enough to stand properly. The clay cores help to improve the soundness of casting. Sometimes, the casting defects, like pipes, spongy surface, and so on, are formed due to the entrapped gas bubbles.

One can identify different stages of processing, finishing and repairing by using instruments. However, for correct identification, one must depend on X-ray radiography that can find out whether the core was complete or partially solid or that the image was cast a single piece or if several separated pieces were cast and soldered together. For casting the molten metal, craftsmen used their own experience and technique.

Some information on the manufacturing techniques is available from various publications. For example, the image of Sultanganj Buddha was cast in two layers. The inner one was in segments, with an earthen mould held together by the 18 mm thick iron bands, now worn down by rust. The outer layer of the copper is now oxidised at different places and has become quite spongy. The casting of the upper part of this image was done in one piece up to the breast, the lower part down to the knees in another and the legs, feet, hands and back were done in several pieces (Mitra 1864: 360-373). Biswas and Sulekha (1996:190) suggest that the outer layer of copper seems to have been cast over the inner one, presumably by the *cire perdue* process. They further identified the composition of non-metallic core as the flammable cinder, originally a mixture of sand, clay, paddy husks and charcoal. In classical Indian literature, some information may be found about the image making, which often describes the casting techniques. The medieval *Shilpa* text, *Manasallasa*, in its sixty-eighth chapter, *Madhuchchistavidanama* describes the lost wax method (Saraswati 1936: 140-141). Most of the images in eastern India were cast using the lost wax technique—a technique that began in the third millennium BCE and continues to the present times among different communities, such as the Dhokras (described in this chapter). Certainly, these techniques have been continuing since the Harappan period.

Manufacturing Techniques of Pal-Sen Images

Manufacturing technique of the Pal-Sen images is highly sophisticated. One of these images is shown in Figure 8.20. We have obtained the detailed compositional analysis of this image by X-ray Fluorescence and X-ray radiographic studies. The composition of these objects is 78.07% copper, 10.41% zinc, 10.59% lead, 0.55% tin and 0.14% iron. The specimen was identified by X-ray radiography to be solid one, and no armature or clay was detected. From the same hoard, we have found an image of the bejeweled Buddha (Fig. 8.21). However, the composition of this image was found to be around 22.77% tin, indicating the use of high tin-bronze. From X-ray study, the specimen was found to be solid, but the bottom was open and no armature or clay was detected in it.

Our knowledge regarding manufacturing process of the Pal-Sen bronzes is limited. Nevertheless, it can be said with reasonable certainty that the finishing stages in the

Fig. 8.20: *Umā-Maheúvara, 10th-12th century, Gangarampur (Courtesy: State Archaeological Museum, West Bengal)*

Fig. 8.21: *Bejewelled Buddha, 10th-12th century, Gangarampur (Courtesy: The West Bengal State Archaeological Museum,Calcutta)*

image-making were excellent. Often gilding was done on the images in two ways. In one of the processes, the gold was dissolved in mercury to make an amalgam. That amalgam was applied on the metal image. In the other process, a very thin sheet of gold was pasted on the image. However, for want of proper analysis, the ancient moulding techniques have not yet been fully revealed.

Iconographic or Stylistic Study

The first important evidence on the use of metal comes from the repousse gold figure from a burial mound of the sixth century BCE from Lauria Nandangarh and two from Piprahwa in the northern part of Bihar. On the stylistic grounds, these were dated to the Mauryan Age (Bandyopadhyay 1981: 5, 14). The specimen from Lauria Nandangarh represents a frontally posed female figure. Whatever may be the iconographic identity of that repousse gold figure, it indicates a technical advancement both in the extraction and processing of metal as also in the fabrication of images. However, one can not overlook the vexing problem about the origin of that relic.

The next important stage is represented by an enigmatic group of Jain bronzes from Chausa in the Buxar District on the western fringes of Bihar. Those bronzes were recovered in CE 1931. These are now housed in the Patna Museum. However, one piece of Chausa origin is lying in a Japanese collection (Pal 1996: 151).

The hoard in the Patna Museum consists of the 16 images of *Tirthankars*, a *Kalpvriksha* and a *Dharmchakra* surmounted on a pillar. The date of these relics is widely debated. However, we are of the opinion that most of the figures can be assigned to the period between third and the early fourth centuries. The *Kalpvriksha* and *Dharmchakra* might be of slightly earlier date. The Jins are somewhat enigmatic in their stylistic affiliations. They probably represent more than one stylistic trend. Some of the Jin figures show undeniable affinity with the later Kushan idiom of Mathura, while others exhibit the features associated with the nascent Gupta traditions of the eastern Madhyadesh. The soft plastic treatment of the body, half-closed eyes in meditation, thick lips, lost details of *Shiraschakra* as indicated by a tenon, the ornamental pillars and the *makar-mukha* figures, all suggest the existence of a typical style close to the fifth century CE. The Mathuraesque features, as noted in some other Jin figures, are the hardened surface treatment, open eyes and smiling lips. This treatment neither approximates the late Kushan-Mathura style nor anticipates the mature Sarnath idiom.

On the contrary, those figures are much alive. On the whole, the Chausa figures reiterate the obvious links with the major stylistic trends of North India, and a growing awareness towards a distinctive local idiom. Probably the chronological limit of the Chausa bronze could be bracketed between the late third and early fourth and the fifth centuries.

Between the fifth and seventh centuries, there seems to be a lull in the production of metal images in eastern India. Barring a few uncertain pieces, like the inscribed Buddha in the Cleveland Museum, the only other definite image, assignable to the seventh century, comes from Deulbadi in the Comilla District of Bangladesh. This image, described as *Sarvani* on the pedestal inscription, was first described by N. K. Bhattasali (Bhattasali 2001: 6-8) in his famous work on the sculptures of Dhaka Museum (now known as National Museum of Bangladesh).

The image represents a standing goddess in a frontal position with eight hands, four on each side, on the back of a couchant lion. Beginning from the top, she holds a discus, a sword, an arrow and a conch shell in her right hands and a shield, a bow, a trident, and a bell in the left, in the same order. She is accompanied by female attendant bearing a flywhisk, on either side. The important feature of this image is the oval rim, linking the main and the subsidiary figures. In sharp contrast to the rigid frontality of the goddess, her attendants are distinguished by an abrupt break of the body axis. The hardened surface treatment and the elongated faces with a weird smile convey a kind of mood, which is difficult to explain.

An image of Surya (Sun-god) in 'octa-metal' of the National Museum of Bangladesh of about 15 cm height can be cited here (Bhattasali 2001: 172). In this image, the god is shown seated inside a one-wheeled car, while seven spirited horses are represented underneath, drawing it. That miniature image seems to be a work of the seventh-eighth century. That image was discovered along with the *Sarvani* image at Deulbadi in Bangladesh.

Of the two most important archaeological sites – Nalanda and Kurkihar – in Bihar, perhaps the former is earlier because of its smaller size and the simpler iconography of the images found at this site. The common types show the image of Buddha seated on a lotus throne in the *dharmchakra mudra*. In this category of images, two deer are shown seated in the centre of *dharmchakra*. The round *prabhamandal* serves as the halo and body aura. The Nalanda images show stylistic affinity with the sculptures of Gupta period. The images of Kurkihar, dated to the late ninth and 10th centuries, indicate a kind of sophistication in the sharp elongation of forms and the striations of robes.

From Bangladesh, the next important bronze image is of the standing Boddhisattva Manjushri, discovered from Salar near Mahasthan, and now preserved at the Varendra Research Museum. It is dated to the seventh-eighth century. The image is a lyrically poised figure, in a gesture of boon-giving by his right hand, and protection by the left (Figure 8.22).

Fig. 8.22: *Boddhisttva Mañjuœri (Courtesy: Vincent Lefevre and Varendra Research Museum)*

Stylistically most of the images, with the high thrown base and the solid stella format, are visually very close to the Buddha images recovered from the Comilla and Sylhet areas of Bangladesh. However, a few pieces indicate an altogether different tradition. For instance, an unidentified figure of a goddess, wearing a decorated headgear secured by a fillet, and with an animal set against a bare solid disc, appears to have a different iconographic and visual feature.

The image of Avalokiteshvar of Pilak is considered to be the earliest of the Tripura bronzes. The deity, standing on the pericarp of a lotus, is set in an elongated halo, crowned by a triangular motif. The edges of the halo are marked by a beaded border, with the tongues of flames at intervals. This figure is assigned to the ninth century. Another bronze image of the south Tripura relates to the transitional phase. The Tulsipahar Vishnu image combines features of the seventh and the late eighth centuries specimens of the south and north Bengal. Some of the elements, like the unadorned lotus base and the plane architrave, supported by the totally undecorated pillars evoke similar response as the iconographic features of the Manir Tat Shiv obtained from the South Twenty-four Pargana District of West Bengal. Again, the configuration of the aureole, with the well-balanced and boldly rendered flame motifs, seems to have evolved out of the halo of the aforesaid Shiv and similar other images. A singularly important feature is the pinning-up device, with which the main figures from the eastern and northern Bengal, Shiv Lokeshvar of Barisal in Bangladesh and the two Vishnu figures probably from Mahasthangarh (Asher 1980: plate 68, 70), could be hung. In the Tulsipahar Vishnu, the penchant for the angular treatment of the faces of main and subsidiary figures is pronounced. One can not fail to notice the pointed, thin and inverted triangle-like shape of the eyes.

The Buddhist bronze images of south Tripura owe stylistically much to Jhewari and related sites of Chittagong. In some of the Buddhist images of Jhewari, the seated Buddha is shown without the backslab or pedestal. This indicates similarities with the Buddha images of Pagan in Myanmar. Compared to Jhewari, the role of Mainamati appears to be less significant. The eastern Indian idiom was redefined in Jhewari.

A standing image of the Buddha, discovered in Kurkihar, Bihar, of the ninth century on a lotus pedestal, the full face is typical of the Devapala period (now preserved at Patna Museum) that is inspired by the Sarnath-Kurkihar archetype, illustrates that change. The lines of drapery are more rigidly defined in the lower part of the hem and the upper robe is given a wavy, fold-like appearance.

Equivalents of the ninth century Buddha are not difficult to locate at Jhewari. The Buddhist images found there have elongated faces and curled lips with meditative smile. A group of Avalokiteshvar and Tara images of the south Tripura show in various degrees the articulation of distinctive elements although rooted in the dominant art style. This distinctiveness manifests itself in such features as the bulging eyes shown by incised lines. The simple rectangular seat, absence of the decorative elements of the stella and such other features suggest that the pieces under consideration cannot be dated later than the 10th century.

Another important one is a bronze of Devi from Hrishyamukh. The goddess stands in a rigid stance on a lotus, her attendants on either side are distinguished by the exaggerated flexion, which is in sharp contrast to the frontality of the central figure. Her longish face conveys a weird mood. The only known bronze of northern Tripura is of Hevajra. That was perhaps imported from the eastern or northern Bengal, rather than cast locally. The Dharmnagar bronzes cannot be properly accommodated within the general evolution process of the metal images in Tripura.

The most colossal bronze image of the Bodhisattva Vajrasattva of this region comes from Mainamati (Bhattacharya 1996a: 137-148; Bhikkhu Sunithananda 2001: 99) has been cited earlier. This two-armed image is seated in the *satvaparyanka asan*. In his right hand, the deity holds the *vishva vajra* and in the left the *vajra-ghanta*. The exquisitely chiselled image is decorated with various ornaments (already shown in Figure 8.17).

Between the ninth and 12th centuries, plastic art as seen in the eastern Indian bronze images was at its zenith. Its basic characteristics are the combination of intentness for achieving rounded forms, multiplicity in floridness, execution of various motifs, profusion of ornamentation and subsidiary figures and the conventionalisation in the treatment of lotuses in seated or standing images. We find the human forms along with plants and animals, and an emphasis on ornamentation on the aureoles and pedestals, with certain floridness. Some of the masterpieces represent the images with their eyes clearly indcitaing the state of yogic meditation. The Buddha images are of various types. One of them is in the famous form of *bhumisparsha mudra*. The other standing Buddha images are found draped with a diaphanous robe and with marked parallel folds. One may also note the beauty of Avalokiteshvar Padmapani. These images were very popular.

Admittedly, there are still serious gaps in our understanding of the regional traditions. The degenerated Dhokra tradition of casting images continued in the eastern India. They are still continuing that tradition in Sikkim and other Buddhist *vihars* in the eastern India. In Bangladesh, Dhamrai was once a centre for brass and bronze castings. A few entrepreneurs are still trying to manufacture images on the traditional pattern.

The Dhokra Process

From the Chalcolithic period onwards, the itinerant metal workers of the Indian subcontinent have been moving from place to place in search of raw materials and supplying metal objects to the society. These indigenes of the central India have been beyond the politics of the country. They have always been isolated and are very conservative. The Dhokras are perhaps the descendant of these itinerant metal workers, who led the traditional way of life and produced cast objects with the cire *perdue* or lost wax process. Such metal casters exist in the isolated pockets of the western part of eastern India. In Chhattisgarh and Orissa, these artisans use *dhuna* – the resinous and aromatic sap of *sal* tree (*shorea robusta)* as a substitute for wax. However, in Jharkhand and West Bengal, these artisans use beeswax.

Though the Dhokra process also follows the lost wax technique, but it is quite different from the process of the Pal-Sen bronzes, characterised by the sophisticated finishing. Normally, the use of chaplet is avoided in the Dhokra process, in which the composition of copper and other elements are not standardised. The wax threads are used widely in decoration, and normally no finishing is done. The former technology (Dhokra) is similar to the modern investment casting process. Let us study it in brief. To start with, the core of the mould is made with fine clay, duly filtered to separate stones and dirt. A paste of fine sand and cow dung in the ratio of 4:1 is made separately. That sand-cow dung paste is mixed with the cleaned and sieved clay, and the mixture is kneaded into dough of the desired texture. A base model of the proposed image is made from that dough. At times, various components (base models) of the proposed image are made in separate pieces, depending upon the complexity of the design. Such a base model is called 'core' in the foundry terminology. The core models are then dried under the sun.

The second step is the preparation of resin or wax recipe for which the *dhuna* (the resinous sap of *sal* tree), vegetable oil and wax are poured in a hot pan so that the entire mixture turns into a liquid. When the wax mixture is cool enough, it is made into a thread, which is similar to the modern practice of extrusion.

The sundried core model is wrapped in the wax thread and a narrow runner-like wax stick is attached to it. The model is then fully covered with the prepared clay leaving the funnel uncovered. This is the mould, and it is left to dry at a convenient place. When dried, the mould is inspected carefully to detect any visible fracture. The next step is making a clay crucible. After it is made, the crucible is attached to the mould with wet clay in such a manner that the wax stick appears exposed in the crucible. This wax stick melts on heating and the gap so formed turns into a runner for the molten metal. When the mould-crucible unit is well dried and found free from all blemishes, it is ready for the final step. In the final operation, a lump of brass, a little amount of zinc and small borax is placed in the crucible. The quantity of brass is around 10 times more than that of the wax used. The mould-cum-crucible is then gently placed in the furnace in such a way that the crucible remains at the bottom of the furnace. Thus, the brass in the crucible is completely melted. The mould-cum-crucible is then tilted with a tong so that the liquid metal from the crucible flows down the runner to fills the gap formed by melted and burnt out wax in the mould. When it is ensured, that the metal has fully filled the gap created by the burnt out wax, the mould-cum-crucible is taken out and allowed to get cool. The mould is then broken and the core material removed. Thus, the Dhokra images are made.

Decorative Metalware of pre-Modern Period

During the 18th and 19th centuries, decorative metalware were widely used for the domestic purposes in the eastern India and Bangladesh. For example, *atardan* (perfume pot), *phuldan* (flower vase), *pandan* (betel box), *besandan* (soap case), *pikdan* (spitoon), *kalamdan* (pen case), *surahi* (high necked pot), hookah-bowl, and so on, were made. These vessels, made of silver and brass, bear excellent decorations.

Several villages of West Bengal are still manufacturing domestic utensils of cast brass and sheet metals. One of those, Ranirghat Village near Nabadwip of the Nadia District may be mentioned here. The artisans of this village manufacture brass objects with the composition of 70% copper and 30% zinc. They are famous for manufacturing brass pitchers (Figure 8.23).

During the 17th century, war drums were widely used in the wars. One of those was known as *nagarah*, shaped like a deep bowl, tapering towards the bottom and wide at the mouth. Those were made of the copper alloys. A good number of such objects are preserved at the National Museum of Bangladesh.

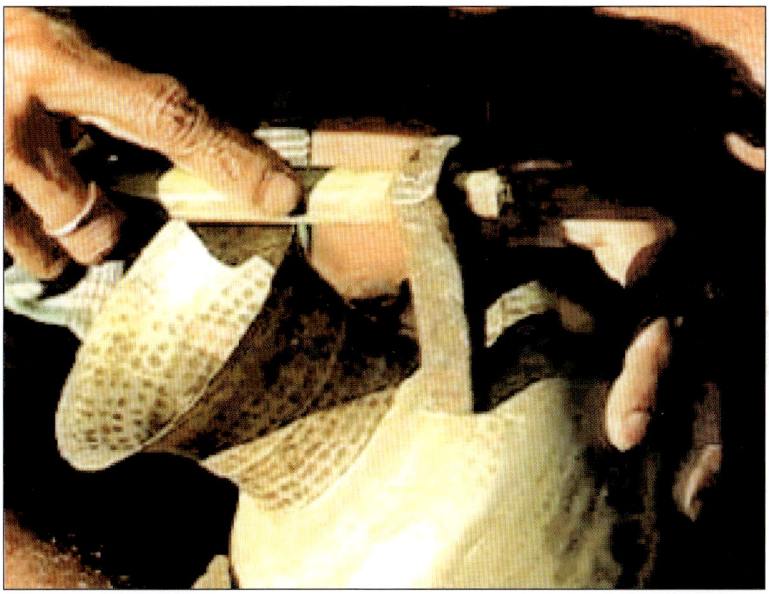

Fig. 8.23: *Manufacturing of brass pitchers at Nabadwip, West Bengal*

Cannons made of Copper Alloys

Most of the cannons of the medieval period were made of iron. However, some of those were also made of brass and bronze. Composite cannons are also known.

In the Bangladesh National Museum at Dhaka, there are seven brass cannons discovered in CE 1909 from Dewanbagh, about seven km from Narayanganj (Roy 2000: 139-143). It may be mentioned here that Dewanbagh was the capital of Manowar Khan, the grandson of Isha Khan. Later on, Manowar Khan, chief of the navy of Sayesta Khan, had the credit of recovering Chittagong from the hands of the Mags of Arakan. One of those seven cannons, the bronze one bears an inscription having the name of '*Raja Kandarpanarayan*' and the name of the maker, '*Rupiya Khan Sang Sreepur*'. It may be mentioned that Sreepur was one of the capitals of the twelve *Bhuians* of the medieval Bengal. The four cannons of that collection belonged to Sher Shah, who defeated Humayun. The muzzles of those cannons bear a tiger-head. The best one of the lot was cast by one Syed Ahmed Rumi in AH 949 (CE 1542-43). An important cannon of that collection belonged to Isha Khan. It is 1.33 m in length and bears a dated Bengali inscription of CE 1593-94 (Figure 8.24).

The two unique cannons of Sher Shah are preserved at the Varendra Research Museum, Rajshahi (Sanyal 1927-28: 1-7; Sharf-ud-din 1927-28). One brass cannons was discovered at Shershahi Village in the Police Station Kaliachak in the Maldah District. Two brass cannons or muskets are available at the State Archaeological Museum, Bhubaneswar. One of them bears a Persian legend. Two unique bronze cannons, 1.96 m and 1.97 m in length are in the Chittagong University Museum. One of those, namely *Sar Jung* ('head of the war') bears an inscription: '*Tope Shah Buland Iqbal Ast*'. Shah Buland Iqbal was a title of Shah Jahan (Hossain 1985: 9-12; 1988: 8-12). One of these cannons is shown in Figure 8.25.

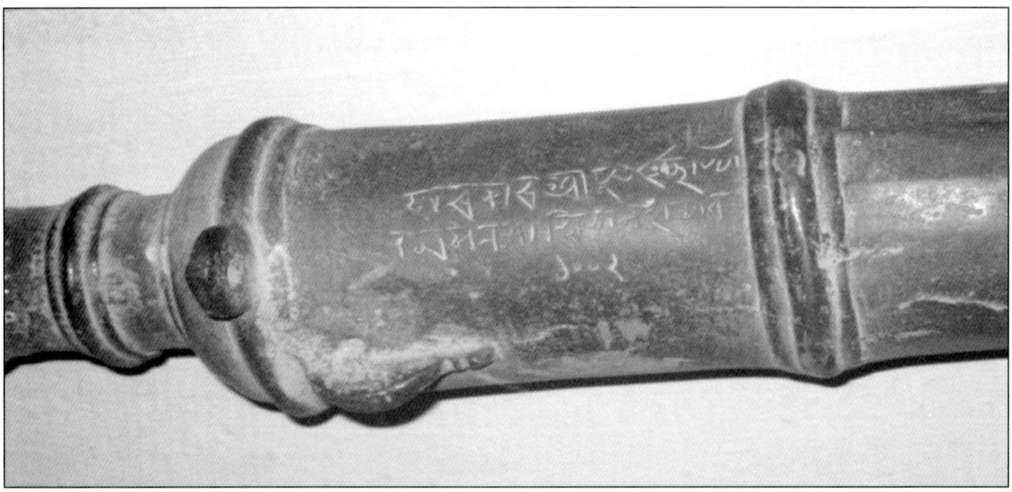

Fig. 8.24: *Brass cannon of Isha Khan (Courtesy: The National Museum of Bangladesh)*

Fig. 8.25: *Sar Jung, the bronze cannon of Shah Jahan*
(Photograph by Ziauddin Chowdhury; Courtesy: The Chittagong University Museum)

In medieval Assam, some unique cannons were made of brass or other alloys of copper. Two of them are preserved in the Assam State Museum at Guwahati and one in the Tai Museum in Sibsagar. One interesting brass cannon of Parikshitnarayan (CE 1603-1613), ruler of the Kochhajo, is also preserved in the former Museum (Figure 8.26).

Maharaja Krishnachandra used brass cannons. One of his cannons, made of brass (no analyses have been made so far), is presently located in the Victoria Memorial Hall, Kolkata (Fig. 8.27). This cannon has a total length of 1.52 m, the diameter of the muzzle is 195 mm and of the muzzle bore is 98 mm. That cannon is of high artistic quality, with the floral decorations and an inscription. That cannon bears the name of the King Krishnachandra Ray and its manufacturer was Brajakishore Das. There are also two brass cannons, made by the same Brajakishore Das, in the State Archaeological Museum, West Bengal (Fig. 8.28 and 8.29). Those two brass cannons were recovered while digging the earth at Garbari-Mangalapota in the Police Station Garbeta in the Medinipur District.

One of the best examples of the composite cannons is known from Fort William. The cannon named as *Tope Zafarbaksh* belonged to Aurangzeb (Figure 8.29). It was

Fig. 8.26: *Brass musket of Gadadhar Simha (Courtesy: The Tai Museum)*

Fig. 8.27: *Brass cannon of Maharaja Krishnachandra (Courtesy: Victoria Memorial Hall)*

Fig. 8.28: *Brass cannon from Garbari-Mangalapota (Courtesy: State Archaeological Museum, West Bengal)*

Fig. 8.29: Tope Zafarbaksh, the composite cannon (Courtesy: Fort William)

manufactured in the CE 1674 (Balasubramaniam and Chattopadhyay 2007: 205-221). Its manufacturing started with the placement of 13 iron staves, possibly over a wooden mandrel. Those iron staves were hooped over with iron rings. Based on the observation of the dented and damaged region just above the trunnion, those iron rings possibly made up most of the thickness of the cannon.

The bottom and side moulds of the cannon were joined together, using iron chaplets, which can even now be noted in its rear part. After finishing the iron assembly, molten bronze might have been poured into the mould. After cooling down the mould, the cannon surface was engraved with inscriptions and designs.

The design and construction of the composite cannon is fascinating. It reveals the skill of the medieval Indian metal smiths in engineering such wonderful devices. Conceiving and fabricating such massive cannons must have required a very good understanding of metallurgy and metallurgical skill. Composite cannons required skills in both wrought iron forge welding and bronze casting technologies.

Bronze Coins

Manipur was one of the important princely states, which issued coins of high tin-bronze or bell metal. Those coins, known as *sel*, were very small in size. The metal for the coins was first cast into small pellets, which were reheated and flattened into irregular circular forms and finished by a punch with a letter on it. There is an example of a *sel* coin (Figure 8.30) with letter *sha* on one side. The reverse side is blank.

Fig. 8.30: *Sel coin of bell-metal, Manipur (Courtesy: N.G. Rhodes)*

Composite Objects

The use of composite metal in various objects is also known besides for the cannons. A plumb bob is used to determine the verticality of a wall in building construction. A bronze plumb bob was discovery in the excavation at Bangarh in West Bengal (Goswami

1948: 33). A pair of composite alloy plummets is preserved in the Jorhat District Museum (Figure 8.31). According to H.N. Datta, such objects were used during the Gupta period in Assam. It is likely that these may be of the Ahom period, when large scale building construction was done.

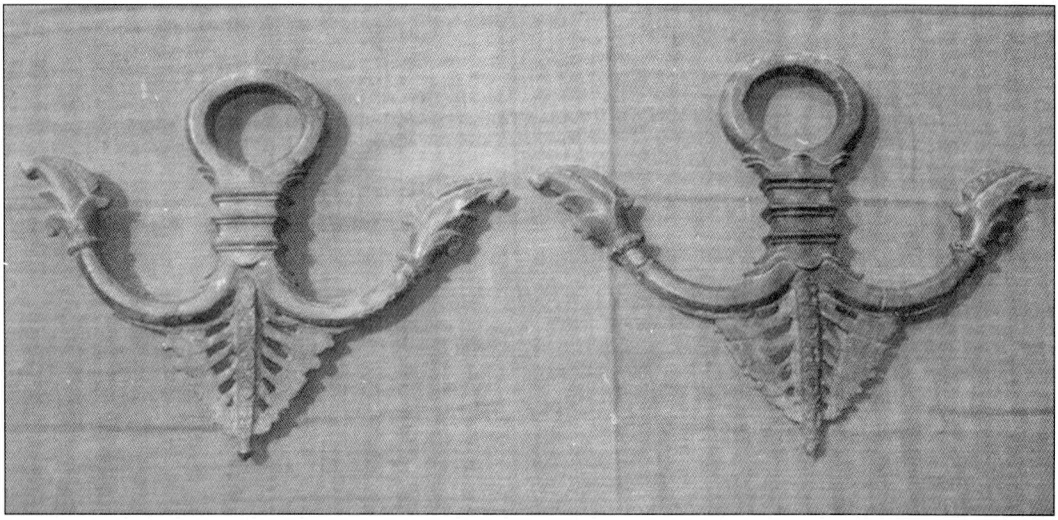

Fig. 8.31: *Plummets, Jorhat District Museum (Courtesy: Dr Hemendra Nath Datta)*

9

CONCLUSION

IN THE PRECEDING CHAPTERS, VARIOUS TECHNOLOGICAL FEATURES of different metals that were used in eastern India through ages have been discussed. Eastern India witnessed a gradual transformation from the Neolithic to the Chalcolithic stage. An overall socio-economic development can be noticed with the invention of farming and firing of pottery. Fire was used in the Neolithic Period to fire earthen wares. Firing of pottery may be said to be the beginning of pyrotechnology, which led to the conversion of ore minerals into metals. The beginnings of metal craft are known from the later Neolithic to the transition of the Chalcolithic phase. This transformation was primarily accentuated by the introduction of copper. From the early NBPW period, during the seventh to sixth BCE, metal smiths learnt that adding other elements improved the strength of copper.

From 300 BCE onwards, the use of additional amount of tin in copper alloys was noticed. With this high amount of tin in the copper alloy, came to be called high tin-bronze, wherein the quatity of tin increased from 15 to 30 percent. Through empirical knowledge of thermo-mechanical process, the smiths could overcome the difficulties caused by alloying.

Iron marked its advent in this part of the country before 1200 BCE. The beginning of iron technology was first noticed in Black-and-Red ware context which at an earlier level is associated with Chalcolithic. A well-developed iron culture was identified among the Asurs of Jharkhand and the Megalithic cultures of Chhattisgarh around 1000 BCE. The manufacture of sponge iron from the lateritic or limonitic iron ores was carried out in the primitive iron-smelting furnaces. The smelting furnaces of this region are commonly called 'bloomery furnaces', for here, solid iron blooms are produced from the solid iron ores. In the beginning, it was pure iron, but later on carburisation commenced in 1000 BCE. Smiths learnt quenching and tempering only in 300 BCE. By controlling the carbon contents and heat treatment process, different types of iron were produced. The razors and sickles must be of very hard material. So smiths first increased the carbon contents (carburisation) by heating for a long time in a charcoal furnace, for heating and forging help the iron to absorb carbon. The finished carburised object in a red hot condition was quenched in cold water. From the megalithic burials, one of the most important discoveries was a ploughshare. The people of the Early Historic period of eastern India used iron extensively. With the use of iron, a radical change took place in the social and economic life of the people in all spheres. Agriculture, urbanisation and trade and commerce; all were transformed, not only with the use of iron chisels for cutting of stone blocks, but also by the direct application of iron beams for structural purposes. In the late medieval period, this part of the country produced marvellous cannons.

From 1000 BCE onwards, an important culture emerged in the western part of this area. The culture, which is identified as the Megalithic was related to the use of large size (mega) stone blocks (lithic). The beginning of megalithic culture was older than the NBPW culture. Such ceramics was also noted in the Gangetic plain. Metallurgy developed here at a much later period. Evidences of metal craft were detected only in the Historic period, similar to the western part. About 600 BCE, an all-round development was witnessed with the use of the sophisticated NBPW. Iron objects of several forms were noticed. Besides the introduction of coins, the people pursued other activities, such as bead making, ivory-carving bronze casting. For clearing of forests and dressing stones, they required developed tools, like axes and chisels. The people of this part of the country achieved that through the carburised iron making.

Copper was introduced during the Neolithic-Chalcolithic transition. In the beginning copper was used in its pure or natural form. When it was mixed with another element, it formed an alloy. This alloy is called bronze. No alloying element was detected in the copper objects of Senuwar in the beginning. In the later Chalcolithic phase, use of tin as an alloying element is known. The origin and subsequent development in the objects of copper hoard has not been satisfactorily explained so far. We have noted the use of copper utensils in the early historic period. Copper in its pure form is still used in everyday religious artefacts at home, and in the monasteries and temples.

The discovery of iron technology entirely changed the life of people in the eastern India. All the stages from the use of wrought iron to the tempered steel are noticed here. The evidence of vanadium in iron objects indicates that smiths knew how to increase the strength of metal. Iron objects had been unearthed from the Megalithic burials and archaeological sites as old as 1200 BCE by the regular excavations. We have found that the residential complex for artisans were in the vicinity of their place of work. Their habitations were located on the outskirts of the site. In the beginning, smelters used low-grade iron ores, but in the course of time, they modified their furnaces to use rich ores.

In eastern India, native gold was known to be associated with the quartz veins and as the gold nuggets in the streambeds. The separation of gold flakes by the indigenes is a wonderful traditional technique. They used to pan for gold twice a year after the rainy season and during the winter. The Doharas of the erstwhile Manbhum had through generations mastered the technique of alluvial gold washing. During the Ahom rule in Assam, from ten to twelve thousand Sonwals (the labourers who collects *sona* or gold) were engaged in gold washing from the sands of Brahmaputra. From Sekta in Manipur, a unique gold mask was discovered. A gold-plated bronze image Bodhisattva Manjushri (*c.* sixth century) was recovered from Balaidhap of Mahasthan.

Silver is a precious metal for the common people of India. This metal was recovered from argentiferous galena. The *Arthshastra* describes the method of purification of silver in a series of crucibles by employing the process of cupellation. Thousands of punch-marked silver coins were discovered. A silver rod was discovered at Bangarh. A bracelet or bangle of silver was discovered in Mahasthan. Several silver ingots, silver bells and bangle pieces were recovered from the monastery cells of Salban *Vihar* of Mainamati. Lalitagiri was one of the silver manufacturing centres. In the Southeast Asia, there are two important sources of silver. One was located at Nan-Chao in Yunnan and the other in the Bawdwin mines of Myanmar.

The earliest evidence of lead in India was detected in the Senuwar excavations, datable to 1950 BCE. Lead was obtained from galena. The presence of lead between the beams indicated that during processing the iron was heated in a lead bath during structural fabrication. This might indicate a major use of lead in the iron industry.

Bronze is widely used in ancient objects. The raw material for bronze is tin. Tin is obtained from cassiterite. The source of tin is scanty in eastern India. The Gond indigenes of Bastar were extracting tin from cassiterite and used it for making ornaments. Brass, an alloy of the copper and zinc, was used for manufacturing utensils and images throughout the ages. Eastern India was also conversant with zinc. However, the supply of zinc was not adequate here. The earliest evidence of brass from Orissa was reported from Kanjipani area of the Keonjhor District of Orissa and at Senuwar of Bihar. That site belongs to the Kushan period.

The people of this part of the subcontinent learnt alloying, first with the small amounts of tin. They also practised alloying with arsenic. Later they developed high tin alloying. They also learnt brass-making, which finally developed into gunmetal. Alloying of copper was developed by the artisans to overcome certain difficulties that they faced while making, shaping and treating the copper artefacts.

Relevant studies that need to be taken up in future

In the foregoing chapters, we have simply discussed the state of our present knowledge. Complete knowledge can only be available with more in-depth studies of the ancient metal objects. The reason for the inadequacy of our knowledge may be due to the fact that during the ancient and medieval periods, most of the precious materials were recycled. Without the proper analyses of materials excavated from various sites and recovered from ancient places, it may be difficult to trace out the origin and development of metallurgy of this region. The committed involvement of the scientists and technologists can contribute significantly in that direction.

The future scholars are expected to study in more detail the traditional manufacturing technologies through the application of archaeometallurgy. The ancient objects in the museum can be studied to great advantage without causing any damage. The non-destructive use of neutron diffraction, Proton Induced X-ray Emission (PIXE) and X-ray fluorescence (XRF) and lead isotope analysis may resolve those complex problems.

GLOSSARY

Alloy: The combination of more than one element. In its natural state, gold is found to be mixed with silver. This alloy is named electrum.

Annealing: When a metal is hammered or forged, it is hardened and often breaks. This hardness can be softened by reheating the material and slowly cooling it subsequently. This process is called annealing.

Austenite: The interstitial solid solution of ferric carbide or carbon in iron. The maximum solubility of carbon in austenite is 2.11 weight percent at 1146 °C.

Black-and-Red Ware: It is a ceramic, mainly of the Chalcolithic period, but has continued even after Early Historic period. It is manufactured on the basis of inverted firing technique, in which the inside surface is black and the outer is red. Paintings in white or black on the outer as well inner surface of the vessels are a dominant feature in this ware.

Boiling point: The temperature at which matter changes from liquid to vapour.

Brass: It is an alloy of copper and zinc.

Bronze: It is an alloy of copper and tin.

Carburisation: When carbon enters iron, it finds a way and occupies some space in its structure. Carburisation is a process of increasing carbon contents in the iron. Pure iron is free from carbon. Excess carbon hardens iron and converts it to steel.

Cast iron: If carbon contents exceed two percent, then carbon resides in the iron as graphite or iron carbide. This iron has a low melting point. In its liquid state, it can be poured into a mould. It takes the shape of the mould cavity on cooling.

Cementite (Fe_3C): This is an inter-metallic compound of iron and carbon, with 6.67 weight percentage of carbon in iron. This is very hard substance.

Compound: It is a combination of two or more elements possessing different properties.

Crystallisation: When a liquid metal is cooled slowly, it turns into grains of crystals on solidification. This formation of metallic grains is called crystallisation.

Ductility: The permanent change in length of the metal specimen with respect to its original length is a measure of ductility of that metal.

Element: It is a pure substance that cannot be decomposed into any simpler substance. Copper is an element, but common salt is a compound made of sodium (an element) and chlorine (another element).

Electron Microscope: The source of illumination in an ordinary microscope is a beam of light. In an electron microscope, the source of illumination is a beam of electrons. These are of two types: Scanning Electron Microscope (SEM) and Transmission Electron Microscope (TEM).

Electron probe micro analyses: Analyses of composition by SEM.

Ferrite: This is almost pure iron, which can accommodate 0.022 weight percentage of carbon at 727 °C. This is body-centered cubic in shape, and capable of absorbing phosphorous.

Flux: This is a substance, like borax, that reduces the melting point of the material

Furnace: It is a source of high temperature to melt, smelt or heat a metal.

Gold plating: This is practised by the Newari artisans. It is a process of applying a quasi-liquid amalgam of gold dust and mercury on the surface of a metallic image. The image is later on heated in the cowdung fire. Thus, an even deposite of gold is obtained all over the image.

Grain: Most materials are crystalline, made of the grains of crystal. Sugar is granular with a fixed shape.

Grain boundary: Interface between two or more grains.

Heat treatment: The treatment of a metal object by heating at a particular temperature and then cooling it in a controlled environment.

High tin-bronze: This is bronze with more than ten percent tin. High tin-bronze or *kansha* usually has around 25% tin.

Hot working: Deformation in the shape of metal by forging or rolling. Metal is heated first to a certain temperature and then subjected to pressure.

Iron Age: The archaeological period associated with iron technology is generally designated as the Iron Age. It also includes the Megalithic period of Chhattisgarh, South India, and other places.

Knobbed Vessel: A vessel made of metal or clay with a lid and a knob.

Metal working: This is hammering of cold metal to change its shape. It is the oldest practice of metal working. Hammering on hot metal to change its shape is called forging.

Martensite: This is formed when a diffusionless transformation from one phase to another occurs. In the case of red-hot iron, when suddenly quenched in water, the carbon entrapped in the iron crystals cannot come out of the lattice. The iron lattice is changed from face-centred cubic to tetragonal shape.

Melting point: This is the temperature, at which a solid substance changes to a liquid state. Solid copper becomes liquid at 1084°C.

Melting: This is the change of state of matter from solid to liquid without any chemical change.

Metallograph: A graphic representation of the structure of a metal or alloy. Microstructure can be seen under a microscope. When the structure is seen with the naked eye or with very low power magnifier, this is called macrostructure.

Mixture: Any material is said to be in the mixture state, if its components can be separated easily.

Neolithic: The time-period during which the early men used polished stone tools. It marks beginning of agriculture. People came in contact with metal at the end of this period.

Normalising: The process of slowly cooling a red hot metal, like iron, in the air.

Northern Black Polished Ware: This distinctive type of pottery was developed around 500 BCE. This deluxe pottery was usually black. However, colours like steel blue, chocolate, golden, and so on, with the shiny surface have also been found in the Gangetic or Eastern Gangetic valleys.

Paleolithic: It is also known as the Old Stone Age, when crude stone tools, like hand axes were used by the primitive people.

Pearlite: It is a lameller arrangement of ferrite and cementite formed during the cooling of austenite; a constituent of steel and cast iron.

Physical metallurgy: It is a branch of metallurgy that deals with the relationship between structures and properties of metals and alloys. It provides a vital link between making, shaping, treating and using of metals and alloys.

Pig iron: This is the product of a modern blast furnace. Its carbon contents are in the ranges of two to four percent.

Proton Induced X-ray Emission (PIXE): A technique to analyse a specimen with the help of proton beams.

Pyrotechnology: Application of heat to convert clay into pottery. The application of heat to the minerals produced metals.

Quenching: The process of cooling hot metal by plunging it into cold water or other liquid.

Radiocarbon Dating: A chemical analysis used to determine the age of organic materials based on their content of the radioisotope carbon -14. It is believed to be reliable for dates up to 40,000 years.

Recrystallisation: This is the nucleation and growth of a new strain of the free crystals from the cold worked metal.

Smelting: It is the process of extracting metals from the ores by heating.

Solidification: The process of cooling a liquid substance into a solid state.

Specific gravity (Sp. Gr.): The ratio of weight of a substance to its equal volume of pure water at 4°C.

Steel: Combination of iron and up to 2% of carbon. Some other elements may also be present.

Tempering: This is the process of bringing metal to a desired consistency, texture, or hardness by first heating and then cooling it gradually.

Toughness: The amount of mechanical energy absorbed by a test piece of metal before it cracks or fails.

Widmanstatten pattern: The change in the microstructure of iron, when it is over-heated for a prolonged time in a furnace.

Work hardening: A state of internal stress in a metal, when subjected to external force, like hammerng.

Wrought iron: Soft iron, free from carbon and occasionally mixed with slag, produced in primitive furnace.

X-ray Fluorescence: The process of determining elemental composition of matter with the help of X-ray.

SELECT BIBLIOGRAPHY

Agrawal, B. B., K. K. Prasad, G. I. S. Chauhan, P. K. Chaudhuri and S. M. Areon. 1998. Evaluation of earlier iron making process and their relevance in Indian context, In *Archaeometallurgy in India* (Ed.) V. Tripathi, Delhi: Sharada Publishing House.

Agrawal, D. P., R. V. Krishnamurthy, Sheela Kusumgar, L. A. Narain and M. N.Sarin. 1974. Alloying in the Copper hoards, *Bulletin of the Museum and Archaeology*: 14.

Agrawal, D. P. 1971. *The Copper Bronze Age in India*. New Delhi: Munshiram Manoharlal.

Agrawal, O. P., Hari Narain and Jay Prakash. 1994. Technical Studies of Silver Punch Mark Coins from Narhan, in P. Singh. 1994. *Excavations at Narhan*: Varanasi: Banaras Hindu University.

Ahmed Bulbul, P. K. Chattopadhyay and N. K. Bhuiyan. 2007. Iron Objects from Wari-Bateshwar: Archaeo-metallurgical Studies. In *Barendra Barennya* Professor A. K. M. Yaqub Ali Felicitation Volume (Eds.), A. K. M. Shahnawaz and R. K. M. Saleh, Dhaka: Somoy Prakashan.

Ahmed, Bulbul. 2001. *Narshingdi zellar Wari-Bateshwar: Akti pratnatattik shamiksha* (Bangla), Writers' Foundation, Dhaka, Bangladesh.

Alam, M. S. and J. F. Salles. 2001. France-Bangladesh Joint venture excavations at Mahasthangarh: *First interim Report 1993-1999*. Dhaka: Department of Archaeology.

Altekar, A. S. and V. Misra. 1959. *Report on Kumrahar Excavations 1951-1955*. Patna: K. P. Jayaswal Research Institute.

Asher, F. M. 1980. *The Art of Eastern India 300-800.* New Delhi: Oxford University Press.

Bagchi, P. C. 1951. *India and China, A thousand years of Sino-Indian Cultural Contact*, Calcutta: China Press.

Balasubramanian, M. N. and K. C. Chandi. 1976. Lead isotope studies of galena from some occurrence in India, *Records of Geological Survey of India*: 107 (2).

Balasubramaniam, R. 2005. Dal Mardan – the Forged Welded iron cannon at Bishnupur, *Indian Journal of History of Science:* 40.3

Balasubramaniam, R. 2007. On the steeling of iron and the second urbanization of Indian subcontinent, *Man and Environme nt: 32* (1).

Balasubramaniam, R. and P. K. Chattopadhyay 2007. Zafarbaksh – the composite Mughal cannon of Aurangzeb at Fort William in Kolkata. *Indian Journal of History of Science:* 42 (2).

Balasubramaniam, R. and N. Mahajan. 2003. Some metallurgical aspects of Gupta Period gold coin manufacturing technology. *Indian Journal of History of Science,* 38 (4).

Balasubramaniam, R. 2008. *The Saga of Indian Cannons*. New Delhi: Aryan Books International.

Ball, V. 1880 *Jungle life in India or the Journeys and Journals of an Indian Geologist,* reprinted as *Tribal and Peasant Life in Nineteenth Century India*. Delhi 1985: Usha Publication.

Bandyopadhyay, B. 2004. *Buddhist centres of Orissa Lalitagiri, Ratnagiri and Udaygiri.* New Delhi: Sundeep Prakashan.

Bandyopadhyay, B. 2007. *Excavations at Udayagiri-2*, New Delhi: Archaeological Survey of India.

Banerjee, R. D. 1911. *Catalogue of Bangiya Sahitya Parishad*, Calcutta: Bangiya Sahitya Parishad.

Behera, P. K. 2002-2003. Excavation at Kumersingha and Kurumpadar – the Iron Age Settlements in the Middle Mahanadi Valley, Orissa: Results of the first Sessions work, *Pragdhara:* 13

Behera, P. K. and P. K. Chattopadhyay. 2004-2005. Iron Objects from the Iron Age – Early Historic Level at Badmal (Dist. Sambalpur, Orissa) Archaeometallurgical Studies, *Puratattva*: 35.

Bhardwaj, H. C. 1987. Review of Metallurgical studies of Ancient Indian Coinage. In *Numismatics & Archaeology.* (Eds.) P. L. Gupta and A. K. Ghosh. Nasik: IIRNS.

Bhardwaj, H. C. 2000. *Metallurgy in Indian Archaeology*. Varanasi: Tara Book Agency.

Bhattacharya, A. K. 1979a. A note on Chemical Analysis of the Alloy, In *East Indian Bronze.* (Ed.) S. K. Mitra. Calcutta: Calcutta University.

Bhattacharya, A. K. 1979b. *A Study in Technique in East Indian Bronzes.* (Ed.) S. K. Mitra. Calcutta: Calcutta University.

Bhattacharya, G. 1996a. Magnificient bronze image of Vajrasatva from Mainamati, Bangladesh, *Journal of Bengal Art:* 1.

Bhattacharya, G. 1996b. A preliminary report on the inscribed metal vase from the National Museum of Bangladesh. In *Explorations in Art and Archaeology of South Asia*. Calcutta: Directorate of Archaeology and Museums, Government of West Bengal.

Bhattasali, N. K. 1922. Nutan Badsahi Amaler Kaman, *Prabashi*. (in Bengali).

Bhattasali, N. K. 2001. *Iconography of Buddhist and Brahmanical Sculptures in the Dacca Museum*. New Delhi: Aryan Books International.

Biswas, A. K. 1996. *Minerals and Metals in Ancient India*. Vol.1. New Delhi: D. K. Printworld (Pvt) Ltd.

Biswas, A. K. and Sulekha Biswas. 1996. *Minerals and Metals in Ancient India*. Vol. 2. New Delhi: D. K. Printworld (Pvt) Ltd.

Biswas, A. K. and W. G. Davenport. 1976. *Extractive Metallurgy of Copper*. Oxford: Pergamon Press.

Blochmann. H. R. 1993. *The Ain-i Akbari* (by Abul-Fazl Allami). (Vol. 1 (Tr.) H. 1873). Calcutta: The Asiatic Society.

Bose, N. K. 2006. *Nirbachita Rachana* (in Bengali), Kolkata: CASTEI.

Bose, P. N. 2005 (First Print 1928). Notes on the Geology and Mineral Resources of Sikhim. In Risley, H. H., *The Gazetteer of Sikhim*. New Delhi: B. R. Publishing Corporation.

Caldwell, K.S. 1920. The result of analyses of certain ornaments found in Assur sites, *Journal of Bihar and Orissa Research Society*: 6.

Campbell, A. 1916. Note on the occurrence of copper celts in Manbhum, *Journal of Bihar and Orissa Research Society*.

Chakrabarti, D. K. 1979. The problem of tin in early India – a preliminary survey. *Man and Environment* : 3.

Chakrabarti, D. K. 1986. Pre-industrial mines of India, *Puratattva* 16.

Chakrabarti, D. K. 1988. The old copper mines of Eastern India. In *The Beginnings of the use of Metals and Alloys*. (Ed.) R. Maddin, Boston: MIT.

Chakrabarti, D. K. 1992. *Ancient Bangladesh*. New Delhi: Oxford University Press.

Chakrabarti, D. K. 1993. *Archaeology of Eastern India: Chhotanagpur Plateau and West Bengal*. Delhi: Munshiram Manoharlal Publishers Pvt. Ltd.

Chakrabarti, D. K. and Nayanjot Lahiri. 1986. Assam-Burma route to China, *Man and Environment*: 10.

Chakrabarti, D. K. and Nayanjyot Lahiri. 1996. *Copper and its Alloys in Ancient India*, New Delhi: Munshiram Manoharlal.

Chakrabarti, D. K. and R. K. Chattopadhyay. 1983. Parihati, a mediaeval smelting site in Midnapur District. *Puratattva:* 12.

Chakrabarti, D. K. and S. J. Hasan. 1982. The sequence at Bahiri (Chandra Hazrar Danga), District Birbhum, West Bengal. *Man and Environment* : 6.

Chattopadhyay, P. K. 2001. Harikela coins of Bengal: Archaeo-metallurgical studies, *Journal of Bengal Art*. Vol. 6.

Chattopadhyay, P. K. 1993-94. Bahiri: a Protohistoric manufacturing center in West Bengal, *Pratna Samiksha* : 2, 3.

Chattopadhyay, P. K. 2001. Harikela coins of Bengal: Archaeometallurgical studies, *Journal of Bengal Art* 6.

Chattopadhyay, P. K. 1995-96. Copper hoards of Eastern India: Analytical Studies, *Pratna Samiksha:* 4, 5.

Chattopadhyay, P. K. 2005. *Metalcrafts of Eastern India and Bangladesh*, Jaipur: Publication Scheme.

Chattopadhyay, P. K. and Nupur Dasgupta. 2005. Ethnological, Historical and Archaeological Records: Tracing the metal craft of some districts of West Bengal and adjacent districts of Bihar, Jharkhand and Orissa. *Man and Environment* 33 (1).

Chattopadhyay, P. K. and Prasanta K. Datta. 2004-05. High-Tin Bronze Craft of Bengal: Archaeometallurgical Studies. *Journal of Bengal Art:* 9&10.

Chattopadhyay, P. K. 2006. *Kansaris* of Bengal: Ethnoarchaeological Studies at Bishnupur, in *Past and Present: Ethnoarchaeology in India* (G. Sengupta, S. Roychoudhury and S. Som (Eds), New Delhi: Pragati Publications. 347-357.

Chattopadhyay P. K., P. K. Datta, V. Vijayan and T. R. Ratray. 2010. Punch marked coins of Bengal: Archaeometallurgical Studies. In *Selected Essays on History & Archaeology*, M. M. Hoque, ATM Atiqur Rahman and Seema Hoque (Eds) Dhaka: CAHR

Chauley, G. C. 2000. Excavated remains at Lalitagiri, a Buddhist site in Orissa. In *Archaeology of Orissa*. Vol. 2. (Eds.) K. K. Basa and P. Mohanty, Delhi: Pratibha Prakasan.

Choudhary, B. K. 2005. Excavations at Panr, *Prajna-Bharat* 11.

Coggin Brown, J. 1916. Further relics of the copper age, *Journal of Bihar Orissa Research Society* 2.

Coggin Brown, J. 1918. Geology and ore deposits of the Bawdwin mines, *Records of the Geological Survey of India*. 48, Calcutta: Geological Survey of India.

Coggin Brown, J. 1923. The Mines and Mineral Resources of Yunnan, *Memoirs of the Geological Survey of India* 11, 7.

Cowell, M. R. and M. M. Lowick. 1988. Silver from the Panjhir mines, In *Metallurgy in Numismatics* 2 (Ed.) W.A. Oddy. London: Royal Numismatic Society.

Craddock, P. T. and N. D. Meeks. 1987. Iron in ancient copper, *Archaeometry* 29 (2).

Das, S. R. 1971. Archaeological discoveries from Murúidâbâd District (West Bengal). Calcutta: The Asiatic Society.

Dasgupta, N. and P. K. Chattopadhyay. 2009. Copper Craft Tradition in the Lower Ganga Valley: Early Historic to Early Medieval Periods. Shahnaj Husne Jahan (Ed.) *Abhijnan: Studies in South Asian Archaeology and Art History of Artefacts* (British Archaeological Reports, International Series S1974), 78-85. Oxford.

Dasgupta, R. 1998. Metal working in Medieval Assam. In *Archaeometallurgy in India.* (Ed.) V. Tripathi, Delhi: Sharada Publishing House.

Dash, R. 1982. The iron from Gudavella and Kharligara, *Journal of the Orissa Research Society* 1 (2)

Datta, A. and P. K. Chattopadhyay. 1986. The problems of copper-hoards in West Bengal – a reappraisal in the light of metallographic and chemical analysis, *Indian Museum Bulletin* 11.

Datta. P. K. 1968. Guns in Mughal India, *Bulletin of the Victoria Memorial.* Vol. II

Datta, P.K. 1986. Technological Aspects of some firearms in Mughal India: 16th to 18th centuries, in *Technology in Ancient and medieval India.* (Eds.) Aniruddha Ray and S. K. Bagchi, Delhi: Sundeep Prakashan.

Datta, P. K. and P. K. Chattopadhyay. 2007. Superior copper metallurgy of Eastern India and Bangladesh in medieval period: From pure copper to high-tin bronzes, *Journal of the Asiatic Society of Bangladesh (Hum.)* 52 (1).

Datta, P. K., P. K. Chattopadhyay and A. Ray 2007. New Evidence for High-tin bronze in Ancient Bengal, *SAS Bulletin* 30(2).

Datta, R and A. K. Datta. 2008. Ancient Vanga and Overseas Trade: A case study of Chandraketugarh. *Journal of Indian Ocean Archaeology.* 5.

De, S. and P. K. Chattopadhyay. 1989. Iron objects from Pandurajar Dhibi: Archaeometallurgical Studies. *Steel India* 12 (1).

Deyell, J. 1983. The China connection: problems of silver supply in medieval Bengal. In *Precious Metals in the later medieval and early modern Worlds*. (Ed.) J. F. Richards. Carolina Academic Press.

Dunn, J. A. 1937. *Memoirs Geological Survey of India.* LXIX. Part 1, Calcutta: Geological Survey of India.

Dutta, M. L. 1982. Spectrographic determination of minor constituents in ancient copper slag, *Transaction of Indian Institute of Metals* 35 (5).

Dutta, M. L. 2005. Emission Spectrography as a scientific tool. In *Science in Archaeology and Archaeo-materials.* (Ed.) A. K. Biswas. New Delhi: D. K. Printworld.

Friend, J. N. and W. E. Thorneycroft. 1924. Examination of iron from Konarak, *The Journal of Iron and Steel Institute* 60 (2).

Gait, E. A. 1897. The Manufacture of Brass and Copper Wares of Assam. *The Journal of Indian Art and Industry* VII, 54.

Ghosh, A. 1989. *An Encyclopaedia of Indian Archaeology*, Vols. 1 and 2, Delhi: Munshiram Manharlal Publishers Pvt. Ltd.

Ghosh, A. K. and P. K. Chattopadhyay. 1982. An early steel implement from Barudih, Bihar province, India: Metallurgical studies, *MASCA Journal* 2(2), University of Pennsylvania 2 (2).

Ghosh, A. K. and P. K. Chattopadhyay. 1981. Identification of new trace element in ancient copper object: fresh light on copper technology. *Science and Culture* 47 (7).

Ghosh, N. C., A. K. Nag and P. K. Chattopadhyay. 1987-88. The Archaeological background and iron sample from Hatigra. *Puratattva* 18.

Ghosh, D. P. 1975. Copper–plate Engravings of Ancient Bengal and the source of south east Asian Art, *Bangladesh Lalitkala* 1,1.

Goswami, K. G. 1948. *Excavations at Bangarh (1938-41)* Calcutta: University of Calcutta.

Hannay, S. F. 1856. Notes on the iron ore statistics and economic geology of Upper Assam, *Journal of Asiatic Society of Bengal* 35.

Haque, E. 2001. *Excavation at Wari-Bateshwar: a preliminary study.* Dhaka: ICSBA.

Haque, E., S. S. Mustafizur Rahaman and S. M. Kamrul Ahsan. 2000. A preliminary report on Wari-Bateshwar trial excavation by ICSBA, *Journal of Bengal Art* 5.

Harunur Rashid, M. 1997. Sculpture in *Mainamati-Devaparvata.* (Ed.) A. B. M. Hussain, Dhaka: Asiatic Society of Bangladesh.

Hossain, S. 1985. Cannon of Shah Jahan with the title Buland Iqbal, *Journal of Asiatic Society of Bengal* 33 (2).

Hossain, S. 1988. *Art and the vintage,* Chittagong: Chittagong University Museum.

Hunday, A. and S. Banerjee 1967. *Memoirs of the Geological Survey of India, Geology and mineral resources of West Bengal*. Calcutta: Geological Survey of India.

IAR: *Indian Archaeology – A Review.* New Delhi: Archaeological Survey of India.

Jaikishan, S. 2009. *Iron and Wootz Steel Industry in Northern Telengana.* Hyderabad: Telengana Jagrithi.

Jamir, T. 2006. A burial site at Jotsoma and the mortuary customs of the Angami

Nagas. In *Past and Present Ethnoarchaeology in India.* (Eds.) G. Sengupta, S. Roychoudhury and S. Som. Delhi: Pragati Publications.

Jamal Hasan, S. 2007. A unique burial system of the Ahoms, In *Kalhar Studies in Art, Iconography, Architecture and Archaeology of India and Bangladesh.* (Eds.) G. Bhattacharya, G. Mevissen, M. Mitra and S. Sinha, New Delhi: Kaveri Books.

Kangle, R. P. 1997. *The Kautiliya Arthashastra* (in 3 Vols.). Delhi: Motilal Banarsidass Publishers Pvt. Ltd.

Khan, I. A. 2004. *Gunpowder and Firearms.* New Delhi: Oxford University Press.

Khan, I. G. 1986. Metallurgy in Medieval India 16th-18th centuries, In *Technology in Ancient & Medieval India*. (Eds.) Aniruddha Roy and S. K. Bagchi, Delhi: Sundeep Prakashan.

Khan, M. R. 2002. Copper using people of Ancient Eastern India and Bangladesh, *Pratnatattva* 8.

Khan, M. R. 2003. *Roots and Migration.* Dhaka: Jinghaful.

Khan, A. 2007. Bengal copperplates: Provenances and preservation data. *Pratnatattva* 13.

Krishnan, M. S. 1955. *Iron ores of India*, Calcutta: Indian Association for the Cultivation of Science.

Kuppuram, G. 1989. *Ancient Indian Mining, Metallurgy and Metal Industries* (in 2 Vols.) Delhi: Sundeep Prakashan.

Kuroda, A. 2009. The Eurasian silver century, 1276-1359: commensurability and multiplicity. *Journal of Global History* 4.

Lal, B. B. 1956. An examination of metal images from Nalanda. *Ancient India* 12.

Lal, B. B. 1949. Sisupalgarh 1948: An early historical fort in Eastern India. *Ancient India* 5.

Leuva, K. K. 1963: *The Asur: A Study of Primitive Iron-Smelters*. New Delhi: Bharatiya Adimjati Sevak Sangh.

Maclaren, J. M. 1904. The Auriferous occurrences of Assam, *Records of the Geological Survey of India.* 31 (4).

Mahajan, M. 2000. *Chhattisgarh: A study in the culture and Historical Geography.* Delhi: Sharada Publishing House.

Mahajan, N. and R. Balasubramaniam. 1997-1998. Scanning electron microscopy study of an ancient silver punch-marked coin with central pentagonal mark, *Numismatic Digest* 21-22.

Majumdar, R. C. 1943. The History of Bengal. Dacca: The University of Dacca.

Majumder, N. G. 1926. A gold plated bronze from Mahasthan, *Modern Review.*

Mallet, F. R. 1874. Geological notes on part of northern Hazaribagh, *Records of the Geological Survey of India.* 7.

Mao, J. 1991. Traditional Craft and technology in Manipur. In *Archaeology of North Eastern India.* (Eds.) J. P. Singh and G. Sengupta. Delhi: Har-Anand Publication

Miah, M. A. H. 1991. Cannons in the subcontinent with a special reference to the historical cannons of Bengal, *Journal of the Asiatic Society of Bangladesh (H)* 36 (1).

Mishra, A. K. 2003. *Ethno-archaeometallurgy of Iron in India,* Delhi: Agam Kala Prakashan.

Mitchiner, M. B. and A. M. Pollard. 1990. *Early South East Asian currency systems.* Napoli, Italia: Instituto Universitario Orientale.

Mitra, D. 1983. *Ratnagiri (1958-61)* Vol. I. New Delhi: Archaeological Survey of India.

Mitra, R. L. 1864. On the Buddhist remains of Sultanganj, *Journal of Asiatic Society of Bengal* 4.

Mohanta, B. K., K. K. Basa, P. K. Chattopadhyay and T. K. Das. 2003. Pre-industrial iron smelting in Mayurbhanj, Northern Orissa: An Ethnohistoric study, *Man and Environment* 28 (2).

Mohanty, P. and Baba Mishra. 2002. Early historic Archaeology of Kalahandi District, Orissa. In *Archaeology of Eastern India New perspectives.* (Eds.) G. Sengupta and S. Panja, Kolkata: CASTEI.

Mukherjee, B. N. 1992. *Coins and currency system in Gupta Bengal,* New Delhi: Harman Publishing House.

Mukherjee, B. N. 1997. Methods of coin making. In *History of Technology in India.* (Eds.) A. K. Bag. Vol. 1. New Delhi: Indian National Science Academy.

Mukherjee, T. N. 1885. Bidri-ware. *Journal of Indian Art* 6.

Murray, E. F. O. 1940. The ancient workers of western Dhalbhum, *Journal of the Royal Asiatic Society of Bengal Letters* 6.

Nayak, D. C. and J. N. Das. 1998. Vanadium ore. In *Geology and Mineral Resources of Orissa.* (Eds.) S. Acharya, N. K. Mahalik and S. Mahapatra. Bhubaneswar: Society of Geoscientists and Allied Technologists.

Neogi, P. 1979. (Reprint) *Copper in Ancient India*, Patna: Janaki Prakashan.

Neogi, P. 2007. (Reprint) *Iron in Ancient India* (Ed.) R. S. Shukla. Delhi: Pratibha Prakashan.

Nigam, J. S. 2000. Notes on the excavations of Udaigiri and Khalkattapatna. In *Archaeology of Orissa.* Vol. 2. (Eds.) K. K. Basa and P. Mohanty. Delhi: Pratibha Prakasan.

O'Malley, L.S.S. 1910. *Bengal District Gazeteers Santal Parganas.* New Delhi: Logos Press.

Oldham, T. 1852. Report of the examination of the districts in the Damoodah valley and Beerbhoom producing iron ore, *Selected Records of Bengal Government VIII.*

Oldham, T. 1856. Preliminary notes on coal and iron of Talcher, *Memoirs of Geological* Survey of India. 1.

Pal, D. C., B. Mishra and H-J. Bernhardt. 2007. Mineralogy and geochemistry of pegmatite hosted Sn-Ta-Nb-, and Zr-Hf-bearing minerals from the southeastern part of the Bastar – Malkangiri pegmatite belt, Central India. *Ore Geology Reviews* 30. Elsevier.

Pal, P. 1996. *The Peaceful liberators Jain Art from India*, Los Angeles: Los Angeles County Museum of Art.

Panda, S. K. 2000. *New perspectives on the history and culture of Orissa*, Calcutta: Punthi Pustak.

Pant. G. N. 1970. *Studies in Indian weapons and warfare*. New Delhi: Army Educational Stores.

Patil, D. R. 1963. *The antiquarian remains in Bihar.* Patna: K.P. Jayaswal Research Institute.

Prakash, B. and K. Igaki. 1984. Ancient iron making in Bastar District. *Indian Journal of History of Science* 19(2).

Prakash, B. and V. Tripathi. 1986. Iron technology in Ancient India. *Historical Metallurgy,* September 1986.

Prasad, B., B. Prakash and N. Ahmad. 1995 Metallurgical study of the silver punch-marked coins. *Journal of Numismatic Society of India* 57 (1, 2).

Ray, Amita and S. K. Mukherjee 1992. Excavation at Mangalkot. *Pratna Samiksha* 1

Ray, H. 1999. *India, South-East Asia and China: Some historical issues.* Calcutta: CASTEI

Ray, R., A. K. Kundu and N. Bhattacharya. 2000. Chalcolithic cultural remains from a site near Kanjipani, Orissa. In *Archaeology of Orissa.* Vol. 1 (Eds.) K. K. Basa and P. Mohanty, Delhi: Pratibha Prakashan.

Rhodes, N. G. and S. K. Bose. 2003. *The Coinage of Assam.* Vol. I. Pre-Ahom Period, Dhubri: Mira Bose.

Rhodes, N. G. and S. K. Bose. 2004. *The coinage of Assa.,* Vol. II. Ahom Period. Dhubri: Mira Bose.

Rothenberg, B. 1978. *Excavations at Timna Site 39 – a Chalcolithic copper smelting site and Furnace and its metallurgy* – IAMS Monograph, No. 1. Archaeo-Metallurgy.

Roy Chowdhury, M. K. 1953. A note on the lateritic iron-ore of the Maikala range, Madhya Pradesh. *Indian Minerals* 7 (3).

Reeves, R. 1962. *Cire Perdue Casting in India.* New Delhi: Crafts Museum.

Rengsi, V. 1991. Traditional Craft and technology of the Mizos, In *Archaeology of North Eastern India,* (Eds.) J. P. Singh and G. Sengupta. Delhi: Har-Anand Publication.

Salles, J. F. 1999. Excavations of Mahasthangarh: new evidence of contacts with the Ganges valley. *Journal of Bengal Art* 4.

Sangma, M. S. 1991. Crafts and technologies of Garos, In *Archaeology of North Eastern India.* (Eds.) J. P. Singh and G. Sengupta. Delhi: Har-Anand Publication.

Santra, T. 1996. Pitaler Rath: Dhatushilper Anupam Nidarshan (in Bengali). *Kaushiki 1996.*

Santra, T. 1998. Banglar Dhatushilpa (in Bengali). *Kaushiki 1998.*

Sanyal, N. B. 1927-28. A note on the addition to the society's Museum, *Varendra Research Society, Annual Report for the year 1927-28.*

Schoff, W. H. 1995. *The Periplus of the Erythrraean Sea,* Delhi: Munshiram Manoharlal Publishers Pvt. Ltd.

Saraswati. S. K. 1936. An ancient text on the casting of metal images, *Journal of the Indian Society of Oriental Art.* Vol.4. No.2.

Saraswati, S. K. 1962. *Early Scuptures of Bengal,* Calcutta: Sambodhi Publications Private Ltd.

Sarma, R. K. 1975. Folk bronzes of Bangladesh. *Bangladesh Lalitkala* 1 (2).

Sen Sarma, S. 2001. *Kautilya's Arthashastra in the light of modern science and technology*, New Delhi: D. K. Printworld (Pvt) Ltd.

Sengupta, G. 1989. Deulbadi Sarvani: a reconsideration. In *Ratna-Chandrika, Panorama of Oriental Studies*, (Eds.) D. Handa and Ashvini Agrawal, New Delhi: Harman Publishing House.

Sharma, A. K. 1994. *Manipur – The Glorious Past*, New Delhi: Aryan Books International.

Sharma, A. K. 2000. *Archaeo-anthropology of Chhattisgarh*, New Delhi: Sundeep Prakashan.

Singer, N. F. 2008. *Vaishali and the Indianization of Arakan,* New Delhi: A.P.H. Publishing Corporation.

Singh, A. K. and D. Kumar (Eds). 2007. *Antichak Excavations Report* (1960-69) Patna: Patna University.

Singh, B. P. 2004. *Early Farming Communities of the Kaimur* (in 2 Vols.) Jaipur: Publication Scheme.

Singh, P. 1999. Rise of cultures in Eastern India. In *The Dawn of Indian Civilisation upto 600 BC*. (Ed). G. C. Pandey. Vol. 1(1). New Delhi: Centre for Studies in Civilizations.

Singh, P. 1994. *Excavations at Narhan*. Varanasi: Banaras Hindu University.

Singh, R., B. Mishra, P. K. Dandsena and N. K. Meher. 2006. Archaeology of Chandrasagar Nala, Dist. Kalahandi, Orissa. *Man in India* 86 (1&2)

Singh, R. N. 2004. Analyses of metal objects. Appendix V. In *Early farming communities of the Kaimur.* (Ed.) B. P. Singh. Jaipur: Publication Scheme.

Singh, R. N. 2007. *Aspects of Archaeometallurgy in South and South-East Asia*. Varanasi: Kala Prakashan.

Sinha, B. K. 1992-93. Excavations at Golabai Sasan, Dist. Puri. Orissa, *Puratattva* 23

Sinha, B. K. 2000. Golabai: a protohistoric site on the coast of Orissa, In *Archaeology of Orissa*. (Eds.) K. K. Basa and P. Mohanty, Delhi: Pratibha Prakasan. Vol. 1.

Sinha, B. P. and L. A. Narain. 1970. *Pataliputra Excavation 1955-56*. Patna: Directorate of Archaeology and Museums, Bihar.

Sinha, B.P. and B. S. Verma. 1977. *Sonpur Excavations (1956 and 1959-1962)* Patna: Directorate of Archaeology and Museums, Bihar.

Sinha, B. P. and S. R. Roy. 1969. *Vaisali Excavations*. Patna: Directorate of Archaeology and Museums, Bihar.

Sinha, R. P. 1999. Rare metal and rare earth pegmatites of Eastern India, *Exploration and Research for Atomic minerals.* 12.

Srinivasan, N. R. 1998. Revival of Rural iron making in Orissa, In *Archaeometallurgy in India*. (Ed.) V. Tripathi. Delhi: Sharada Publishing House.

Sundaram, C. V., B. Raj and C. Rajagopalan. 1999. History of Metallurgy in India, In *Chemistry and Chemical Techniques in India*, New Delhi: Centre for Studies in Civilizations.

Sunithananda, B. 1999. Bangladesher Baudhha Vaskarya, (in Bengali). Dhaka: Asiatic Society of Bangladesh.

Syiemlieh, D. R. 1988. Khasi iron culture and iron trade with Sylhet in the late eighteenth and early nineteenth centuries. *Proceedings of North East India History Association,* Kohima 1987.

Tarafdar, M. R. 1995. *Trade, technology and society in medieval Bengal*. Dhaka: International Centre for Bengal Study.

Tewari, R., R. K. Srivastava, K. K. Saraswat and K. K. Singh. 1999-2000. Excavations at Malhar, District Chandauli (U.P.), *Pragdhara* 10.

Upadhyay, P. and V. Tripathi. 2006. Gold washing in Eastern India, in *Past and Present: Ethnoarchaeology in India*, (G. Sengupta, S. Roychoudhury and S. Som (Eds). New Delhi: Pragati Publications.

Upadhyay, P. 2007. *Minerals and Mining in Ancient India*, Varanasi: Kala Prakashan

Verma, B. S. 2007. *Chirand Excavation Report*, Patna: Directorate of Archaeology

Vijan, V., T. R. Routray, P. K. Nayak and D. K. Basa. 2005. Studies on the composition of ancient Indian punch-marked silver coins. *X-Ray Spectrometry* 34.

Vijan, V., T. R. Routray, P. K. Nayak and D. K. Basa. 2005. Non-Destructive analysis of ancient punch-marked silver coins by Proton Induced X-Ray Emission studies, *Ancient Sciences and Archaeology*. (Ed.) M. D. Sampath. Delhi: Bharatiya Kala Prakashan.

Watson, E.R. 1907. *Iron and Steel work in the province of Bengal,* Calcutta: Bengal Secretariat Book Depot.

Watters, T. 1996. *On Yuan Chwang's Travels in India AD 629-64.* New Delhi: Munshiram Manoharlal Publishers Pvt Ltd.

Wheeler, T. S., J. D. Muhly and R. Maddin. 1979. Mediterranean trade in copper and tin in the late bronze age. *Annali*: *Instituto Italiano Di Numismatica* I-II.

Yule, Lieutenant H. 1842. Notes on the iron of Kasia Hills. *Journal of Asiatic Society of Bengal* 11.

Yule, P. 1985. *Metal work in the Bronze age in India.* Prahistorische Bronzefunde, ableitung XX, band 3, Munchen: C. H. Beck'sche Verlagsbuchhandlung.

Yule, P. 2001. Addenda to the copper hoards of the Indian subcontinent: Preliminaries for an interpretation. *Man and Environment* 36 (2).

Yule, P. and B. K. Rath 2000. Sankarjang: a metals period burial site in the Dhenkanal uplands of Orissa. In *Archaeology of Orissa*, Vol. 1 (Eds.) K. K. Basa and P. Mohanty. Delhi: Pratibha Prakasan.

Yule, P. and M. Thiel-Horstmann. 1985. The Prehistoric metal objects in the S. C. Roy collection, Ranchi, *Man in India* 65 (2).

Yule, P., A. Hauptmann, and M. J. Haughes. 1989. *The copper hoards of the Indian Subcontinent: Preliminaries for an interpretation.* Mainz: Romisch-Germanisches Zentral Museum. Mainz.

Yule, P., B. K. Rath and K. Hojgarrd. 1989. Sankerjung ein metalizei-thicher Besta-ttengsplatzim Dhenkanal vorgebirge ostindiens. *Anthropos* 84.

INDEX